This first volume of *Cambridge M*
the most outstanding lyrical pl
eleventh and twelfth centuries, the period of the finest flowering of
medieval Latin drama. Newly edited and translated, the texts are given in both Latin and English, with detailed notes and apparatus to aid interpretation. They are selected to represent the range of dramatic achievement between about 1050 and 1180, when the use of sung play-texts, within a context of liturgical ceremony as well as for entertainment, was at its peak. The plays chosen are boldly inventive and compellingly imaginative, revealing the depth and range of medieval dramatic power. Included are works from France, Germany, and Spain, a piece by Hildegard of Bingen, and the Passion Play from the *Carmina Burana*.

Cambridge Medieval Classics 1

Nine medieval Latin plays

Cambridge Medieval Classics

General editor

PETER DRONKE, FBA

Professor of Medieval Latin Literature, University of Cambridge

This series is designed to provide bilingual editions of medieval Latin and Greek works of prose, poetry, and drama dating from the period *c.* 350–*c.* 1350. The original texts are offered on left-hand pages, with facing-page versions in lively modern English, newly translated for the series. There are introductions, and explanatory and textual notes.

The Cambridge Medieval Classics series allows access, often for the first time, to outstanding writing of the Middle Ages, with an emphasis on texts that are representative of key literary traditions and which offer penetrating insights into the culture of medieval Europe. Medieval politics, society, humour, and religion are all represented in the range of editions produced here. Students and scholars of the literature, thought, and history of the Middle Ages, as well as more general readers (including those with no knowledge of Latin or Greek) will be attracted by this unique opportunity to read vivid texts of wide interest from the years between the decline of the Roman empire and the rise of vernacular writing.

Opening titles

1. Nine Medieval Latin Plays, translated and edited by PETER DRONKE
2. Hugh Primas and the Archpoet, translated and edited by FLEUR ADCOCK
3. Johannes de Hauvilla, *Architrenius*, translated and edited by WINTHROP WETHERBEE

Other titles in preparation

Prodromic Poems, translated and edited by MARGARET ALEXIOU and MICHAEL HENDY
Adelard of Bath, *Quaestiones Naturales* and *De Eodem et Diverso*, translated and edited by CHARLES BURNETT
Dante, *De Vulgari Eloquentia*, translated and edited by STEVEN BOTTERILL
Dante, *Monarchia*, translated and edited by PRUDENCE JAMES
Digenis Akritas, translated and edited by ELIZABETH JEFFREYS
Nigel of Longchamp, *Speculum Stultorum*, translated and edited by JILL MANN
Dhuoda, *Liber Manualis*, translated and edited by MARCELLE THIÉBAUX
Gregory of Nazianzus, Autobiographical Poems, translated and edited by CAROLINNE WHITE
Peter Abelard, The Theological and Polemical Letters, translated and edited by JEAN ZIOLKOWSKI

Nine medieval Latin plays

TRANSLATED AND EDITED BY
PETER DRONKE
University of Cambridge

CAMBRIDGE UNIVERSITY PRESS
Cambridge, New York, Melbourne, Madrid, Cape Town, Singapore, São Paulo

Cambridge University Press
The Edinburgh Building, Cambridge CB2 8RU, UK

Published in the United States of America by Cambridge University Press, New York

www.cambridge.org
Information on this title: www.cambridge.org/9780521395373

© Cambridge University Press 1994

This publication is in copyright. Subject to statutory exception
and to the provisions of relevant collective licensing agreements,
no reproduction of any part may take place without the written
permission of Cambridge University Press.

First published 1994
This digitally printed version 2008

A catalogue record for this publication is available from the British Library

Library of Congress Cataloguing in Publication data
Nine medieval Latin plays / translated and edited by Peter Dronke.
    p. cm. – (Cambridge medieval classics: I)
Contents: Sponsus – Officium stelle – Tres filie – Tres clerici –
Verses pascales de tres Maries – Versus de pelegrino – Danielis ludus –
Ordo Virtutum – Ludus de passione.
Includes bibliographical references
ISBN 0 521 39537 2
1. Christian drama, Latin (Medieval and modern) – Translations into English.
I. Dronke, Peter. II. Series.
PA8165.N56   1994
872'.03080382–dc20   93–45669 CIP

ISBN 978-0-521-39537-3 hardback
ISBN 978-0-521-72765-5 paperback

Contents

Preface	page	ix
List of abbreviations		xii
Introduction		xv

Eleventh-century plays   1

    I *Sponsus*   3
        The Bridegroom, from Limoges
    II *Officium stelle*   24
        The Play of the Star, from Freising
    III–IV *Tres filie*   52
        Tres clerici
        The Three Daughters, and *The Three Students*, from Hildesheim

Twelfth-century plays   81

    V–VI *Verses pascales de tres Maries*   83
        Versus de pelegrino
        Easter Verses of the Three Maries, and *Verses about the Stranger*, from Vic
    VII *Danielis ludus*   110
        The Play of Daniel, from Beauvais
    VIII *Ordo Virtutum*   147
        The Play of the Virtues, by Hildegard of Bingen
    IX *Ludus de passione*   185
        The Passion Play, from the *Carmina Burana* (Bressanone?)

Preface

My aim in this book is to present a richly varied and inviting group of the Latin lyrical plays of the eleventh and twelfth centuries, editing them afresh from the manuscripts and providing line-by-line translations that do not evade the detailed questions of meaning. The edition is addressed to lovers of drama and poetry as much as it is to scholars.

The introductory, textual and explanatory notes that accompany each play are exceptionally full for a volume in the Cambridge Medieval Classics. This was necessary because of the sheer number of problems of text and interpretation that are still outstanding. At the same time, in order to keep the material surrounding the plays within manageable scope, I have formulated certain judgements perhaps too apodictically: for, to have commented in adequate detail on scholarly controversies, or to have added extensive allusions to secondary literature, would have placed an intolerable strain on the format of the volume. For a similar reason, while I was aware of the existence of previous English translations of four of the nine plays here edited, I chose not to consult these: such consultation would inevitably have led to further discussion of minutiae, and hence to a more cluttered book.

In two respects the present volume is more limited than I originally planned. It was intended from the outset to provide, along with the texts and translations, a new edition of the music of the plays, insofar as this was extant and transcribable. Sadly, the musicologist who agreed to undertake this had to withdraw from the project unexpectedly, at a point when all other aspects of the volume were already complete. For the present, then, I would refer readers to the following existing musical editions, to complement the play-texts below:[1] for I (*Sponsus*), the music of which survives nearly complete, the transcription by Raffaello Monterosso in Avalle 1965,[2] pp. 123–30; for V–VI (*Verses pascales de tres Maries* and *Versus de pelegrino*), of which only part of the music is

---

[1] I am leaving out of consideration adaptations of medieval Latin plays for modern performance: in these, the music as presented tends to go beyond what can be deduced from the manuscripts.

[2] References are given in full in the list of abbreviations below.

preserved, that of Anglès, pp. 276–8 and 281; for VII (*Danielis ludus*), both that of W. L. Smoldon[3] and that of Mathias Bielitz;[4] for VIII (*Ordo Virtutum*), finally, that of P. Barth, M. I. Ritscher and J. Schmidt-Görg.[5] It should be noted that, especially in the case of the plays V and VIII, there are important differences between the texts as printed in this volume and those given under the melodies in the musical editions. It is from the manuscripts of these two plays, moreover, that I have chosen the four facsimile pages for this book (plates I–IV) : these will give readers an impression of the shape of certain melodies as well as of the original texts.

The music of the plays III–IV (the Hildesheim *Tres filie* and *Tres clerici*) is missing; it is unlikely that the music of II (the Freising *Officium stelle*) will ever be fully transcribable. On the problems involved in reconstructing the music of IX (the *Ludus de passione* among the *Carmina Burana*), there is a challenging essay by Thomas Binkley.[6]

While much fundamental work on the extant music of the plays still needs to be done, the present, textually oriented volume will fulfil its purpose if it reveals something of their dramatic artistry and imaginative range. The situation is a little as with Hofmannsthal's libretti in our century: while these were naturally destined for their operatic settings, and many aspects can come fully alive only in a first-rate performance, there are other, equally fascinating aspects, many subtleties of characterisation and scenic invention, which will show themselves first and foremost through close attention to the poet–dramatist's language.

The second part of the original plan that could not be realised in this volume was a new edition of the mid-twelfth-century *Play of Antichrist* (*Ludus de Antichristo*). I had worked intensively on the text in the principal manuscript in Munich (Clm 19411), but was quite unable to obtain photographs of the second, fragmentary manuscript, in the Austrian Benedictine abbey of Fiecht,[7] which I felt it was necessary to collate. Both my own requests and those most kindly made on my behalf, by colleagues at the Monumenta Germaniae Historica, proved fruitless. I hope, however, that this obstacle will not remain insuperable,

---

[3] *The Play of Daniel: A Medieval Liturgical Drama* (London 1960; 2nd edn. rev. D. Wulstan, London 1976).
[4] Bulst 1989 (the 'Notentext' presents a revision of Coussemaker's edition of 1860).
[5] Hildegard von Bingen, *Lieder* (Salzburg 1969), pp. 165-205.
[6] 'The Greater Passion Play from Carmina Burana: An Introduction', in *Alte Musik. Praxis und Reflexion*, ed. P. Reidemeister, V. Gutmann (Winterthur 1982), pp. 144-57.
[7] Cf. J. Riedmann, 'Ein neuaufgefundenes Bruchstück des "Ludus de Antichristo"', *Zeitschrift für Bayerische Landesgeschichte* 36 (1973) 16-38.

and that a later volume of the Cambridge Medieval Classics will have a new critical bilingual edition of the *Play of Antichrist* – the most ambitious political-religious drama of the period – as its centrepiece, accompanied by further examples of high achievement in twelfth- and thirteenth-century Latin drama, together with the music of the plays when this survives.

I should like to express my warm thanks to the British Academy for the generous research grants that enabled me to work with the manuscripts in Wiesbaden, Munich and Vic, and to have help with the preparation of electronic copy for this volume. In preparing this for me, Sarah James showed great patience and skill in getting the more complex Latin verse-forms onto the page, and in matching these line by line with the translations – to her, too, a heartfelt thanks.

It is a pleasure, finally, to record my gratitude to Monsignor Miguel Gros and the Museu Episcopal at Vic, for supplying a microfilm and allowing the reproduction of Plates I and II, and to Dr Wolfgang Podehl and the Hessische Landesbibliothek, for permission to reproduce Plates III and IV.

Cambridge, 25 March 1993   P.D

Abbreviations

AH	Analecta Hymnica Medii Aevi, ed. Guido Maria Dreves, Clemens Blume (55 vols., Leipzig 1886–1922)
Anglès 1935	Higini Anglès, La Música a Catalunya fins al segle XIII (Barcelona, repr. 1988)
Arlt 1970	Wulf Arlt, Ein Festoffizium des Mittelalters aus Beauvais in seiner liturgischen und musikalischen Bedeutung (2 vols., Cologne)
Avalle 1965	Sponsus. Dramma delle vergini prudenti e delle vergini stolte, ed. D'Arco Silvio Avalle. Testo musicale ed. Raffaello Monterosso (Milan–Naples)
1984	It teatro medievale e il Ludus Danielis (Turin)
1987	'Secundum speculationem rationemve (Il "Ludus Danielis" di Beauvais)', Helikon XXII–XXVII (1982–1987) 3–59
Blaise	Albert Blaise, Dictionnaire latin-français des auteurs chrétiens (2nd edn, Turnhout 1962)
Bulst 1989	Hilarii Aurelianensis Versus et Ludi, Epistolae, Ludus Danielis Belouacensis, ed. Walther Bulst †, M. L. Bulst-Thiele. Anhang, Notentext: Mathias Bielitz (Leiden)
CB	Carmina Burana
Bischoff 1967	Bernhard Bischoff, Carmina Burana. Einführung zur Faksimile-Ausgabe der Benediktbeurer Liederhandschrift (Munich)
Bischoff 1970	Carmina Burana, I 3, ed. Otto Schumann†, Bernhard Bischoff (Heidelberg)
Dronke 1962	Peter Dronke, 'A Critical Note on Schumann's Dating of the Codex

	Buranus', *Beiträge zur Geschichte der deutschen Sprache und Literatur* 84 (Tübingen) 173–83
Steer 1983	'"Carmina Burana" in Südtirol', *Zeitschrift für deutsches Altertum* 112, 1–37
Vollmann 1987	*Carmina Burana. Texte und Übersetzungen*, ed. Benedikt Konrad Vollmann (Frankfurt am Main)
CC CM	Corpus Christianorum, Continuatio Mediaevalis
Coussemaker 1860	Edmond de Coussemaker, *Drames liturgiques du moyen âge* (Paris)
Dronke 1977	Peter Dronke, *The Medieval Lyric* (2nd edn, London–New York)
1984	*The Medieval Poet and his World* (Rome)
1986	*Poetic Individuality in the Middle Ages. New Departures in Poetry 1000–1150* (2nd edn, London)
1991	*Latin and Vernacular Poets of the Middle Ages* (Aldershot)
1992	*Intellectuals and Poets in Medieval Europe* (Rome)
1993	'Amour sacré et amour profane au moyen âge latin: Témoignages lyriques et dramatiques', in *Du récit à la scène (XIIe–XVe siècle)*, ed. Jacqueline Cerquiglini (in press, Geneva)
Drumbl	Johann Drumbl, *Quem quaeritis? Teatro sacro dell'alto medioevo* (Rome 1981)
Fassler 1992	Margot Fassler, 'The Feast of Fools and *Danielis Ludus*: Popular Tradition in a Medieval Cathedral Play', in *Plainsong in the Age of Polyphony*, ed. Thomas Forrest Kelly (Cambridge)
Hardison	O. B. Hardison, Jr, *Christian Rite and Christian Drama in the Middle Ages* (Baltimore 1965)
Hesbert	R. J. Hesbert, *Corpus antiphonalium officii: III Invitatoria et antiphonae* (Rome 1968);

	IV Responsoria, versus, hymni et varia (Rome 1970)
Hofmann-Szantyr	J. B. Hofmann, Anton Szantyr, *Lateinische Syntax und Stylistik* (Munich 1965)
Jones, *Liturgy*	Charles W. Jones, *The Saint Nicholas Liturgy and its Literary Relationships (Ninth to Twelfth Centuries)*, with an Essay on the Music by Gilbert Reaney (Berkeley–Los Angeles 1963)
Lexicon	*Lexicon Latinitatis Medii Aevi* (Turnhout 1975)
MGH	Monumenta Germaniae Historica
Mlat. Jb.	*Mittellateinisches Jahrbuch*
Norberg	Dag Norberg, *Introduction à l'étude de la versification latine médiévale* (Stockholm 1958)
Novum Glossarium/NG	*Novum Glossarium Mediae Latinitatis*, ed. Franz Blatt *et al.* (Copenhagen 1957–)
PL	Patrologia Latina
Rankin 1990	Susan Rankin, 'Liturgical Drama', in *The Early Middle Ages to 1300* (New Oxford History of Music II), ed. Richard Crocker, David Hiley (Oxford–New York)
Simon 1991	*The Theatre of Medieval Europe. New Research in Early Drama*, ed. Eckehard Simon (Cambridge)
von den Steinen, *Notker*	Wolfram von den Steinen, *Notker der Dichter und seine geistige Welt* (2 vols., Berne 1948)
Tobler–Lommatzsch	A. Tobler, E. Lommatzsch, *Altfranzösisches Wörterbuch* (10 vols., Berlin–Wiesbaden 1925–76)
Women Writers	Peter Dronke, *Women Writers of the Middle Ages: A Critical Study of Texts from Perpetua († 203) to Marguerite Porete († 1310)* (Cambridge 1984)
Y	Karl Young, *The Drama of the Medieval Church* (2 vols., Oxford 1933)
ZfrP	*Zeitschrift für romanische Philologie*

Introduction

The purpose of this volume is to make accessible nine of the most imaginative medieval Latin religious plays composed in the eleventh century and the twelfth. Surprising as it may seem, the editing and interpreting of these plays is still something of a pioneering venture. Most of those who read medieval literature, for love or scholarship or both, must have a general impression that, as regards the Latin drama, all the editorial groundwork has been done. Notably the two imposing volumes of Karl Young's *The Drama of the Medieval Church* (1933)[1] would seem to offer a definitive corpus of texts.

Nonetheless, since O. B. Hardison's critique of Young's methods, in his *Christian Rite and Christian Drama in the Middle Ages* (1965), we know that this corpus is problematic in at least one important aspect. It was arranged so as to inculcate a certain view of how the plays evolved, and this arrangement entailed the flouting of all chronological order. In ordering the plays, Young always proceeded from the simplest forms to the most complex – even when, as was often the case, the complex plays were preserved in early manuscripts and the simple in much later ones. Thus the assumptions – implicit in the ordering, and often made explicit in Young's discussion – about how the diverse dramatic genres developed tended to be highly misleading.

Yet this was by no means the only weakness in Young's monumental project. On closer inspection, it turns out to be much less comprehensive than might appear at first sight, and in the presentation of certain genres there are quite serious lacunae. Thus for instance, while Young knew and edited the 'great Passion-play'[2] that is preserved among the *Carmina Burana*, he was unaware of the equally wide-ranging and original Passion-play from Monte Cassino, wholly different in concep-

---

[1] Full references for works alluded to in the Introduction can be found in the list of abbreviations (pp. xii–xiv).
[2] This term, which has no manuscript authority, has been used by scholars to distinguish the play that is freshly edited below (IX) from the *Ludus breviter de passione* (CB 13*) – as it is called in the Codex Buranus rubric – which was added to the codex in the late thirteenth century. The *Ludus breviter* is a play that uses almost exclusively biblical phrasing.

xv

tion and detail – a play that still awaits a reliable edition.[3] Some genres, too, are missing from Young's corpus: he seems not to have known Hildegard of Bingen's allegorical drama, *Ordo Virtutum* (VIII below), and by overlooking this, as well as the other ranges of allegorical dialogues in his chosen period, he tended also to ignore the presence and functions of allegory in plays that he did edit.

Young transcribed his texts with considerable accuracy. A fresh look at his manuscripts, however, still leads to quite a few new readings and new perceptions. Particularly in cases where Young's text remained fragmentary – as in the Freising *Play of the Star* (II) and the pair of plays from Vic (V–VI) edited below – the use of an ultraviolet lamp can add numerous readings, so that these plays can now be presented in full.

Young's transcriptions, it should be added, even when they were very accurate, were transcriptions rather than editions. That is, they remained close to being diplomatic texts; they included scarcely any discussion of corrupt passages or of difficulties, and few attempts at emendation. The plays in his volumes lack not only translation but textual commentary; at times they still bristle with desperate, but unremarked, cruces; it would seem that detailed interpretation simply lay outside Young's concern.

The most serious lacuna in Young's collection is the complete absence of the music of the plays, which often survives together with the play-text in the manuscripts. The music is likewise missing in a later major corpus: Walter Lipphardt's ambitiously conceived edition of Easter ceremonies and Easter plays (*Lateinische Osterfeiern und Osterspiele*, 9 vols., 1975–91). In fact, in order to find a scholarly edition of a group of medieval Latin plays together with their music, one has to look back many generations behind Lipphardt and even behind Young, to a work published in 1860: Edmond de Coussemaker's *Drames liturgiques du Moyen Age*. Even here, however, the texts are not translated, and when they are incomprehensible they are neither emended nor discussed.

This means that, in the longer term, a wholly new corpus of medieval Latin drama is needed, with all the plays freshly edited from the manuscripts, ordered as accurately as possible by time and place, with philologically sound texts and translations that genuinely confront the

---

[3] The text of D. M. Inguanez, *Un dramma della Passione del secolo XII* (2nd edn, Montecassino 1939), is still the best available. I have briefly noted some of the defects in 'Laments of the Maries', in Dronke 1992, pp. 474 f. Cristina Dondi (Milan), who has worked on the text of this play with me, has collated the MS afresh and is preparing a critical edition.

problems of meaning, along with textual and explanatory notes setting out the difficulties that remain. Wherever the music survives in legible form, this should be edited with the text, in an edition as scholarly as that devoted to the words.

With the present volume I make no claim to initiating such a corpus: only to offering a small sample of bilingual texts, in a way that I hope will be both adequate to the needs of specialists and attractive to non-specialists.

The nine texts included here have been chosen to show something of the range of dramatic achievement in the Latin plays that survive from c. 1050 to c. 1180 – the period of their finest flowering. All the plays in this volume were sung, not spoken, though the music has not always been preserved. While the sung Latin plays nearly always treat religious themes, there was also a tradition of spoken plays that existed alongside them, plays that were more often secular than religious in content. Some of these spoken plays – from the 'Altercation between Terence and his Critic' in the ninth century to *Pamphilus* c. 1100 or *Babio* c. 1140[4] – likewise show a high degree of dramatic and verbal artistry. They have been excluded here, because to do any kind of justice to spoken as well as sung drama would require an extremely bulky volume.

By concentrating on fully-fledged plays, I have also had to exclude examples from the range of 'borderline' compositions that relate as much to liturgical ceremony as to drama. These have received an almost inordinate amount of scholarly attention – and controversy – in the last half-century.[5] If one accepts that the boundaries between ceremony and play were not immutable, and that some pieces could be oriented in the one direction or the other, depending on the mode and context of their performance, it should also be recognised that the artistic peaks among the eleventh and twelfth-century play-texts are clearly sited in the region of drama. This does not mean that such plays exclude all that belongs to liturgical ceremony. On the contrary, some of the most skilled dramatic composers also integrated ceremonial elements. The authors especially of the four plays edited here that concern events in the life of Christ – Epiphany (II), Passion (IX), and

---

[4] The 'Altercation' is conveniently available in E. K. Chambers, *The Medieval Stage* (2 vols., Oxford 1903), II 326–8; the best texts of *Babio* and *Pamphilus* are those of A. Dessì Fulgheri and S. Pittaluga, in *Commedie Latine del XII e XIII Secolo* (Genoa 1976 ff.), II 129–301, III 11–137. On the modes of performance of these pieces, see esp. Dronke 1991, chs. II ('A Note on *Pamphilus*') and IV ('Narrative and Dialogue in Medieval Secular Drama').

[5] See most recently *The Theatre of Medieval Europe*, ed. E. Simon (Cambridge 1991), esp. chs. 2–3.

Resurrection (v–vi) – chose to work with two complementary styles. With all their bold inventiveness in the greater part of their plays, they deliberately retained certain sacred moments set amid their free dramatic inventions, moments that keep the words *in illo tempore*, unchanged or scarcely changed from their origins in gospel or liturgy. The melody too, in such cases, is often unchanged from that used in a long-hallowed ceremony.

The retention of such moments within plays does not, however, warrant any simple conclusions about the relations between liturgy and drama. This much-debated topic is not directly relevant to the compositions edited here. Suffice to say that, even if in the case of certain other works that survive it may be possible to trace the actual growth of a play from a liturgical ceremony, such a growth is out of the question for any of the plays in this volume. For these at least, the most illuminating perspective is that of Johann Drumbl, who in his book *Quem quaeritis* (1981), as rich in new insights and challenges as it is in learning, begins with the concept of 'the alien theatre' (*das fremde Theater, il teatro estraneo*). Where the received opinion was that early medieval drama is a kind of 'natural' extension of worship, and is totally impregnated by its sacred function, Drumbl sees all that is dramatic in it as entering from without. What the surviving texts show us, he argues, is not liturgical question and answer gradually approaching the condition of drama, but if anything the contrary: a range of attempts by the Church to 'normalise' dramatic impulses, to diminish their distinctive qualities in order to bring them back closer to liturgical practice. The great number of ceremonies at the borders of the drama – of which the *Quem quaeritis* dialogues sung at Easter and Christmas are the best known – do not, Drumbl suggests, 'help us to study the development of medieval dramatic writing, but are, on the contrary, documents of its lack of success. The real medieval dramatic tradition ... can often be traced not in these documents, which show us "adapted" [i.e. liturgically oriented] versions, but in the space that the reformers, who transmitted these "liturgical" versions of medieval drama to us, consciously left aside'.[6]

When we look at the four eleventh-century plays chosen for this volume, it is at once evident that they were conceived in that space which was 'left aside'. To consider the four together is to become aware of what a fullness of theatrical creation, what a multiplicity of poetic-dramatic techniques and effects, was already possible by the eleventh

[6] Drumbl p. 366.

century – a period, that is, when not one among the numerous *Quem quaeritis* compositions contained even as many as ten lines of dialogue.

The diptych of St Nicolas plays from Hildesheim introduces us to a genre for which earlier testimonies are lacking – the genre that from the thirteenth century onwards is known as the 'miracle play' (*miraculum*), portraying not episodes from the Old or New Testament but the life and wonders of a saint. Were the Hildesheim plays the very first *miracula*, or must we reckon with earlier experiments in this genre that have not survived? By chance we know through an English testimony that *miracula* were familiar in England already around 1100. In 1119, the *Gesta Abbatum S. Albani* tell us, a monk named Geoffrey was elected Abbot of St Albans. The chronicler relates that, when Abbot Geoffrey had been a young schoolmaster in the nearby town of Dunstable, he had tried to stage a 'play of St Catherine' (*ludus de sancta Katerina*). In order to provide fine costumes for the players, he had borrowed some splendid copes from the monastery. When a fire broke out and the vestments in his care were burnt, Geoffrey offered to make reparation by becoming a monk himself.[7]

It is only through this – precious and quite fortuitous – testimony that we know of the existence of a play of St Catherine in the time of Abbot Geoffrey's youth. Quite possibly plays about saints were not a rarity before 1100, even if their texts were not copied in durable form, on parchment, and hence earlier examples have not survived. At all events the Hildesheim dramatist does not have the air of a 'beginner'. His strophes may appear innocent, yet they are *faux-naïf* rather than simple: there are touches of subtle, humorous complicity with the audience which suggest that this early dramatist has something of the cultivated mock-innocence of the author of *Aucassin et Nicolette*.

He took inspiration from hagiography, and perhaps from a lost earlier tradition of performed *miracula*. But it is also likely that, some important differences notwithstanding, he received a stimulus to his plays from another direction. The Nicolas plays were planned for musical performance in Hildesheim cathedral, though sadly their music is not extant; the verses, composed almost wholly in lyrical strophic forms, could not aspire to the lively freedoms of spoken dialogue. Yet this playwright's themes – the three daughters, and the three students[8]

---

[7] Rolls Series 28, iv, 173 (a section written by Matthew Paris); cf. R. M. Wilson, *The Lost Literature of Medieval England* (London 1952), p. 215.

[8] For the plot of the three students, no older source in hagiographic legend has been found. It is not likely, however, to be an entirely free invention of the Hildesheim dramatist (see below p. 56).

– tantalisingly recall themes in the spoken plays of Hrotsvitha of Gandersheim in the later tenth century.[9] Like the three sisters – Agape, Chionia and Hirena – in one of Hrotsvitha's plays, or Sapientia's three daughters in another, the three young people in each of the Nicolas episodes are seen as the potential, or actual, victims of a more brutal world. It is not only the ordeals of the triads of the young and guileless, in the two Hrotsvitha plots and the two Nicolas ones, but the contiguity of comedy and tragedy in the unfolding of those plots, that makes the resemblance striking. In the year 1007 the proudly independent foundation of Gandersheim had been assigned to the diocese of Hildesheim, and since then had owed obedience to its bishop, whose cathedral was only some thirty kilometres away. Hrotsvitha by then was probably no longer alive; moreover, she had never written *lyrical* dialogues, and had written for a court and not a church. Yet that the first dramatist we know of who brought non-biblical episodes into church performances was close to Hrotsvitha in themes and outlook, as well as geographically, must give pause for thought.

A brief indication of the nature of the bilingual play, *The Bridegroom* (*Sponsus*), from Limoges, will reveal a further range of the eleventh century's imaginative possibilities in drama. The manuscript containing the *Sponsus* stems from the end of the century, but one can see that the play is somewhat older: the vernacular verses in it, originally Provençal, have undergone some linguistic remodelling at the hands of the Limousin copyist. Most scholars speak of these vernacular verses as 'glosses' or '*farcitures*' of the Latin text, which they assume must have been the original. But this assumption can and should be questioned. For the Provençal verses have even greater poetic power than the Latin ones, and are never dramatically superfluous or discardable. I do not believe there was ever an original version of this play purely in Latin, which was later amplified by vernacular 'glosses'. Rather, this is the integral conception of a single dramatist, and one who could express himself more tellingly in his own native idiom than in the language of high culture he had assimilated. Besides, I think it was particularly his non-clerical, vernacular audience who had lively experience and expec-

---

[9] Cf. my observations in the introduction to *Rosvita, Dialoghi drammatici*, ed. F. Bertini (Milan 1986), pp. xl–xli. The two relevant plays by Hrotsvitha are today generally known as *Dulcitius* and *Sapientia*, but the titles she herself gave them are, respectively, 'The Passion of the Holy Virgins (*Passio sanctarum virginum*) Agape, Chionia and Hirena', and 'The Passion of the Holy Virgins Fides, Spes and Karitas' (cf. *ibid.* pp. xx–xxi). A third play of Hrotsvitha's, *Gallicanus*, mentioned by C. W. Jones (*Liturgy* p. 101), does not, as he claims, 'involve three sisters-german who struggle under threats of a fate worse than death'.

tations of lyrical dialogue: in the same manuscript, for instance, we encounter a delicate Annunciation piece, *Mei amic e mei fiel*, composed wholly in Provençal, in which the strophes of Gabriel's attempts to persuade Mary and those of Mary's replies are formed as a subtle spiritual counterpart to the wooing-dialogues of profane vernacular *pastorelas*.[10] Early vernacular dramatic dialogue, that is, should not always be imagined in a humble role such as that of glossing: it could already achieve much in its own right.

The play of the *Bridegroom* shows a confluence of learned and popular streams. Symbolically the night of the drama is both the night of the Easter vigil and that of the bridal wake in the parable of the Wise and Foolish Virgins: it is the hour of redemption, but also the hour of the final judgement. The Bridegroom is symbolically both Christ in the Harrowing of Hell and the *Sponsus* in the Song of Songs: he can open the gates of limbo, as of the divine bridal chamber. He does not, as in the gospel parable, come accompanied by a bride: no, each of the ten maidens can become his *Sponsa*. Yet five of them lose this chance through oversleeping: *Dolentas, chaitivas, trop i avem dormit!* – 'We, wretched in our grief, have slept too long!' In this refrain, and in the moving pleas and plaints of these maidens, as in the harsh and ugly replies of their wise sisters – 'Don't bother us any more with your begging ... you sluggards ... you shan't get a thing (*no·n auret pont*)' – we perceive a human empathy, indeed partisanship, of the poet for the victimised ones, which surely did not come to him from the side of theology or exegesis, and which lends his interpretation of the parable an unusual dramatic force. Was it really so terrible to sleep too long? How can it be that the Bridegroom does not pardon such a fault? The *Sponsus* dramatist would have understood perfectly the reaction of Margrave Frederick of Thuringia, who in the year 1321 saw the Eisenach play about this parable:

> When he saw and heard that the five Foolish Virgins were barred from eternal life, and that Mary and all the saints interceded for them and this was of no avail ... then he was beset by doubt and moved to great anger, and said: 'What then is Christian faith, if God will not have mercy on us at the prayers of Mary and of all the saints?' ... And he was so shattered by his long anger, that for three years he took to his bed.[11]

The dramatist of our bilingual *Sponsus* shapes his material with effortless freedom. He is aware of several exegetic traditions and touches upon them, though without ever committing himself to a particular

---

[10] Cf. Dronke 1977, pp. 50 f., 237.
[11] *Deutsche Dichtung des Mittelalters*, ed. M. Curschmann, I. Glier (Munich 1981), III 689 f.; cf. MGH *Scriptores* XXX 1, 448.

exegete; he does not teach, he *shows* the symbolic depths of his theme. He recognises what seems rebarbative in the parable – yet he refuses to gloss it over or (at least overtly) to judge. He stresses all that is humanly unbearable and tragic, and sees no theodicy in the background, that might make it less so; and precisely because of this fearlessness of vision his play is individual and moving.

The fourth of the eleventh-century plays, the Freising *Play of the Star*, shows still another astonishing range of new techniques. These are discussed in some detail in the introductory note to the play (pp. 24–31 below). Among the salient innovations are: the use of a sung prelude, composed so as to be accompanied by mime; the attempt to characterise the protagonists by the way they speak – the disdainful messenger, the impatient, overweening and furious Herod, the sardonic, sinister shield-bearer; the use of classical allusions and citations to bring certain parallels to mind: the Magi arriving as serene and dignified strangers, like Aeneas and his retinue, at a foreign court, or Herod working himself into a rage like Catiline in the Roman Senate; the symbolic superimposition of the present – the revelry of the 'Feast of Fools' of the youngest clergy, the day of the Innocents, December 28 – on the past, Herod's grim massacre of the young boys, the Innocents, in his kingdom; and throughout the play, the alternation of two kinds of language – the one hieratic, the other, freely formed, here often in the guise of rhyming ('leonine') hexameters. It is these last that, along with the classical reminiscences, indicate that such a play must have arisen in, and been first performed for, a highly cultivated milieu. If the Freising play is the culmination of the eleventh-century experiments, a fragment from Metz, copied soon after the year 1000, already shows the dramatist of a Magi play freely creating rhymed hexameters: there, in complete contrast to Freising, these reveal Herod as well as his messengers speaking with perfect courtliness.[12] To cite Drumbl once more, about the oldest versions of the *Play of the Star*:

> The composition with which the history of the theatre in the early Middle Ages takes its beginning shows itself as the product of the *schola*, and we do not know whether it was originally destined for liturgical use. Unexpectedly the study of the diffusion of the *Play of the Star* has taught us that what we can study of medieval theatre is not its origin, but only the moment at which it enters and becomes a part of 'culture'.[13]

---

[12] On the dating, see Drumbl p. 293, who also prints the text (from Y II 448).
[13] Drumbl p. 326.

Introduction xxiii

Perhaps we can pursue this suggestion a little further. The towns where the *Play of the Star* is attested naturally had cathedral schools, and one could suppose these plays to be in the first instance the products of such schools. Yet it may also be significant that some among these towns – notably Metz, Regensburg, Freising – had close relations with the *Imperium*, and in particular with the Ottonian dynasty.[14] And it is precisely at the Ottonian court, as we learn for instance from the *Vita* of Bruno of Cologne, brother of Otto the Great, that the plays of Terence were avidly read; it is there, too, that Hrotsvitha of Gandersheim found 'favourers' (*fautores*) for her own – Christian-Terentian – plays. At that same court, Claudia Villa recently showed, three young princesses – Adelheit, Hedwich and Matthilt – set their names at the close of a handsome Terence manuscript (today Oxford Bodley Auct. F. 6. 27), and described themselves as 'well-bred girls' (*curiales adolescentule*).[15] Does not all this prompt the surmise that the Ottonian Renaissance, which fostered Hrotsvitha's dialogues, also lay behind another impulse to unite classical and Christian language – as we see it in the *Stella* plays from the Metz fragment onwards? They may well be viewable in their beginnings as 'co-productions' of some of the major cathedral schools and an exceptionally cultivated imperial court; their first audiences may well have included not only scholars but the Ottonian princes and their entourage.

How, then, did all these dramatic possibilities, that we can richly document in the course of the eleventh century, develop? Rather than risk any new contribution to a general theory of origins, I should like to signal at least a small number of specific testimonies from earlier centuries that to my mind give interesting pointers.

It is among the many great merits of Drumbl's book that he empha-

---

[14] Thus for instance, at the very time in which the Metz Magi fragment was copied, the inhabitants of Metz address verses to Henry II, who succeeded Otto III in 1002, and who received his early education from Abraham, Bishop of Freising: Metz implores Henry's help against his brother-in-law, Bishop Thierry I, who had driven out the city's beloved Bishop Adalbero II (*Ursus nobilis*) in 1005. The verses are printed in MGH *Poetae Latini* v 494; cf. R. R. Bezzola, *Les origines et la formation de la littérature courtoise en Occident* I (Paris 1958) 269.

The existence of no fewer than eleven Magi plays in eleventh-century MSS indicates that the genre had developed in the previous century. When Otto the Great, in 961, 'celebrated the birth of the Lord in the city of Regensburg', as the contemporary chronicler, Adalbert of Magdeburg, relates (*Quellen zur Geschichte der Sächsischen Kaiserzeit*, ed. A. Bauer, R. Rau, Darmstadt 1977, p. 214), it seems to me altogether possible that he witnessed there a Magi play such as that preserved in fragmentary form in a Regensburg MS of c. 1050 (Y II 445; for the date and the St Emmeram provenance, cf. Drumbl p. 306).

[15] C. Villa, *La 'Lectura Terentii'* I (Padua 1984), Pl. 1 and pp. 99–120. On Hrotsvitha and the Ottonian court, see esp. *Women Writers*, ch. 3.

sised the importance for the history of medieval drama of an unusual passage in an early commentary on Horace's *Ars poetica*.[16] The manuscript, Vienna 223, is of the eleventh century, but scholars generally assign the commentary itself to the ninth.

In the *Ars poetica* (179–87) we read:

> On the stage, an event is either acted or related. What is taken in by hearing is less vivid to the spectator's mind than what is brought before his trusty eyes, what he can see for himself. Yet you will not put on the stage things that should be done behind the scenes, and you will keep from the spectator's eyes much that an eloquent tongue can readily narrate: don't let Medea slaughter her children before the audience, or let impious Atreus cook human flesh on the open stage, or let Procne be turned into a bird there, or Cadmus into a snake.[17]

The commentator writes:

> Every event is either acted on the stage, by the characters who have been brought on, and also related – as in the case of Herod's banquet (for there we have both: it includes acting as well as relating) – or again, the actors only relate certain events.[18]

This would suggest that the ninth-century commentator was familiar with a dramatic representation of Herod's banquet (*cena Herodis*) that featured both mimetic and narrative moments. (Theoretically we cannot rule out that this passage in the commentary is a later interpolation, nearer the time of the manuscript, but there is no positive reason

---

[16] Drumbl pp. 327 f.; cf. also I. Pagani, 'Il teatro in un commento altomedievale ad Orazio', in *Il contributo dei giullari alla drammaturgia italiana delle origini* (Centro di studi sul teatro medievale e rinascimentale, Atti del II Convegno di Studio, Rome 1979), pp. 51–61.

[17] *Aut agitur res in scaenis aut acta refertur.*
Segnius irritant animos demissa per aurem
quam quae sunt oculis subiecta fidelibus et quae
ipse sibi tradit spectator: non tamen intus
digna geri promes in scaenam, multaque tolles
ex oculis, quae mox narret facundia praesens;
ne pueros coram populo Medea trucidet,
aut humana palam coquat exta nefarius Atreus,
aut in avem Procne vertatur, Cadmus in anguem.

[18] Vienna, Öst. Nationalbibl. 223, fol. 7v:

Omnis res aut agitur in scenis, propter personas introductas, et refertur – ut in cena Herodis (nam ibi utrumque: <et agitur et> refertur) – aut acta tantum referunt.

The complete commentary was edited by J. Zechmeister, *Scholia Vindobonensia ad Horatii Artem Poeticam* (Vienna 1877), whose completion for sense (<*et agitur et*> *refertur*) I have adopted above, but whose edition also makes many unwarranted minor departures from the MS.

for supposing this.) I would interpret the allusion to the 'banquet' scene rather differently from Drumbl, who argues that the words *cena Herodis* are simply an orthographic variant of *scena Herodis*: that is, he would see this passage as alluding to Herod's 'scene' – namely, in an earlier milieu, to a scene in a Magi play such as we know from the eleventh century. It seems to me preferable, however, to take the manuscript reading, *cena*, at face value: the allusion in that case must be to a play about Herod's feast, featuring Salome's dance and the beheading of John the Baptist (perhaps it was this action which, with Horatian decorum, was related by an actor and not staged). My reasons for upholding the manuscript reading are: first, in Mark's gospel (6, 21), the day of Salome's dance is explicitly the day that Herod arranges a *cena* for his birthday. Second, it seems to me likely that it was Horace's mention of the grim feast of Atreus, in this very passage, that stimulated the commentator to recalling the equally grim feast of Herod. Third, it appears in a slightly later passage that the Vienna commentator distinguished carefully between *cena* and *scena*:[19] where Horace enjoins (192) that 'a fourth character should not try to intervene by speaking' (*nec quarta loqui persona laboret*), the commentator writes:

> A fourth character should not try to intervene in a single given scene (*scena*). Horace is not, however, denying that many characters may speak in the course of a comedy. But this [i.e. more than three speaking in one scene] may be compared to a banquet of questionable taste (*dubie cene*): for, just as there you hesitate what you would soonest take to eat, so in a sense here [one is bewildered] if there are several changes of the characters. What I call a scene (*scena*) comprises only one change of characters.[20]

Ninth-century art, moreover, includes quite an abundant iconography of Herod's banquet and Salome's dance: the *scena* of this *cena* was not rare in the manuscripts.[21] So it seems to me more probable that

---

[19] Even if in some passages the Vienna copyist has confused the two words (see the quotation in n.20 below).

[20] Fol. 8r:

Nec laboret quarta persona loqui in <s>cena una simplici. Non tamen negat quin in comedia loquantur multe persone, que comparari potest dubie cene, quia sicut ibi dubitas quid potissimum sumas, ita quodammodo hic cum sint varietates personarum. <S>cenam unam voco unam varietatem personarum.

Here the MS has *cęna* in the first line, *Cęnam* in the last. The copyist's use of *e caudata* is irregular and inconsistent throughout.

[21] Cf. *Lexikon der christlichen Ikonographie* VII (1974) 184. The depiction in the Liuthar Gospels (from Reichenau, c. 990) is particularly vivid and brilliant: cf. L. Grodecki, F. Mütherich et al., *Die Zeit der Ottonen* (Munich 1973), Pl.127. There is also a striking decree, by William, Bishop of Orléans, in 867, telling priests, if they attend a banquet, 'not

we have in the Vienna Horace commentary an early testimony to the existence of a Herod-play that was not a Magi play, one different in its plot from any that have come down to us. As with the lost *Ludus de sancta Katerina* that Geoffrey of St Albans directed before becoming a monk, it is a fascinating reminder of how much must have failed to survive, and of how much imaginative effort is needed to in some measure reconstruct the prehistory of medieval Latin drama.

An even more archaic testimony pointing in this direction can be found in a celebrated manuscript, 'The Book of Cerne' (Cambridge Univ. Libr. ʟʟ. i. 10), from the beginning of the ninth century, itself a copy of an eighth-century Northumbrian manuscript.[22] Here, after the Passion and Resurrection chapters from the four gospels, a collection of hymns, prayers and meditations, and the psalms for the liturgical hours, comes a unique composition which appears to have something of drama about it. It is a remarkable representation of the Harrowing of Hell. It is written in fifty-five lines, on three pages; some passages, written wholly in red or beginning in red, which are italicised below, can be interpreted either as moments of explanatory narrative or as stage-directions. I should like to try, by way of an abridged citation, to give some impression of the nature of the piece as a whole. –

> *This is the prayer of the countless crowd of holy ones*
> *who were kept in hell in captivity.*
> *With tearful voice and obsecration they implore the Saviour,*
> *saying, when he descends to the underworld:*
>> You have come, redeemer of the world:
>> you have come, you whom we awaited in longing, day by day,
>> you have come, you whom Law and prophets proclaimed would be here for us!
>> ... Release the dead who are hell's prisoners! ...
>
> *At once, at the Lord's command, all those of old who were just,*
> *... their chains unshackled,*
> *clasping the Lord Saviour's knees*
> *in humble supplication, were shouting with ineffable joy:*
>> Lord, you have smashed our chains –
>> in your presence we shall offer a sacrifice of praise ...
>
> *But Adam and Eve were still not released from their chains.*
> *Then Adam, with mournful and wretched voice, cried out to the Lord saying:*

to let dancing-girls perform disgraceful *ludi* in their presence, in the manner of the daughter of Herodias' (*Nec saltatrices in modum filiae Herodiadis coram se turpes facere ludos permittant*, PL 119, 739).

[22] Cf. most recently D. Dumville, in *Journal of Theological Studies* n.s. 23 (1972) 374–406. There is a diplomatic text by A. B. Kuypers, *The Book of Cerne* (Cambridge 1902).

> Have mercy on me God, have mercy on me in your great mercy ...
> I erred like a sheep that had been lost.
> Unshackle my chains, because your hands made me and formed me ...

Then, as the Lord shows mercy, Adam, unshackled,
clasping the knees of Jesus Christ:
> My soul, bless the Lord,
> and all my inner being, bless his holy name! ...

Still Eve persists in her weeping, saying:
> You are just, Lord, and your judgement is unswerving,
> for I suffer this deservedly,
> since, when I was in honour, I did not understand ...
> Do not turn the face of your mercy away from me,
> do not, in anger, shun your handmaid![23]

---

[23] Fols. 98v–99v:
> *Hoc est oratio innumerabilis sanctorum populi*
> *qui tenebantur in inferno captivitate.*
> *Lacrimabili voce et obsecratione salvatorem deposcunt,*
> *dicentes, quando ad inferos discendit:*

5 Advenisti, redemptor mundi:
   adveniti, quem desiderantes cotidie sperabamus,
   advenisti, quem nobis futurum lex nuntiaverat et prophetae!
   ... Solve defunctos captivos inferni! ...

   Statim, iubente domino, omnes antiqui iusti,
10 ... *resolutis vinculis,*
   domini salvatoris genibus obvoluti
   humili supplicatione, ineffabili gaudio clamantes:
       Disrupisti, domine, vincula nostra:
       tibi sacrificamus hostiam laudis...

15 *Adam autem et Eva adhuc non sunt desoluti de vinculis.*
   Tunc Adam lugubri ac miserabili voce clamabat ad dominum dicens:
       Miserere mei, deus, miserere mei in magna misericordia tua ...
       erravi sicut ovis quae perierat.
       Resolve vincula mea, quia manus tuae fecerunt me et plasmaverunt me ...

20 *Tunc, domino miserante, Adam e vinculis resolutus,*
   domini Iesu Christi genibus provolutus:
       Benedic, anima mea, dominum,
       et omnia interiora mea, nomen sanctum eius! ...

   Adhuc Eva persitit in fletu, dicens:
25   Iustus es, domine, et rectum iudicium tuum,
       quia merito haec patior,
       nam ego, cum in honore essem, non intellexi ...
       Ne avertas faciem misericordiae tuae a me,
       et ne declines in ira ab ancilla tua!

I follow the MS, adding my own line-divisions, line-numbering and punctuation. Lines 9–12 are in black in the MS (these instructions begin in red, a line earlier); similarly 15 is in red but 16, the continuation, in black. At 7, the MS has *lux*; before 22 (in red), *Tunc domino Iesu Christi provolutus*.

This is the last extant line of the Latin text; a later, Anglo-Saxon homily that is cognate with it indicates that there was a 'happy ending' for Eve also.

What was the function of this piece in the eighth century? David Dumville, who last discussed it in some detail, suggested that there are two basic ways of interpreting the red ink that distinguishes the narrative passages from the rest: 'The first is that this gives a clear indication of the part of a narrator in a liturgical work intended for performance by three soloists (narrator, Adam, Eve) and full choir (the *antiqui iusti*). Alternatively, the red-written sections are rubrics or "stage directions" in our earliest surviving example of Christian dramatic literature, written specifically to be acted.'[24]

Whether this text was performed more like an oratorio or more like a religious play of the later centuries is scarcely decidable on the evidence that remains. It seems to me significant, however, that the lines in red, too, are in *rhythmic* prose, like the chorale of the just and the laments of Adam and Eve. So on balance I think it probable that the 'stage-directions' were also sung – that here, as later at the opening of the Freising *Play of the Star*, a narrator had what might be called a directorial function.

Among the extant apocryphal texts about Christ's Harrowing there is none, to my knowledge, in which Adam and Eve must wait till the last and are brought to the brink of despair: in the well-known texts and iconography they are always the first to be released. Again we must reckon with lost traditions – perhaps with oral or popular ones, that were seldom written down.

The final testimony towards the development of medieval Latin drama that I wish to consider is the lyrical dialogue of Rachel, composed probably in the 860s, by the greatest Latin poet of the earlier Middle Ages: Notker the Stammerer, or Notker the Poet († 912),[25] who spent his life at the monastery of St Gall. Unique among the forty sequences[26] in Notker's cycle is the evocative, enigmatic dialogue between Rachel and the voice that tries to console her:

---

[24] Dumville (cit. n.22) p.381.
[25] See the outstanding study and edition by W. von den Steinen, *Notker der Dichter und seine geistige Welt* (2 vols., Berne 1948).
[26] The poetic-musical form of *Quid tu, virgo* is that of a classical sequence: apart from the prelude (1) and coda (7), each pair of half-strophes (2a–b, 3a–b...) has an identical syllabic and melodic structure, but one that is distinct from the other pairs. For an edition of the melody, see G. Vecchi, *Poesia latina medievale* (Parma 1958), Pl. IV.

1 Why do you weep,

2a maiden mother, 2b whose face gives
beautiful Rachel,   Jacob delight?

3a As if your older sister's 3b bleary-eyedness would attract him!

4a Mother, dry 4b How do you think your
your streaming eyes! tear-cracked cheeks become you?

5a 'Alas alas alas, 5b Since I am bereft
why do you accuse me of my son, the only one
of pouring out who took care of me
my tears in vain, in my poverty,

6a Who would not yield to enemies 6b and who would have helped
the paltry plot of ground his many blockish brothers
Jacob acquired for me, whom, sad to say, I bore?'

7 Is he to be mourned, then,
who has conquered heaven's kingdom,
and who with frequent prayers
helps his poor brothers
in God's sight?[27]

---

[27] London, BL Add. 19768, fols. 18v–19r (old foliation, pp. 30–1):

1 *Quid tu, virgo*

2a *mater, ploras,* 2b *cuius vultus*
Rachel formosa, *Iacob delectat?*

3a *Ceu sororis anniculæ* 3b *lippitudo eum iuvet!*

4a *Terge, mater,* 4b *Quam te decent*
fluentes oculos! *genarum rimulæ?*

5a *Heu, heu, heu,* 5b *cum sim orbata*
quid me incusatis fletus *nato, paupertatem meam*
incassum fudisse, *qui solus curaret,*

6a *qui non hostibus cederet* 6b *quique stolidis fratribus,*
angustos terminos *quos multos, pro dolor,*
quos mihi *extuli,*
Iacob adquisivit, *esset profuturus?*

7 *Numquid flendus est iste,*
qui regnum possedit celeste,
quique prece frequenti
m<i>seris fratribus
apud deum auxiliatur?

My text is based on an early MS, copied at the monastery of St Alban at Mainz between 936 and 962 (cf. von den Steinen, *Notker* II 157), taking account of the editions by von den Steinen (II 86) and D. Norberg, *Manuel pratique de latin médiéval* (Paris 1968), pp. 176 f., but with my own punctuation. The Mainz MS has *profuturis* at 6b 4, *mseris* at 7, 4.

xxx   Introduction

Notker's primary allusion, the one familiar to all medieval Christians, is to the close of Matthew's gospel account of the slaughter of the Innocents (2, 17-18): 'Then was fulfilled what was said by the prophet Jeremiah (31, 15): "A voice is heard in Rama, loudly lamenting and keening: it is Rachel lamenting her children, refusing to be comforted, because they are no more."' It was to Notker's dialogic recreation of this moment that two dramatists who portrayed the massacre of the Innocents responded by incorporating his sequence as the climax of their plays. In late-eleventh-century Freising, only a decade or two after the Magi play, an independent 'play of Rachel' (*Ordo Rachelis*) was composed, in which Rachel, emblematically every Jewish mother who lost her child at Herod's command, first sings a *planctus* in rhyming hexameters. Then, the stage directions say (Y II 120), 'A woman comforter (*consolatrix*) shall approach', who sings the first three strophes of Notker's composition. 'At this point', says the next rubric, 'the *consolatrix* shall wipe Rachel's eyes' – that is, as she sings strophe 4. The words 'Then Rachel shall rejoin' introduce Rachel's lament (sts. 5–6), and the play concludes with 'the *consolatrix* approaching her and uttering' the final strophe. In the twelfth-century Fleury playbook, similarly, Notker's words are given their scenic interpretation as the climax of a series of laments in rhymed hexameters. Here Rachel has 'two *consolatrices*' (Y II 112), who 'gather her up as she faints' in her sorrow, later 'lifting the children upright' (*esupinantes infantes*) as they sing the final strophe to comfort her.

The Fleury playwright makes explicit that Rachel is not consoled by what the *consolatrices* say: she 'flings herself on the children', singing: 'My spirit is anxious within me, my spirit is troubled within.' Then, says the rubric, 'the *consolatrices* shall lead Rachel away', and this play concludes with a further scene – the return of the holy family from Egypt.

To convey the whole poetic density of Notker's brief composition would require a full-length essay. He touches lightly upon other ranges of symbolic association: thus for instance 'maiden mother' can suggest both Mary and Ecclesia; Jacob, who looks askance at the bleary-eyed older sister, Leah, preferring the lovely Rachel (cf. Genesis 29), suggests the traditional figura of Christ favouring Ecclesia over Synagoga. Moreover, Notker destines his sequence liturgically not for the feast of the Innocents but for general use on feasts of martyrs. What matters to him most is the sense of human waste that hedges the death of any martyr, anyone who is young and brave and not like his 'blockish brothers'. Unlike the later dramatists, Notker does not introduce a *consolatrix*: the voice that tries to comfort Rachel is deliberately not identified. Nor are we given any hint as to whether Rachel is consoled by the voice's final intimation, that her child – the martyr – has reached heaven and can help mankind from there. On the contrary, each of the three segments of dialogue – the attempted consolation, Rachel's lament, the reply – is left open-ended: each ends not in an affirmation but a question. Notker has juxtaposed two conflicting ways of looking, two convictions that he does not try to reconcile. In his sequence, as in the play of the *Bridegroom*, we reach the borders of tragedy: we are left with the sense of a human, or divine, injustice that no theodicy can make palatable.

We know how Notker's lyrical dialogue was performed dramatically in eleventh-century Freising and twelfth-century Fleury; we do not know how it was first performed, at St Gall in the 860s. We may conjecture that there were two soloists, and that they sang the melancholy music unaccompanied. That they enacted two rôles, with gesture and mime, is not demonstrable and perhaps not even probable. Yet that this lyrical dialogue – alone, without the setting of an *Ordo Rachelis* – was not only a masterpiece in itself but a signpost to some of the profoundest possibilities in medieval drama, seems to me beyond doubt.

The evidence both of the eleventh-century plays and of the earlier testimonies is so many-sided that I believe it should rule out any monolithic answer to the question of the beginnings of medieval Latin drama. Even if one can still (all too often) hear the quasi-mechanical repetition of answers according to which, for instance, everything dramatic grows out of the liturgy, or every dialogue grows out of the *Quem quaeritis* tropes, does not the complexity and variety of the surviving early texts demand something less simple-minded, something pluralistic, by way of explanation? Not one of the texts mentioned till now can be seen as having developed out of a trope of the *Quem quaeritis* kind. That some of the texts were composed in a liturgical context is clear. It is evident in the case of Notker's *Rachel* sequence, and highly probable in that of the *Harrowing of Hell* in the Book of Cerne. Here, however, we perceive not only a piece destined for performance in church,[28] presumably during the Easter vigil, but also a human

---

[28] Clifford Flanigan's claims (in *Literary and Historical Perspectives of the Middle Ages*, ed. P. W. Cummins et al., Morgantown 1982, p. 231) – that the texts in the Book of Cerne constitute 'a collection of private devotions', and that the Harrowing of Hell composition 'presupposes no music' – are not supported by any evidence. The notion that the Harrowing of Hell piece was read and used simply as a private prayer would be hard to make plausible.

element, an empathy with the despairing Eve, which, like that of the *Sponsus* playwright with the Foolish Virgins, can have owed little to official theology; perhaps it owed something to lost popular-apocryphal traditions, perhaps it was the product of one unusual author's creative imagination.

Alongside these impulses, we have noted those from the world of popular hagiographic legend (for the Nicolas plays) and from the classicising, scholastic world (for the *Play of the Star*). Even if this latter world helps to account only for certain subsidiary aspects of the religious drama and its language, the guiding presences of Vergil and Sallust, Terence and Horace should not be altogether forgotten.

That I have here stressed the poetic and dramatic variety discernible in eleventh-century plays does not in any way imply that the twelfth-century dramatists were less inventive than their predecessors. In the diptych of Resurrection plays from Vic (V–VI), for instance, we can see particularly clearly the distinction between the words *in illo tempore*, of biblical or liturgical provenance, and the far longer passages where the dramatist's imagination runs free. It is he who creates the figure of the Merchant, and his conversation with the three Maries who come to visit him, as well as a long lyrical dialogue, in virtuoso form, between Mary Magdalen and an Angel; it is he who likewise recreates Mary Magdalen's failure to recognise the risen Christ in terms of a moment in the Song of Songs, to which he gives new lyrical form. After 87 verses that have no earlier parallel, this dramatist inserts the archaic exchanges of the trope *Quem quaeritis*; and into his unparalleled recognition-scene he inserts words from John's gospel. There is no way that his dramatic inventions can be derived from his traditional material. It is a juxtaposition of wholly diverse kinds of language and techniques, and a perfect illustration of how the large dramatic parts are, in Drumbl's expression, 'alien' to the brief liturgical–biblical ones.

A still more far-reaching creative freedom marks Hildegard of Bingen's *Play of the Virtues* (VIII, c. 1150). Her scenario is not tied to any biblical or hagiographic plot: it is freshly improvised, even if with some cognisance of Prudentius' poem depicting the battle of virtues and vices, his *Psychomachia* (c. 400). Yet where Prudentius' plot is didactically predictable, Hildegard's holds surprises till the close. At the same time she creates a wholly individual poetic and musical style, the concentrated language fusing allegory, figura and symbolism, and each melodic pattern expressing a distinct range of emotions.

The two other twelfth-century plays in the volume – the Beauvais *Play of Daniel* (VII, c. 1140) and the *Passion Play* from the Codex Buranus

(IX, c. 1180) – have certain features in common. Like Hildegard's *Ordo*, they are on a large scale, with a playing-time of over an hour. Unlike her play, each of these two is conceived in terms of two contrasting 'acts'; they are, moreover, furnished with fairly explicit stage-directions (see the introductory notes, pp. 110ff., 185ff.). It is only in plays from this period onwards that we are at times fortunate enough to have some detailed instructions about staging: we can reconstruct a great deal imaginatively, for instance, about how the Anglo-Norman *Mystère d'Adam* must have looked,[29] or the Bavarian *Ludus de Antichristo*;[30] somewhat less, though still a certain amount, about the two plays edited here. It would be possible in the case of other plays, where such instructions are lacking, to supply more or less plausible conjectural ones – as has been done in certain popular editions intended to adapt medieval plays for modern performance. However, it seemed preferable, for the purposes of this volume, not to intrude editorially: to concentrate on providing the most precise editions and translations possible, confining indications of action – when they are missing from the Latin text, but are nonetheless essential for understanding the text – to the explanatory notes.

Both *Daniel* and the *Passion Play* have moments in the vernacular, yet these are used in very different ways. In *Daniel* they are brief snatches only, elegant and witty flourishes in French, that carry little of the essential meaning of the play. The Beauvais author, like his predecessor at Freising, was composing essentially for a cultivated élite. As in the Freising *Play of the Star*, there are allusions to the revelries of the boys during a Feast of Fools, accompanied by adroit interpenetration of past and present. Yet the *Daniel* playwright also has something of Hildegard's capacity for playing with figural relationships, so that not only the Feast of Fools but also the New Testament adds a further dimension to the deeds of the Old Testament personages. We glimpse the Daniel of the past as *figura Christi*, as a deliverer in the Christian world and a source of joy in the world in which the players live.

In the *Passion Play*, the passages in German are extensive: they carry much of the dramatic meaning and are among the play's most exhilarating and moving creations. In this respect the *Carmina Burana* play is a fitting successor to the *Sponsus* from Limoges. The *Sponsus* is a play that the German-speaking dramatist is unlikely to have known; but

---

[29] *Le Mystère d'Adam (Ordo representacionis Ade)*, ed. P. Aebischer (Geneva–Paris 1964).
[30] *Ludus de Antichristo*, ed. G. Vollmann-Profe (2 vols., Göppingen 1981). On the fragment of a second MS of the play, the discovery of which was signalled in 1973, see above, p. x.

(whether or not at firsthand) he *had* come to know of the Merchant and his strophes from Vic. He adapted these to a very different Merchant scene, not with the three Maries but with Mary Magdalen and her girlfriends. This Mary is first exuberant in her celebration of human love and joy, and then penitent – as impulsive in her repentance as in her sensuality. As in his first act – that of the Magdalen – this playwright borrows from Vic, so in his second – that of Mary the mother – he draws two of her three *planctus* from French learned sources; the third *planctus*, in a simpler form and in a German of touching directness, seems to be his own.

Is he less inventive, then, than the earlier playwrights chosen for this volume? His powers of invention can be seen above all in the way he has formed the scenes of Mary Magdalen's love-life, and in the greater synthesis – the contrast and complementarity of the two Maries who are his heroines – that he has achieved. His taking over certain strophes from others is standard practice in medieval Latin drama, especially from the thirteenth century onwards; yet his total achievement is such that we may well, in his case, call to mind T. S. Eliot's shrewd distinction: 'Immature poets imitate; mature poets steal.'[31]

Each of the plays chosen for this volume thus presents some notable examples of dramatic innovation. Further details about this are given in the introductory notes to the individual plays. These include, for each play, a brief discussion of the style, meaning and structure, of the versification,[32] and of the manuscript in which the play is preserved.

[31] *Selected Essays* (London 1932), p. 206.
[32] In the analysis of Latin versification, I have used the simple but effective system of notation devised by Dag Norberg, in his *Introduction à l'étude de la versification latine médiévale* (Stockholm 1958). In medieval Latin rhythmic verse, what is of particular note is both the number of syllables in a line, or segment of a line, and the place of the principal stress. This will nearly always be on the second-last (paroxytone) or third-last (proparoxytone) syllable, either of the line or the segment. Norberg notes the paroxytone stresses as p, the proparoxytone ones as pp. He uses + to indicate caesuras. Thus for instance at the opening of the *Sponsus* (I), the verses

> Adest spónsus,   qui est Chrístus –   vigilate, vírgines! –
> pro advéntu   cuius gáudent   et gaudebunt hómines

would be noted as 4p + 4p + 7pp lines. The strophic form that occurs later in the *Sponsus*, as well as in the Hildesheim Nicolas plays (III–IV) and the Vic *Verses pascales* (V) –

> Cara míchi   pignora, fílie,
> opes pátris   inopis húnice
> et solámen   mee misérie,
> michi mésto   tandem consúlite!

would be noted as 4 x (4p + 6pp). On the other hand, if the stress-pattern in the first half of such lines as these is not wholly regular, as in the *Sponsus* –

A note on editorial practice

In the plays edited, all indications of speakers and all rubrics are reproduced from the manuscripts. Only those in angle brackets – < > – have been supplied editorially. These have been kept to an essential minium.

Italics are used: for rubrics; for non-Latin words; for refrains; and for emendations. The context should in each case make the reason for the italics clear.

In the texts, u and v are distinguished; proper names, and personifications, are capitalised; contractions in the manuscripts are expanded. Apart from this, manuscript spellings are not normalised. Unclassical forms that might cause readers difficulty, notwithstanding the facing translations, have an entry in the explanatory notes.

Capital letters are sometimes set at the beginnings of verses, especially if such capitals occur in the manuscript. But none of the manuscripts used for this volume is wholly consistent in this procedure, and I have at times alternated capitals with lower-case openings, particularly if this helped to indicate the articulation or movement of the poetry.

In the rubrics, the copyists often vary between future indicatives and present subjunctives. I have resisted the temptation to make such tenses consistent, and have on the whole rendered both constructions by availing myself of 'shall'.

Nos vírgines que ad vos vénimus
negligénter oleum fúdimus

– where the one line is 4pp + 6pp, but the next is 4p + 6pp, Norberg prefers to note the form simply as 4 + 6pp. This notation will be exemplified and, it is hoped, further clarified, in the brief sections on versification below.

Eleventh-century plays

I Sponsus
The Bridegroom, from Limoges

Style, meaning and structure

The *Sponsus*, composed probably c. 1050/60, is a decade or two older than the Freising *Officium stelle*, and some three decades older than the Nicolas plays from Hildesheim. Thus within the space of one generation we can observe original dramatic achievement of very diverse kinds in diverse regions – southern France, Bavaria, and Saxony. In the general introduction (pp. xx–xxii) I have tried to give a first impression of the human and symbolic vision of the *Sponsus* dramatist; this will be complemented here by some more detailed indications concerning style, meaning and structure in his play.

The prevalent scholarly opinion, of which the most distinguished exponent is D'Arco Silvio Avalle,[1] is that the vernacular parts of the *Sponsus* were composed later than the Latin ones – that they were added by another hand to the original, wholly Latin, text, as 'glosses' for the benefit of the unlearned in the audience. I know of no concrete evidence in support of this view, and should like to outline briefly an interpretation that, if valid, would support the contrary – that this play shows a fully unified imaginative conception, elaborated bilingually by a single author (naturally for the sake of an audience, or congregation, that included unlearned people as well as learned).

The five opening strophes (1–10) lack a rubric in the manuscript; but their wording shows that they must be sung by a human protagonist (not, as some have thought, by Angel Gabriel) – most probably by the personified Ecclesia, speaking to as well as for humanity. At the very start of her song comes one of the few moments of explicit allegory in the play: the bridegroom of the gospel parable (Matthew 25, 1–13) is identified with Christ. The command *vigilate* (1), with which the parable closes and which directly follows here, reminds that he who comes as loving bridegroom will also come as judge at the end of time. Similar commands to keep watch (*Videte, vigilate et orate ... Vigilate ergo ...*

---

[1] *Sponsus*, ed. D'A. S. Avalle (with Italian translation), music ed. R. Monterosso (Milan–Naples 1965).

Vigilate) run refrainlike through the passages in which Christ warns of the world's imminent end in Mark (13, 33–7) and Luke (12, 35–40).

Yet in their primary meaning these strophes evoke a joyous advent, not the final, terrifying one. Christ is coming as (in Paul's phrase) the second Adam, the liberator who by his harrowing of hell undoes the harm that the first Adam caused. The moment being celebrated and re-enacted is that of the Easter vigil: the crucifixion and redemption have just been accomplished, and the freeing of hell's captives, by the loving divine bridegroom of human souls, is about to occur.

The transition to the plot of the parable, in the vernacular strophes of Gabriel that now follow (11–27), is a subtle one, though the defective rubric (*Prudentes*, nothing more) makes what happens somewhat difficult to grasp. Ecclesia's message had been addressed to all the maidens – emblematically we could say, to every soul. They can either heed or ignore her: they can alertly welcome the liberating bridegroom, like the biblical ancestors in the harrowing, or else sleepily fail to respond to his arrival. As Avalle valuably noted, already St Jerome indicated an interpretation of the parable in Matthew along these lines, seeing the ten maidens as exemplifying 'solicitous and sluggish human beings: some are always watching for the Lord's coming, others, surrendering to sleep and to inertia, do not think the judgement will take place'.[2]

Though there is no rubric to inform us, the text implies that in the course of Ecclesia's strophes, or else between hers and Gabriel's, the Foolish Virgins have mimed their surrender to sleep and to inertia; thus when Gabriel sings he is left addressing the Wise Virgins only. This is one of the playwright's significant departures from the gospel text, where all ten Virgins fall asleep (Matthew 25, 5); that here only the Foolish do so is strongly suggested not only by the play-text but also by an explicit instruction at this point in the medieval German dramatisation of the parable: 'Then let all the Foolish have a feast, lie down, and fall asleep.'[3] The culpable sleepiness of these maidens – in effect, their torpid indifference to the message of the redemption – has another consequence of which the gospel text knows nothing: there they had not thought to take oil with them in order to greet the bridegroom; here in the play they come provided with oil, but spill it negligently – in their drowsiness, that is, they must handle or set down their lamps so carelessly that these topple over. This is a visual dramatic invention comparable to that of the artists who, in fourth-century catacomb

---

[2] Avalle p. 18; Jerome, *Adversus Jovinianum* II, PL 23, 322.
[3] *Das Eisenacher Zehnjungfrauenspiel* 116c, ed. M. Curschmann, I. Glier, *Deutsche Dichtung des Mittelalters* III (Munich 1981) 274–306, at p. 281.

paintings, depicted the Foolish Virgins holding overturned, extinguished lamps: these are ways of *showing* that the lamps are empty, more vivid than the simple forgetting to bring oil implied by the prose narrative.

There is, to my knowledge, no tradition of Gabriel addressing the Wise Virgins: this may be a contribution of the playwright's own, enriching his symbolic contexture. Gabriel is first and foremost the angel of the annunciation to Mary, and Mary, often identified with the beloved in the Song of Songs, is the celestial bride *par excellence*. All the maidens can, like her, become the loved consorts of the divine bridegroom, and Gabriel's declaration to them re-enacts that first annunciation. It should be noted that with his strophes the play has reached a later moment in time: Gabriel, like Ecclesia, alludes to events of Christ's life and death, but in his discourse the harrowing is already over, 'And he has risen! Scripture affirms it' (24). Gabriel concludes by warning that the second coming is near. His vernacular refrain – 'Don't fall asleep!' – is the counterpart to the eschatological *Vigilate* of the gospels.

After Gabriel's strophes, the Foolish Virgins wake up again, and notice that their lamps had capsized while they were sleeping (28ff.). They realise that, bereft of light, they will be unworthy to greet the bridegroom. There are many allegorical and moral interpretations of the oil they lack and for which they now ask their sisters[4] – but the playwright does not dwell on these; he concentrates wholly on the maidens' remorse and anxious pleas for help. The only hints of allegorical meaning in their strophes are 'this journey' (32) – which is both the bridal wake and the course of earthly life – and 'the place on high' (36) – both the 'high table' of the wedding-feast and the court of heaven. But what dominates the strophes of the Foolish Virgins is their vernacular refrain, *Dolentas, chaitivas, trop i avem dormit!* – one of the most haunting lines in all Provençal poetry – in which they express their never-ceasing self-accusation and naked despair.

Their wise sisters answer (43ff.), refusing them with a scornfulness that has no counterpart in the gospel narrative. Their tone and attitude cannot, in my view, be accounted for in terms of theology or allegories: it is a human and dramatic aporia. At most, we can relate it to Christ's frightening predictions that, as the end of the world draws near, 'A brother will deliver his brother to be killed, and a father his son, and children will rise up against their parents and afflict them with death ... but whoever endures to the end will be saved' (Mark 13, 12–13). In the

---

[4] Cf. Dronke 1986, pp. xx–xxiii.

moments before the second coming, that is, it is everyone for himself. Yet this playwright gives full emotional weight to the vulnerable victims, and shows the ugliness of the well-provided, who can 'endure to the end'. At the same time he faces the harshness of the parable without extenuation: he dwells on it unflinchingly, or even heightens it, establishing a keen tension between the human perspective and the divine. He lets the Foolish Virgins show a contrition and repentance for their negligence (54–6) that has no equivalent in the gospel, and that, if it were thought through in theological terms, would ensure their pardon. He then gives an even more contemptuous vernacular strophe to the Wise Virgins (63–5), who, as they see their sisters making their way to the Merchants, are determined to be rid of these importunate siblings once and for all.

The Merchants, who are barely mentioned in the parable, are presented with sympathy and deftly characterised by their speech. Their vernacular strophes carry the action forward (note that there is no Latin here which they could conceivably be 'glossing'). They are courteous and concerned, but recognise that they cannot help these maidens. Once more there is an elusive hint of allegory: speaking perhaps more wisely than they know, the Merchants tell that it is a divine, not human, aid which their customers need (67–70). Yet they are optimistic, and believe that this divine aid can be mediated by sisterly love, if they beseech their sisters once more 'in God's glorious name' (72). The Merchants' two utterances, taken together, suggest that here the dramatist is playing upon the well-known Patristic interpretation of the lamp-oil as the oil of charity. But the Foolish Virgins realise it is hopeless to beg yet again (75–9); their sense of doom is implicitly an indictment of the wise sisters, who – the Merchants are sure – could help them, but who will not. The dramatist here stretches the tension between the unfolding of human character and the inexorable unfolding of the parable to the limit.

In the dénouement, the transformation of loving bridegroom into pitiless judge is complete. The poetic language brings this out in a remarkable way. When the Foolish Virgins implore, 'let the gate be opened for us' (81), and are turned away by Christ, the wording suggests a dramatic reversal of the moment in the Song of Songs (5, 6) when the bride says:

> I opened the latch of my gate for my beloved,
> but he had turned away and gone past.

I would suggest further that the dramatist recalled the bride's anguished words in her next verse (5, 7):

> The guards who patrol the city found me,
> they struck me and wounded me . . .

and found there the hint for his own grim counterpart (which is not in the gospel) – the demons' seizing of the rejected Virgins. They, who began by ignoring the annunciation of the divine bridegroom, end by becoming the antitype of the divine bride.

Christ's Latin words, banishing them (83–4), are in the same metre as Ecclesia's at the opening, and were presumably sung to the same melody. In that opening Christ had been the joyously awaited *sponsus*; now he curses those who, through negligence or torpor, had not welcomed him then. His curse (85–7), in the vernacular, once more goes far beyond the gospel parable – it is freely improvised from Christ's threats about the judgement later in Matthew's chapter (25, 41): 'Depart from me, you accursed ones, into the eternal fire which was prepared for the devil and his angels.'

Here in the play devils appear on stage for the first time (as far as the extant records show) – not to languish in the fire themselves but to plunge the rejected maidens into it. If the performance took place in a church where, below the *aula* – the sanctuary that is an image of heaven – steps led down to the crypt, a lit brazier placed in the crypt could readily have evoked the eternal fire. But what of the original impact of this final moment, in which five maidens are hurled down? Did it bring the play to a fearsome, cathartic close, or bring relief from the dreadful final words by a visually grotesque, outrageous climax (comparable perhaps to that of *The Jew of Malta*), in which serious and comic aspects become inseparable? The dramatic texts and testimonies that survive from the eleventh century are too scant to provide a basis for a decision. Yet the nature of later vernacular dramatisations of this parable might speak for the second, serio-comic alternative.

The German play from Eisenach, composed around 1300, and the late medieval Dutch play are both on a much larger scale than the *Sponsus* (they comprise 576 and 812 verses respectively).[5] While in the German play the spoken dialogues are framed by sung Latin responsories, the Dutch is (except for one song) entirely in speech. In all three plays, the Foolish Virgins and not the Wise are dramatically in the foreground: in the *Sponsus* they are given seven strophes while the Wise have three, and the proportions in the later plays are even more striking: the longest scene in the German, the concluding one, consists wholly of the lamentations of the rejected Virgins (383–576); in the

---

[5] For the German play, see note 3 above; the Dutch, *Het Spel van de V vroede ende van de V dwaeze Maegden*, is ed. by M. Hoebeke (2nd edn, The Hague 1979).

Dutch, far the most elaborate scene is that of the Foolish Virgins' feast (83–308). It is artistically more exciting to depict vice than virtue, as William Blake well noted:

> The reason Milton wrote in fetters when he wrote of Angels & God, and at liberty when of Devils & Hell, is because he was a true Poet and of the Devil's party without knowing it.[6]

It is hardly too much to say that in the *Sponsus* the Foolish Virgins are not only the protagonists but the heroines: what the parable shows as the dread aspect of divine justice, the dramatist insists on showing also as a human tragedy, of five soft, helpless young women undone by 'the stamp of one defect'. He stands apart from the northern dramatists in that he does not moralise. They, by contrast, frankly present their plot as an *exemplum*, a cautionary tale – though the German also has moments of keen human poignancy. Yet it is noteworthy that, despite all the moralistic emphasis in the German and Dutch plays, the sins of the Foolish Virgins, on account of which they are condemned to hell's torment, are hardly more heinous than the oversleeping in the *Sponsus*. In the German, the first Virgin, sure that 'God does not want the sinner's death', and that there's time enough to appeal to his mercy later, summons her companions to play with ball and dominoes (*spelsteyne*): 'we want to take joy in our young life ... we want to get away from these old churchmice' (78–88). They 'dance with great delight' (100a), and they have a banquet, after which they drowse off – nothing worse. In the Dutch play, where the five have become personified vices, the first, Time-Wasting, invites her sisters – Recklessness, Pride, Vainglory, and Tittle-Tattle – to a feast of waffles and spiced *clareyt* (206–7). Their antics (such as Pride's insistence on being shown reverence by the rest) are comic but never sinister. Is the moral of these plays, then, that if you take pleasure in being young, playing, dancing and feasting, you will be damned? I suspect that the Germanic authors too treated the parable subversively: like the Provençal dramatist's human tragedy, their cautionary tales could call official notions of theodicy in question. Is it conceivable that – as in the Eisenach play – Mary could intercede with Christ for such lighthearted sinners, but be refused? Or – as in the Dutch – that girls could be banished from heaven for enjoying waffles and *clareyt*? Such thoughts must have crossed the minds of the authors, not just of the marquis of Eisenach (see above, p. xxi).

In these later texts, the language used by the devils is hedged by

---

[6] *The Marriage of Heaven and Hell*, ad init.

ironies: in the German, when Christ condemns the Foolish Virgins, Beelzebub comments: 'Jesus is making a good speech in our play! I'll have the chains fetched...'; Lucifer then complains about sinners having to go to hell – if the devils need sulphur and pitch in order to torment them, they themselves must live with that stench (305–6, 315 ff.). In the Dutch play, the devils speak in a low, often comic, register, full of exclamatory and abusive outbursts, and of black humour: one demon, Quadenraet (Evil Counsel), says to the maidens: 'We'll teach you how to sing us little songs, to which we'll dance and leap up joyously!' (749 f.).

We cannot simply extrapolate from these later texts to the dramatic mode of treating the demons at the close of the *Sponsus*. Yet just as in the eleventh-century Freising play (II) Herod already has something of the 'fearsome-comic' aspect which Robert Weimann defined brilliantly in the context of later, vernacular Herod plays,[7] it is at least possible that our earliest demons, like Herod, showed something of the ambiguous, apotropaic effect, the *furchtbare Komik*, on which later centuries relied in the dramatic portrayal of evil.

Language and versification

Avalle, in his detailed analysis of the language of the vernacular parts of the *Sponsus*, showed that the play was copied in the region of Limoges. He also showed that the Limousin copyist was transcribing a vernacular not of his own region but of southwestern France. This fact, along with the corruptness of the text as transmitted, does not in my view permit a *late* eleventh-century dating for the composition: if the oldest part of the Saint-Martial codex, which includes the *Sponsus*, was copied towards the end of the century, the play itself will probably have been composed a good generation earlier.

Avalle's musical collaborator, Raffaello Monterosso, allowed himself an unhappy comment on the play's language: for him the music is vastly superior to the text – the melodic phrases in their variety 'redeem the anonymous poet's colourless paraphrase of the gospel text from its generic inexpressiveness'.[1] The many departures from the gospel text signalled above hardly suggest a 'colourless paraphrase' – rather, a passionate, controversial rethinking of the biblical narrative. The expressiveness of the language deserves perhaps a further comment. I

---

[7] *Shakespeare und die Tradition des Volkstheaters* (Berlin 1967), pp. 111–21.
[1] Avalle p. 120.

believe the dramatist, while well-versed in Latin rhythmic composition, showed his most expressive artistry in his first language, in his vernacular lines. No one who has responded to the play is likely to forget its two compelling refrains: *Gaire no·i dormet! – Dolentas, chaitivas, trop i avem dormit!* A closer look at Gabriel's strophes (11–27) reveals their succinctness and force – how much the playwright can compress into these, with not a trace of didactic heaviness. The terse, irate vernacular strophe of the Prudentes (63–5), and the gentle solicitude revealed in the Merchants' strophes (67–74), vividly establish character by way of speech; the final curse of Christ (85–7) forms a true climax, of a savageness unmatched in the biblical Latin of the parable.

The author uses basically two verse-forms. Ecclesia (1–10) and Christ in his Latin words (83–4) are given couplets of the form 4p + 4p + 7pp, one of the types of rhythmic imitation of the classical trochaic *septenarius* (cf. Norberg p. 114). The remaining Latin strophes consist of verses of the type 4 + 6pp, which is first found in the refrains of late antique and Merovingian hymns (cf. Norberg p. 152). Strophes composed wholly of 4 + 6pp verses, with or without refrain, appear to become widespread only in the eleventh century, and those in the *Sponsus* may be among the earliest extant. Avalle (p. 47) observes that the conjunction of strophes of 4p + 4p + 7pp lines with a refrain that is 4 + 6pp can be found in a famous late antique hymn on the day of judgement, *Apparebit / repentina / dies magna domini* ('Suddenly will appear the great day of the Lord'), which has the refrain *In tremendo / die iudicii* ('On the dread judgement-day'), and that it may well have been this hymn that prompted the dramatist's choice of his two measures for a play with an eschatological theme.

The vernacular verses are generally in the form 4 + 6: that is, they are a counterpart to the Latin 4 + 6pp lines, but without their heavier proparoxytone stress near the close. There are also some irregularities: the first half of the Provençal line may have five syllables (cf. 13, 16) or three (cf. 87), the second half may have seven (cf. 85–7). Gabriel's refrain has six syllables,[2] that of the Fatue has twelve (6 + 6).

The strophic use of 4 + 6pp verses is seen again in Hildesheim (III–IV) and Vic (V), and once more, briefly, in the *Carmina Burana* Passion-play (IX). In the Eisenach play of the ten maidens come some Latin lines (168a) which the editors print as prose, as if they were one of the liturgical responsories, but which in fact form a non-liturgical strophe,

---

[2] It seems a little strained to call Gabriel's strophes 'pseudo-Sapphic' (Avalle p. 48), particularly since one of these strophes has four verses, not three, before the refrain.

closely related by its wording and refrain to those from Vic (see below p. 92). The second Foolish Virgin sings:

> Sed eamus   oleum emere,
> preter quod nil   possumus agere.
> Qui caret hoc,   carebit glorie.

And the others reply with the refrain:

> *Heu, quantus est noster dolor!*[3]

As Latin strophes are not found elsewhere in the Eisenach play, this one has probably been incorporated from another, earlier Latin play of the ten maidens which has not survived (or perhaps, has not yet been traced in MSS).

The manuscript

The manuscript which today is Paris Bibliothèque Nationale lat. 1139 consists of several originally separate collections of liturgical and paraliturgical compositions. These were assembled at Saint-Martial de Limoges, and belonged to the abbey at least from 1265. The oldest part of the codex was written in the last years of the eleventh century (thus Guy de Poerck,[1] and Charles Samaran, cited by Avalle pp. 10 f.). It consists of two sections, written by two distinct principal hands. Fols. 32r–79v contain verses, tropes, and plays, fols. 80r–118r chiefly sequences and Kyries. Over the great majority of the texts there is Aquitanian neumatic notation. Apart from the *Sponsus*, there is a brief play of the Innocents on fols. 32v–33r, and the earliest extant play of the Prophets on fols. 55v–58r.

The fullest descriptive account of the contents of the manuscript is still that of Spanke (1931).[2] In the section fols. 32r–79v, in which one unsigned fascicule, a kind of appendix, has been displaced,[3] the language of the vernacular compositions (which include the Annunciation-lyric with dialogue, *Mei amic e mei fiel* – see above, p. xxi)

---

[3] 'But let us go to buy the oil – there's nothing else we can do. Whoever lacks this oil will lack (heaven's) glory. *Alas, how great is our grief!*' Similarly at 236a there comes a clearly non-liturgical Latin rhyming quatrain (though *regni* in the fourth verse is hypermetric), that presumably likewise stems from the lost Latin play of the ten maidens postulated above.
[1] *Scriptorium* 23 (1969) 298–312 (the best codicological study of the MS).
[2] 'St Martial-Studien I', repr. in Hans Spanke, *Studien zur lateinischen und romanischen Lyrik des Mittelalters* (Hildesheim 1983), at pp. 6–23.
[3] Cf. Sarah Fuller, *Musica Disciplina* 33 (1979) 7–10.

shows that the scribe is from the northern Limousin. That is, there is a strong presumption that he was working at Saint-Martial itself, or else at a convent not far away (cf. Avalle pp. 10, 27). The music of the *Sponsus* survives with the text, except for the final section (80–7 in the edition below).

53r **Sponsus**

<Ecclesia>
53v Adest sponsus, /   qui est Christus –   vigilate, virgines! –
pro adventu   cuius gaudent   et gaudebunt homines.

Venit enim   liberare   gentium origines,
quas per primam   sibi matrem   subiugarunt demones.

5   Hic est Adam   qui secundus   per propheta dicitur,
per quem scelus   primi Ade   a nobis diluitur.

Hic pependit   ut celesti   patrie nos redderet
ac de parte   inimici   liberos nos traheret.

Venit sponsus,   qui nostrorum   scelerum piacula
10 morte lavit   atque crucis   sustulit patibula.

<Gabriel>
   <ad> Prudentes
Oiet, virgines,   aiso que vos dirum:
aiseet presen   que vos comandarum –
atendet un espos,   Iesu salvaire a nom:
54r   Gaire no·i / dormet!

15 Aisel espos   que vos hor atendet
venit en terra   per los vostres pechet,

All who have studied the *Sponsus* agree there are flaws in the text as it has come down to us. The assessment of those flaws, and of where to emend, regularise or normalise, is particularly delicate: each problematic word or spelling, each possible lacuna, must be judged afresh, and each editor will settle for different compromises. Avalle's edition, in which these questions are meticulously discussed, goes a long way towards eliminating unnecessary changes: this is one of the many ways it supersedes earlier editions, including those of L. P. Thomas (1951) and Karl Young (Y II 362–4). The text offered above is much indebted to Avalle's insights; I have, however, occasionally retained a MS reading he rejected (e.g. 55 *que*), or judged that an emendation was, after all, needed, or at least helpful: e.g. even if retaining the verb-form *de* for *det* (58) is philologically defensible (cf. Avalle pp. 57 f.), to print *de*<t> seems to me an aid to understanding.

    F. Bossy, 'Les vierges sages et les vierges folles, drame liturgique en parlange (sic) du XIe siècle', *Aguiaine, Revue de recherches ethnographiques* XIV, 5 (1980) 344–65, does not print a variant version or independent treatment of the theme of this play: his is simply another edition of the *Sponsus*, with reference to older editions but without cognisance of Avalle 1965. I am indebted to Edouard Jeauneau for procuring for me a photocopy of Bossy's work.

P: Paris, BN lat. 1139, fols. 53r–55v

A: *Sponsus*, ed. D'A. S. Avalle, music ed. R. Monterosso (Milan–Naples 1965)

10/11 PRUDENTES (Gabriel ad *om*.) P
12 aiseet] aise& P *The reading is not wholly certain, and A inclines to read* aisex, *emending to* Eiset

The Bridegroom

Ecclesia
Here is the bridegroom, who is Christ – keep watch, maidens! –
he in whose advent mankind takes joy and will take joy.

For he is coming to free the ancestors
over whom, through the first mother, the demons seized power.

5 This is the Adam whom the prophet called second,
through whom the first Adam's guilt is washed away from us.

He hung to restore us to our heavenly home,
and to pull us – free – away from the Fiend's side.

The bridegroom is coming, who has washed the stains of our guilt
10 by his death, and has endured the gallows of the cross.

Gabriel
    to the Wise
Listen, maidens, to what we shall tell you:
go forth at once when we command you to –
attend a bridegroom (Saviour Jesus is his name):
    Don't fall asleep!

15 That bridegroom whom you shall now attend
came on earth for your sins' sake,

16   *Sponsus*

            de la virgine   en Betleem fo net,
            e flum Iorda   lavet e bateet.
                    Gaire <no·i dormet!>

20   Eu fu batut,   gablet e laideniet,
     sus e la crot   batut e claufiget,
     *e*u monumen   desoentre pauset.
                    Gaire <no·i dormet!>

     E resors es!   la scriptura o dii.
25   Gabriels soi,   eu <m'a> trames aici;
     atendet lo,   que ia venra praici!
                    Gaire <no·i dormet!>

     Fatue
     Nos virgines   que ad vos venimus
     negligenter   oleum fudimus:
30   ad vos orare,   sorores, cupimus
     ut *ad* illas   quibus nos credimus –
          dolentas, chaitivas, trop i avem dormit!

54v Nos co/mites   huius itineris
     et sorores   eiusdem generis;
35   quamvis male   contigit miseris
     potestis nos   reddere superis!
               Do<lentas, chaitivas, trop i avem dormit!>

     Partimini   lumen lampadibus,
     pie sitis   insipientibus,
40   pulse ne nos   simus a foribus
     cum vos sponsus   vocet in sedibus.
               Dole<ntas, chaitivas, trop i avem dormit!>

     Prudentes
     Nos precari,   precamur, amplius
     desinite,   sorores, otius –
45   vobis enim   nil erit melius
     dare preces   pro hoc ulterius!

---

[18] buteet P (*A* reads bateet, *assuming an archaic Merovingian open form of* a)
[21] batut] *A's emendation to* pendut (*'hanged') seems unnecessary*
[22] Deu P (*em.* A)
[25] m'a *om.* P (*suppl.* A)
[29] fundimus P (*em.* A)
[31] et PA

of the maiden in Bethlehem was he born,
in the river Jordan washed and baptised –
   Don't fall asleep!

20 He was beaten, slandered and cursed,
high on the cross beaten and fixed with nails,
in the tomb he was then placed.
   Don't fall asleep!

And he has risen! Scripture affirms it.
25 I am Gabriel: he has sent me here.
Watch for him, for now he will soon be near!
   Don't fall asleep!

The Foolish
We maidens who are approaching you
have spilt our oil carelessly:
30 sisters, we want to appeal to you
as the ones in whom we trust –
   we, wretched in our grief, have slept too long!

We are your companions on this journey
and sisters of the same blood;
35 though things have turned out badly for us, pitiful,
you can restore us to the place on high!
   We, wretched in our grief, have slept too long!

Share with us the light from your lamps,
take pity on us – we have been foolish –
40 lest we be driven from the gates
when the bridegroom calls you to your places.
   We, wretched in our grief, have slept too long!

The Wise
We beseech you, do not beseech us
any longer, sisters, from now on –
45 for you shall fare none the better
by begging for this more!

<Fatue>
    Dolentas, <chaitivas, trop i avem dormit!>

<Prudentes>
Ac ite nunc,   ite celeriter,
ac vendentes   rogate dulciter
50 ut oleum   vestris lampadibus
dent equidem   vobis inertibus!
<Fatue>
    Do<lentas, chaitivas, trop i avem dormit!>

A misere,   nos hic quid facimus?
55r vigilare   numquid po/tuimus?
55 hunc laborem   que nunc perferimus,
nobis nosmed   <illum> contulimus!
    Dol<entas, chaitivas, trop i avem dormit!>

Et de<t> nobis   mercator otius
quas habeat   merces, quas sotius:
60 oleum nunc   querere venimus
negligenter   quod nosme<d> fudimus.
    Dol<entas, chaitivas, trop i avem dormit!>

<Prudentes>
De nostr'oli   queret nos a doner? –
no·n auret pont: alet en achapter
65 deus merchaans   que lai veet ester!
<Fatue>
    Dol<entas, chaitivas, trop i avem dormit!>

Mercatores
Domnas gentils,   no vos covent ester
ni loiamen   aici a demorer:
cosel queret,   no·u vos poem doner –
70 queret lo Deu,   chi vos pot coseler.

---

[55] que] A's emendation to quem seems unnecessary. The corruption is more likely to be in 56, which, without the illum I have supplied, would be the only hypometric Latin verse in the play.
[56] nosmed contulimus PA
[58] de<t>] de PA
[61] nosme PA (but cf. 56)   fundimus P (em. A)

The Foolish
> We, wretched in our grief, have slept too long!

The Wise
But go now, go quickly
and ask the vendors gently
50 to give some oil for your lamps –
as indeed they should – to you sluggards!
The Foolish
> We, wretched in our grief, have slept too long!

Ah what are we doing here, in our pitiful state?
Could we not, after all, have stayed awake?
55 We who now endure this anguish,
we ourselves have brought it on ourselves!
> We, wretched in our grief, have slept too long!

If only the merchant will give us quickly
the goods he has, and his colleague too:
60 now we are on our way to seek the oil
that we ourselves spilt carelessly.
> We, wretched in our grief, have slept too long!

The Wise
You're asking us to give up some of *our* oil?
You shall have none: go and buy some
65 from the merchants you see standing there!
The Foolish
> We, wretched in our grief, have slept too long!

The Merchants
Gentle ladies, it's not right that you should stand
or wait here a long time:
you are seeking aid we cannot give you –
70 seek it of God, who can come to your aid.

20   *Sponsus*

    Alet areir   a vostras sinc seros
    e preiat las,   per Deu lo glorios,
    de oleo   fasen socors a vos:
55v faites o tost,   que ia venra l'espos! /

    Fa<tue>
75 A misere,   nos ad quid venimus?
    nil est enim   illut quod querimus –
    fatatum est,   et nos videbimus,
    ad nuptias   numquam intrabimus!
        Dol<entas, chaitivas, trop i avem dormit!>

        Modo veniat sponsus.

80 Audi, sponse,   voces plangentium,
    aperire   fac nobis ostium
    cum sotiis: prebe remedium!

    Christus
    Amen dico,   vos ignosco,   nam caretis lumine,
    quod qui per*d*unt   procul pergunt   huius aule l*i*mine.

85 Alet, chaitiv*a*s,   alet, malaüreas:
    a tot iors mais   vos so penas liureas!
    en efern   ora seret meneias!

        Modo accipiant eas demones
        et precipitentur in infernum.

[79/80] modo veniat sponsus *in margin* P, *but also (wrongly) above 83 in text*
[84] perdunt] pergunt P (*em.* A)   limine] lumine (*em.* A)
[85] chaitiuns (?) P

Go back again to your five sisters
and beg them, in God's glorious name,
to bring you relief from their own oil:
do it soon, for now the bridegroom will come!

The Foolish
75 Ah to what end have we come, in our pitiful state,
since our seeking is of no avail?
It is fated, and we shall see it —
we shall never go in to the wedding-feast!
> *We, wretched in our grief, have slept too long!*

> *Now let the bridegroom arrive.*

80 Oh bridegroom, hear our voices filled with weeping,
let the gate be opened for us
as for our companions: grant us this remedy!

Christ
Amen I say, I know you not, for you have no light:
those who lose it must go far from the threshold of this court.
85 Away with you, wretches, away with you, luckless ones:
for ever more suffering shall be your lot!
Into hell you shall now be led!

> *Now let demons take them,*
> *and let them be hurled into hell.*

Explanatory notes

1   MS indications of who is singing are somewhat erratic. While 11–27 are sung by Gabriel (cf. 25), the first person plural forms in 1–10 (6 *nobis*, 7–8 *nos*, 9 *nostrorum*) show that these are sung by one who is human and speaks on behalf of humanity. An only slightly later fresco from Pedret (now in the Museum of Catalan Art, Barcelona), depicting the personified Ecclesia with the five Prudentes, suggests that she is the singer here (though other possibilities – e.g. a chorus of redeemed souls – cannot be excluded). The relevance of the Pedret fresco was first noted in the edn of L. P. Thomas, *Le 'Sponsus'* (Paris 1951), p. 45.

5   Cf. Paul, I Corinthians 15, 45–7.

10/11   As the sense shows that 11–27 are sung to, not by, the Prudentes, the rubric should probably read '<Gabriel to> the Wise': that is, while 1–10 were addressed to both the Wise and the Foolish Virgins, the Foolish have meanwhile fallen asleep.

15   Editors have been divided over whether this verse begins the second vernacular strophe or should be considered, along with 'Don't fall asleep!', as part of the refrain. The alternation of three- and four-line strophes throughout the play speaks in favour of the first solution.

27/8   After Gabriel has concluded, the Foolish Virgins wake up again and see that during their sleep their lamps have overturned.

47   (also 52, 66) While the use of the refrain by the Fatue is clear at 32, 37, 42, 57, and 62, scholars have disagreed about the interpretation at 47, 52, and 66, after speeches of the Prudentes. Some have emended *avem* to *avet* on these three occasions, making the Prudentes accuse the Fatue ('You grieving, wretched ones have slept too long!'); others have argued that the Prudentes too can accuse themselves of not having been perfectly watchful. I would venture a different suggestion. It is important to remember that in the MS there is no rubric whatever between 43 and 66. This means that, since the copyist was careless about indicating who was to sing, the decisions must here be made editorially. The sense shows that 43–6, 48–51, and 63–5 must be assigned to the Prudentes, and 53–62 to the Fatue. But is there any reason not to assign the refrain at 47, 52 and 66 to the Fatue as well? That is, they would renew their plangent outburst each time the Prudentes reproach and reject them. This seems the most effective solution dramatically, and eliminates the need for emendation.

48–9   ite... vendentes] Cf. Matthew 25, 9.

78	ad nuptias... intrabimus] Cf. Mathew 25, 10.
81	Cf. esp. Song of Songs 5, 6.
83	Amen dico, vos ignosco] Cf. Matthew 25, 12.
84	'this court': *aula* can mean both the sanctuary of the church where the play is performed and, symbolically, the court of heaven.

II *Officium stelle*
The Play of the Star, from Freising

The medieval Latin plays that portray the journey of the Magi are known by various names, including 'The Play of the Star' (*Ordo stelle, Officium stelle*), 'The Play of the Three Kings' (*Officium regum trium*), and 'The Play showing Herod' (*Ordo ad representandum Herodem*). There are no fewer than eleven such Magi plays preserved in eleventh-century manuscripts (cf. Drumbl p. 306). They stem from France (the earliest extant, from Metz, copied soon after the year 1000), Germany (Lorsch, Regensburg, Freising), Belgium (Malmédy), Austria (Münsterschwarzach), and Hungary (Györ). They range from brief fragments to the ambitiously conceived and executed play from Freising – nearly 140 lines in the present edition – that marks the culmination of the diverse eleventh-century experiments in this genre. The playwright builds on the texts of his predecessors and integrates some of their lines in his own composition. Yet in verbal and dramatic inventiveness, subtlety of allusion and symbolic power, he goes beyond them.

This has not been apparent hitherto, for two reasons. One is that Young printed the Freising play after five twelfth- and thirteenth-century plays on the same theme – whose authors were often only too happy to take over the Freising dramatist's innovations. Young himself repeatedly refers to these as twelfth-century innovations – that they in fact belong to Freising c. 1070, and are due to the artistry of one particularly gifted playwright, does not emerge from his book. The other reason is that, despite some fine work towards recovering the badly erased Freising text, Young printed it with many passages of dots, giving the impression that it remained hopelessly fragmentary, in a state such that it could hardly be evaluated as a play at all. In what follows the Freising play is given complete.

Style, meaning and structure

The Freising Magi play is notable for the variety of its techniques. The opening instructions (1–6) are sung, possibly by a soloist expositor, or, more probably, by the choir that intervenes to sing at several later

moments in the play, beginning with the *Gloria* of the angelic host
(11–12). The music over the lines of instruction shows beyond doubt
that these were intended for singing. The hortative subjunctives ('The
King shall mount...') indicate that the actions mentioned in these lines
were not conceived as mere reportage but were composed to be accompanied by mime.

The rôle of such moments, of instruction or narration, to clarify or
provide a background for dialogue, is perhaps most familiar from
modern 'epic theatre'. Yet it was likewise an accepted, and not
infrequent, medieval technique. The author of the secular *'comedia'*,
Ovidius puellarum (c. 1080), a close contemporary of the Freising
dramatist and quite possibly also from south-western Germany (cf.
Dronke 1991, chs. II and IV), writes a piece that is three quarters
dialogue and one quarter narrative. In the vernacular, the Anglo-
Norman *La Seinte Resureccion* (c. 1150) is the first extant play to have a
rôle for a narrator, who in his verses describes the setting of the scenes
and marks the transitions between them.

I have divided the Freising play into twelve scenes, to help show its
articulation. The first introduces Herod and the prospect of his tyranny.
Scene II brings us to the Angel and the Shepherds, Scene III to the Magi
arriving in Jerusalem; with Scene IV we are back at Herod's court. The
playwright shapes his brief episodes skilfully. If the Freising play was, as
seems wholly probable, performed in the cathedral, the scenic arrangement will have been as follows. Before the high altar, in the East
(symbolically the region where 'God doth live'), there would be the crib,
with the attendant midwives and the divine child. But the Magi, witnesses to that child, are also 'from the East' (*Eoi*); they will thus have
entered from the choir, near the altar. The North (symbolically Lucifer's
region) would be the aptest location for Herod's palace. He has a throne
(*solium*), on a raised platform, that is approached by steps (he must
'ascend' in order to mount his throne). The Magi make their way to
Herod's palace via 'the citizens of Jerusalem' – i.e. they journey from the
choir, towards the north transept, passing through the audience in the
nave, who become, momentarily, the citizens whom they address. We
may, finally, assume another platform, for the Shepherds, near the
south transept, from where they make their way to the crib (at the close
of Scene II); thus, when they return (in Scene X), their path crosses that
of the Magi, approaching the crib from Herod's side, from the north
transept.

For the Angel and the Shepherds (II), the dramatist uses hieratic
words, words *in illo tempore*: two antiphons, followed by the *Gloria*. So,

too, for the Magi's first appearance (III): their opening words about the star and their resolve (13–18) are unvarying from play to play. These are here followed by their question to the citizens (19–23), which is not part of this older tradition of dialogue, but is again couched in high liturgical language.

At Herod's court things are very different. There, in a profane realm, the dramatist gives free rein to his invention: it is a realm where speech can turn into classical and 'leonine' (rhyming) hexameters, where the author places classical echoes with knowing wit, where he portrays arrogance and rage and attempted cunning ironically, at moments even comically. His first irony lies in a juxtaposition: the Magi have just asked about the newborn *rex Iudeorum* (21); the Messenger who runs to Herod with news of their arrival greets him as *rex Iudeorum* (24). The expression – a key one in the play – is loaded.

We see how this dramatist can define his characters through the way they speak: he shows the Messenger's disdain (*tres viri ignoti ... regem quendam queritantes*, 26–8) and Herod's impatient, overweening nature (*iam iam citus, impero*, 29) from the start.

The next scenes (V–IX) move between a vestibule or antechamber of the palace – from which the Magi are summoned to the King and to which they are sent back – and Herod's throne-room. The Messenger (30–2) interrogates the Magi in words that echo the *Aeneid*, where the Arcadian Prince Pallas questions the newly arrived Aeneas and his men (*Aen.* VIII 112–14). The contrast between Aeneas' welcome in King Evander's palace and that of the Magi in Herod's, in the scenes that follow, has been carefully planned, and some at least of the audience will have known their *Aeneid* well enough to appreciate the implied contrast.

In Scene VI, a Shieldbearer (later to be revealed as an evil counsellor) offers the King a solemn formulaic greeting (37). Herod at once turns to his Messenger: again his impatience emerges in the parenthetic, half-threatening *vives* ('as you shall live', 38), and in the way he cuts short the Messenger's news: it is not just 'unknown men' but kings who have come to call on him.

Scene VII opens with the Messenger's pompous, discourteous hexameter to the Magi: he apes his master in insisting that everyone should hurry to do his bidding (41). In this scene and the next, the Freising dramatist then takes over a shaping of dialogue that had been previously established: Herod's first questioning of the Magi ends with their declaration of their three symbolic gifts (*mystica munera*) – gold, frankincense and myrrh – which already Irenaeus in the second century had explicitly interpreted as prophetic tokens of recognition, respectively, of Christ's kingship, priesthood–godhead, and mortality (cf. Y II 32).

Thereupon the Magi are dismissed: we know this because they are called back at the end of the next scene (90). The King (59) asks his knights to fetch the *scribe* ('scribes' in the technical sense of qualified interpreters of the Law). They, when questioned, point to Micah's prophecy (65–9) – the words themselves (70–2) are sung as an antiphon, presumably by the choir. Then the dramatist again invents freely (73–80): he gives Herod two leonine hexameters, the first sarcastic about the prophet, the second filled with fury at the *scribe* themselves. He hurls down their book as he dismisses them, and asks advice from his nobles instead. The Shieldbearer, speaking on their behalf (76–9), suggests giving gifts to the Magi now, so as to obtain more information from them later (his last words, 'that you too may know what to adore', can hardly be other than ironic). Herod asks him to summon the Magi once more, in a verse – 'Vassal, bring the foreign tyrants back – be quick about it!' – that epitomises his arrogance and short temper, and compels us to see these in a comic as well as a grim light.

The King, it would seem from the interview that follows (IX), has not taken his Shieldbearer's advice about mollifying the Magi, in order to make sure that they return. There is no more mention of the gifts he had recommended (77): Herod, as this dramatist shows him, seems intent only on discountenancing his royal guests by the insolence of tone of his questions. The first Magus he still addresses in a hexameter, albeit a discourteous one; the second and third Magus get only the most brusque form of address imaginable. Serenely they ignore this: each answers Herod in a majestic hexameter; their replies bring out more and more the contrast between these great kings and the petty tyrant who assumes that, as kings, they too must be *tyranni* by nature (82–7). The scene, so individually developed, closes, however, with the hallowed words adapted from Matthew, as Herod commands the Magi to find out more and then report back to him (88–90).

Most of the dialogue in the next two scenes (X–XI) had already been shaped when the Freising dramatist wrote. Yet he seems to be the first to imagine a meeting and dialogue between the Shepherds returning from the crib and the Magi approaching it (93–6) . This 'charming invention', as Young calls it (II 59), is not first attested in twelfth-century Sicily, as he suggests, but in eleventh-century Freising. The question to the Magi (97–9), here sung by 'an Angel, from afar' (perhaps from an upper gallery above the choir), is one that had been given to the

Midwives in other eleventh-century Magi plays; here the Midwives are left with no more than a brief summons to the Kings (104–6). The reasons for this diminution of their rôle can only be surmised.[1]

When the Magi have offered their symbolic gifts and been warned by the Angel, returning to the East avoiding Herod's palace in the North (107–17),[2] the finale (XII) is once more set in Herod's court and once more provides the Freising dramatist ample scope for his inventive powers. As before (30–2) he had adapted a scene from the *Aeneid*, so now he presents Herod, raging that he has been mocked and outwitted by the Magi, in terms of the Roman conspirator Catiline, whose story was widely known from Sallust. Catiline, accused of treason in the Roman Senate, stormed out, saying 'Since I am hounded by enemies on every side, I'll quench my blaze of rage by a cataclysm!' Again some at least of the audience will have recalled the original context of the line (119) and seen the point of the allusion. (The words, which this playwright was the first to use, became almost classic in later Magi plays.) It is the Shieldbearer who now eggs Herod on to murder the children (120–3), and Herod after giving the order (124), elaborates it more sinisterly in words adapted from the early Christian hymn on the Innocents by Prudentius.

The close of the play (129–36), unparalleled in either earlier or later Magi plays,[3] is a brilliant piece of symbolic invention. As soon as the children, the Innocents, have been killed by the Shieldbearer and his men, there comes the instruction 'Let the boys in the King's procession sing these verses.' The hexameters that follow are a triumphant paean.

---

[1] The account of Christ's birth in the second-century *Protoevangelium Iacobi*, which in the fifth century was adapted in the widely diffused Latin 'Gospel of pseudo-Matthew', mentions two midwives, Zelomi and Salome, whom Joseph sends in to Mary (ps.-Matt. XIII 3–5; cf. *Protoev.* XIX–XX). Salome, who doubts Mary's virginity and whose hand withers as she probes Mary's womb, is healed when she adores the Christ-child, and then joyously proclaims his birth and his wondrous powers. Such popular texts had had their detractors since the time of St Jerome – as Hrotsvitha, whose earliest verse legend, *Maria*, is based on pseudo-Matthew, was well aware (see her Preface, ed. Homeyer, p. 37; the episode of the midwives, *Maria* 588–629, *ibid*. pp. 70 f.). A century before Hrotsvitha, Notker in his Christmas sequence, *Natus ante saecula* (ed. von den Steinen, *Notker* II 12), had alluded to the folktale only to modify it or even gently to dismiss it: Mary 'is surrounded, instead of midwives, by angels singing "Glory to God" in harmony' (*quam circumstant obstetricum vice/concinentes angeli/gloriam deo*). The Freising dramatist, playing down the rôle of the midwives and stressing that of the angel, would seem to have had an intuition, or sense of decorum, similar to Notker's.

[2] The beautiful antiphon *O regem celi* (114–17) also occurs in the play from Györ (Drumbl p. 304), which is roughly contemporary with that of Freising, but not in other eleventh-century plays.

[3] Except that a twelfth-century playwright at Bilsen (Belgium) borrowed these verses for the opening of his *Ordo Stelle* (Y II 75).

Just as Herod thinks he has killed all the little boys and stamped out the rival King, the mutiny breaks out in his own palace: it is Herod's own page-boys who, in his royal procession, proclaim the rival King, the true *rex Iudeorum*.

At the same time the boys' celebration of the 'yearly feast' (*dies annua*, 130), with its festive songs and dances (*odas, festa, choreas*, 134), has a further, contemporary meaning that goes beyond the biblical events. December 28, the yearly feast of the Innocents, was one of the days on which the Church permitted a Feast of Fools (*festum stultorum*), in which the youngest *clericuli* took leading rôles. It was a day on which play with every kind of freedom was allowed, and a boy was invested with the sceptre of authority who could, in jest, turn the established world upside-down. In that sphere of play, the boys of the cathedral school are the Innocents, and Herod – chosen from their number – is the Lord of Misrule: a King, but only for the feast's duration. The boys, pretending to sing the praises of their false King, are implicitly giving that homage to the true one. Thus the massacre of the Innocents is here concluded in a symbolic ritual reversal: it resolves itself in play. When the play is done, we are finally told (136/7), these same boys shall sing *Letabundus*[4] – the sequence that is both a celebration of the true King's birth and, in its later part, a challenge to Synagoga (the personification of Judaism) to recognise that King, whom both the pagan Sibyls and Synagoga's own prophets had foretold.

The Freising playwright and his predecessors

From Drumbl's fine outline of the diverse forms of the *Ordo Stelle* (pp. 294–340), we can see that ten versions are either earlier than or approximately contemporary with the Freising play,[1] for which (pp. 336–7) he proposes a date a generation before the end of the eleventh century, i.e. *c.* 1070. His analysis makes clear that already at the beginning of the eleventh century, in Metz, it was customary to introduce leonine hexameters into a Magi play: the brief Metz fragment (Y II 443) includes seven such hexameters, none of which is taken up in Freising. The only eleventh-century Magi play at all comparable in scope with Freising is that from Compiègne (Y II 53–6), which does

---

[4] For a complete text and translation of *Letabundus*, see *The Penguin Book of Latin Verse*, ed. F. Brittain, pp. 183–5.
[1] I am leaving out of account the additions to the Zagreb (Györ) MS, which are slightly later than the second half of the eleventh century (cf. Drumbl pp. 302–3), and the Einsiedeln MS, which is s. XI/XII (cf. Drumbl p. 306).

include among its leonine verses two that also occur here (Freising 44–5). With the help of Drumbl's evidence, it is possible to answer a question which he did not himself consider: what does the Freising play contain that is *not* to be found in any of the other eleventh-century examples ? In this way we can circumscribe the dramatic and poetic individuality of its author.

Briefly, his principal innovations appear to be the following:

(1) The prelude: Herod's entry, taking counsel, and edict (1–6).
(2) The scene between the Angel and the Shepherds (7–12).
(3) The Magi's address to the citizens of Jerusalem, and the ironic echo of their phrase *rex Iudeorum*, of Christ, in the Messenger's greeting of Herod (19–24).
(4) The to-and-fro of Herod's court: the Messenger scurrying between Herod and the Magi – he is always told to make haste – his scornful account of the three strangers, his Vergilian questioning of them, and their measured reply (25–40); the complex shaping of brief scenes involving the Messenger is unparalleled in earlier or indeed in later Magi plays.
(5) Herod's rage at the prophecy, his overbearing interrogation of the Kings, and their serene replies (73–87).
(6) The meeting between the Magi coming to Christ, and the Shepherds, on their way home (93–6). (This seems to have been copied a generation later at Einsiedeln, Y II 447.)
(7) Herod expressing his fury at the Magi's deception in the words of Catiline – this too was copied at Einsiedeln – and then in words borrowed from Prudentius (119, 125–8).
(8) The jubilant hexameters sung by the 'Innocents' – who are both page-boys at Herod's court in the past and celebrants of the *Festum puerorum*[2] in the present (129–36).
(9) The singing of the sequence *Letabundus*, rather than of a traditional *Te deum*, at the close of the play (137 ff.).

It is possible that further early texts may still be discovered which could cause this analysis of innovations to be modified in one or other detail; yet there is enough here to indicate that, while the Freising playwright incorporated older elements in his piece, and was not the

---

[2] On this feast, see esp. E. K. Chambers, *The Mediaeval Stage* (Oxford 1903) I 274–371, and, most recently, P. G. Schmidt, 'The Quotation in Goliardic Poetry: The Feast of Fools ...', in *Latin Poetry and the Classical Tradition*, ed. P. Godman, O. Murray (Oxford 1990), pp. 39–55.

first to include hexameter dialogue, in sheer dramatic inventiveness he stood head and shoulders above his predecessors.

Text and versification

My debt to Young's text of the Freising play (II 92–7) is considerable, especially in the completing of a number of illegible lines (see the textual notes below). Some words and letters must still have been legible when Young used the manuscript (before 1933), which are no longer so today; on the other hand, with the help of an ultraviolet lamp I have been able to recover certain words and letters that eluded him. Yet notwithstanding Young's great merits with regard to this text, I disagree with him on a fundamental point: in my view, the words of the play are entirely recoverable and nowhere fragmentary.

According to Young (II 92 n.5), the text 'is very defectively preserved'; thus he used 'dots, representing passages for which no restoration is offered', as well as 'pointed brackets, enclosing passages that may be restored with certainty or reasonable probability'. On no fewer than eight occasions, however – at 28/9, 37/8, 39/40, 43/4, 46/7, 118/19, 119/20, 136/7 – Young printed dots where in fact there are *no* further letters or words in the manuscript (the ultraviolet lamp shows this beyond doubt). Thus on these occasions he gave the impression that the text was irrecoverable, when it was indeed complete.

On the four other occasions where Young printed dots – at 38, 39, 73, 74/5 – it seems to me that plausible completions can be suggested, and that with the lamp some further letters can be deciphered, even if not with certainty, that suggest the way towards the completions. If this is correct, then we do in fact have the full text of the Freising play; only a handful of words must be regarded as conjectural rather than as definitively established.

In the text below, the classical hexameters, including incomplete hexameters, have been inset; leonine hexameters also have a space between the rhyme at the caesura and the second half of the line. The lines of the remainder of the play are not in a strict rhythmic or metrical form, though they make considerable use of rhythmic parallelism, homoioteleuton, assonance and rhyme.

The manuscript

This play was copied on the outer leaf (fol. 1r) of a collection of homilies of the Fathers (Bede, Gregory, Augustine and others) destined to be read on the feasts of saints during the Church year. These begin on fol. 1v, with a *lectio* for the vigil of St Andrew (November 29). Near the close of the 126 leaves come two homilies (fols. 122v, 124v) for the feasts of Mary's Nativity (September 8) and St Corbinianus (September 9): Mary was the patron of Freising's cathedral, and Corbinianus, whose remains were brought there in 765, was traditionally held to have been Freising's first bishop. The homiliary, according to the 1873 catalogue,[1] is a composite, written in hands of the ninth to tenth centuries. It is one of the Freising cathedral manuscripts that in the early nineteenth century were taken to Munich, into what today is the Bavarian State Library.

The play copied on the front of the first leaf, which is much rubbed and worn away at the edges, was added, presumably in the cathedral scriptorium, c. 1070. It was written in a small, neat and regular hand, in two columns; neums were inserted throughout, except in the final section (129 ff. in the text below).

---

[1] *Catalogus Codicum Latinorum Bibliothecae Regiae Monacensis*, ed. C. Halm, G. Thomas, W. Meyer I 3 (Munich 1873), 81 f.

<*Officium stelle*>

I

<*Chorus:*>
Ascendat rex, et sedeat in solio.
Audiat senten<tia>m.
Ex se ipso querit consilium.
Exeat edictum
5 ut pereant c<on>tinuo
qui detrahunt eius imperio.

II

Angelus inprimis:
Pastores, annuntio vobis gaudium magnum,
<quia natus est vobis hodie salvator mundi, alleluia>!

<*Pas*>*tores:*
Transeamus Bethlehem et videamus hoc verbum
10 <quod factum est, quod fecit dominus et ostendit nobis>.

Cho<*rus*>:
Gloria in excelsis deo,
et in terra pax h<ominibus> b<one> v<oluntatis>!

III

Magi procedunt. Primus:
Stella fulgore nimio rutilat,

<*Secundus:*>
Que regem regum natum monstrat,

M: Munich, Bayer. Staatsbibl. Clm 6264a, fol. 1r
Y: K. Young, *The Drama of the Medieval Church* (2 vols., Oxford 1933), II 93–7

Title: *missing in* M. *On designations of Magi Plays, see above p.* 24. Officium stelle *is apt here because of* Expleto officio *(136/7) below.*
³ querit] *sic* M querat Y
⁸, ¹⁰ *On these completions of the antiphons, see the explanatory note ad loc.*
¹² h.b.v. M
¹²/¹³ procedunt] *I have expanded contractions such as* proced, dic̄, resp̄, *in the directions, as indicatives and not as subjunctives* (procedant Y).

The Play of the Star

I

Choir:
Let the King mount and sit upon the throne.
Let him listen to opinion.
From himself he takes counsel.
Let an edict go forth
5 that those who detract from his sovereignty
shall perish instantly.

II

The Angel, opening the scene:
Shepherds, to you I am proclaiming a great joy –
that born to you today is the Saviour of the world, alleluia!

The Shepherds:
Let's make our way to Bethlehem and see this word
10 that's come about, that the Lord has brought about and shown us.

Choir:
Glory to God in the highest,
and peace on earth to men of good will!

III

The Magi appear. The first:
The star is glowing with surpassing brightness,

The second:
the star that shows the King of kings is born,

<T>ercius:
15 Quem venturum olim prophetie signaverant.

<Magi insimul:>
Eamus ergo et inquiramus eum,
offerentes ei munera:
aurum, thus et mirram.

<Ad c>ives <Hierosol>im<itanos>:
Dicite nobis, o Hierosolimitani cives,
20 ubi est expectatio gentium,
noviter natus rex Iudeorum,
quem, signis celestibus agnitum,
venimus adorare?

IV

Internun<tius> currens:
Salve, rex Iudeorum!

Rex:
25 Quid rumoris affers?

In<ternu>ntius:
Assunt nobis, domine, tres viri ignoti,
ab oriente venientes,
noviter natum regem quendam queritantes.

Rex:
    Que sit cau<sa vie>   iam iam citus, impero, quere.

V

Inter<nuntius ad m>agos:
30   Que rerum novitas aut que vos causa subegit
    ignotas temptare vias?
    Qui genus, unde domo? pa<cemne huc> fertis <an arma>?

<M>agi respondent:
Chaldei sumus; pacem ferimus;
regem <re>gum quer<im>us,

[15/16] Magi insimul] *sic* Y *(M is illegible today)*
[28/9] Rex... Y – *but no further letters or words in M*

The third:
15 he whom prophecies of old signalled would come.

The Magi, together:
Let us go, then, and seek him out,
offering him gifts:
gold, frankincense and myrrh.

To the citizens of Jerusalem:
Tell us, citizens of Jerusalem,
20 where is the one awaited by the nations,
the newly-born King of the Jews,
he whom, revealed by heavenly signs,
we are coming to adore?

IV

A Messenger, running:
Hail, King of the Jews!

The King:
25 What sort of news do you bring?

The Messenger:
My Lord, we have three unknown men here,
coming from the East,
pestering us about some newborn king or other.

The King:
Ask the reason for their journey – quickly now, I command it!

V

The Messenger to the Magi:
30 What new event or what cause has impelled you
to venture on strange routes?
Who are you, and where from? Do you bring peace or war?

The Magi answer:
We are astrologers: we bring peace;
we are seeking the King of kings,

35 que\<m n\>at\<um\> esse stella indicat
que fulgore ceteris clarior rutilat.

VI

Arm\<iger\> ad regem:
Vive, rex, in eternum!

Rex:
    Quid \<rumor\>is habes?   que fers \<mi\>hi nuntia, vives?

Internuntius:
    Rex, miranda fero: tres reges, ecce, matu\<rant\> –

Rex:
40 Ad nos vocemus, ut eorum sermones audiamus.

VII

\<Inter\>nunti\<us\>:
    Regia vos man\<data\> vocant: \<non\> segniter ite!

\<Internuntius preced\>ens:
En magi veniunt,
\<et\> regem regum natum stella duce requirunt.

Rex:
    Ante venir\<e iube\>,   quo possim singula scire:
45   Qui sint, cur veniant,   quo \<nos rumore requir\>ant.

\<Magi ad\> regem:
\<Salve, princep\>s Iudeorum!

Rex:
    \<Que sit causa vie?\> qui \<vos? vel unde\> venitis?
    Dicite!

[37/8] Rex... Y – *but no further letters or words in M*
[38] fers... nuntia Y
[39] ecce... Y
[39/40] Rex... Y – *but no further letters or words in M*
[41/2] Internuntius precedens] *I adopt Y's plausible completion.*
[43/4] Rex... Y – *but no further letters or words in M*
[44–5] *These lines can be completed on the basis of the Compiègne play (Y II 60).*
[46/7] Rex... Y – *but no further letters or words in M*
[47–50] *The completions can be made on the basis of the Malmédy fragment (Y II 445).*

35 who has been born, as a star reveals
that glows more radiantly than all the rest.

VI

The Shieldbearer to the King:
King, live for ever!

The King:
What sort of news do you have? What report are you bringing
me, as you shall live?

The Messenger:
King, I bring amazing news: look, it is three kings who hasten –

The King:
40 Let us call them to us, to hear what they have to say.

VII

The Messenger:
You are summoned by royal command: do not be slow to go!

Preceding them, the Messenger says:
Now they are coming, the astrologers,
and they are seeking a newborn King of kings, with a star as their guide.

The King:
Command them to come forward, that I may learn each thing:
45 who they are, why they have come, through what rumour they sought
us out.

The Magi to the King:
Hail, Prince of the Jews!

The King:
What is the cause of your journey? Who are you, and where do you
come from?
Speak!

\<Mag\<i\>:
Rex \<est causa vie; reg\>es \<sum\>us ex \<Arabitis\>,
50   huc \<venientes\>.

Rex:
Regem quem queritis, natum esse quo signo didicistis?

\<Magi\> respondent:
\<Illu\>m natum esse didicimus in oriente, stella monstrante.

Rex econtra:
Si illum regnare creditis, dicite nobis.

Magi res\<pondent\>:
Hunc regnare fatentes, cum mysticis muneribus
55   de terra longinqua adorare ven\<imus\>:

Primus:
Auro regem;

Secundus:
Thure sacer\<do\>te\<m\>;

Tercius:
Mirra mortalem.

VIII

Rex ad milites:
H\<uc\>, symmiste mei,
60   disertos pagina
scribas prophetica
\<vo\>cate.

Milites ad scribas:
Vos, legis periti, a rege vocati,
cum prophetarum libris properando venite.

[50/1] Rex] *The second column in M begins with this word.*
[52] Illum] *Completed from the Compiègne play (Y II 60).*
[55] ven\<imus\>] While there is space for *venimus*, and the neums for the whole word can be seen, only *ven* is legible.
[59] symniste M

The Magi:
A King is the cause of our journey; we are kings from Arabian lands,
50 making our way here.

The King:
That King you seek – by what token did you learn he was born?

The Magi answer:
We learnt he was born, in the East, when a star revealed it.

The King rejoins:
If you think he is already reigning, tell us.

The Magi answer:
Affirming that he reigns, we, with symbolic gifts,
55 from a far-off region are coming to adore him –

The first:
As a King, with gold;

The second:
As a priest, with frankincense;

The third:
As a mortal, with myrrh.

VIII

The King to his Knights:
My companions, call
60 the interpreters, well-versed
in the pages
of prophecy.

The Knights to the Interpreters:
You, experts of the Law, called by the King,
come swiftly, bringing the books of the prophets.

Rex ad scribas:
65 O <vos> scribe, interrogati,
dicite si quid de hoc puero scriptum habetis in libris.

Respondent scribe:
Vidimus, domine, in prophetarum libris
nasci Christum in Bethlehem, civitate David,
Pro<pheta> sic vaticinante:

Antiphona:
70 Bethlehem, <non es minima in principibus Iuda,
ex te enim exiet dux qui regat populum meum Israel;
ipse enim salvum faciet populum suum a peccatis eorum>.

Rex ad scr<ibas>:
   H<oc fuit? hunc finem>   spectat prudentia rerum?
   Vadite cum vestris,   qui digni vatibus estis!

Et proiciat librum.

Rex ad pro<cer>es:
75   Consilium nobis,   proceres, date laudis, honoris.

Armiger ad r<egem>:
   Audi que facias, rex: audi pauca sed apta:
   Eois des dona magis, nec mitte morari,
   Ut, noviter nato   quem querunt rege reperto,
   Rex, per te redeant, ut et ipse scias quid adores.

Rex ad armigerum:
80   Adduc externos   citius, vassalle, tyrannos!

IX

Armiger ad magos:
   Regia vos mandata <vocant: non segniter ite>!

Rex ad magos: ad primum:
   Tu mihi responde,   stans primus in ordine – fare!

---

[73] H<oc fuit? hunc finem>] *The verse can probably be completed as in the twelfth-century French Herod play ed. by Solange Corbin, Mlat. Jb. 9 (1973) 43–52, v. 19 (p. 46). Y printed* H...nem, *but between* H *and* nem *there is space for eleven or twelve letters.*
[74/5] Rex ad ... Y – *but some letters of* proceres *can be made out*
[81] mandata <vocan>t. Y *No letter after* mandata *is visible in M today, but I assume the words are a cue for a complete repetition of 39.*

The King to the Interpreters:
65 You interpreters, now you are being questioned:
tell us if in the books you find anything written about this boy.

The Interpreters answer:
We saw, my Lord, in the prophets' books,
that Christ is born in Bethlehem, the city of David.
This is how the prophet foretold it:

Antiphon:
70 Bethlehem, you are not the least among the leaders of Judah,
for from you will issue a Prince who shall rule my people, Israel,
for he will save the people from their sins.

The King to the Interpreters:
Was it this? Is this the outcome seen by foresight?
Be off with your prophets – they are all you're fit for!

And let him hurl down the book.

The King to his Nobles:
75 Nobles, give us advice worthy of praise, of honour.

The Shieldbearer to the King:
Hear what you shall do, Sire: hear these words, few but fitting:
give gifts to the Magi from the East, and let them not delay,
so that, when they have found the newborn King they seek,
they may return your way, Sire, that you too may know what to adore.

The King to the Shieldbearer:
80 Vassal, bring the foreign tyrants back – be quick about it!

IX

The Shieldbearer to the Magi:
You are summoned by royal command: do not be slow to go!

The King to the Magi: to the first:
Answer me, you there standing first in the row – speak!

Respondet primus:
    Impero Chaldeis,   dominans rex omnibus illis.

Ad secundum:
Tu ai, unde es?

Respondet secundus:
85   Tharsensis regio   me rege nitet Zoroastro.

Ad tercium:
Tu tercius, unde es?

Respondet tercius:
    Me metuunt Arabes,   mihi parent, usque fideles.

Rex consilio habito dicit:
Ite <et> de puero dilienter investigate,
et invento redeuntes mihi renuntiate,
90 ut et ego adorem eum.

X

Magi aspicient<es> stellam cantent:
Ecce stella in oriente previsa
iterum precedet nos lucida!

Magi ad pastores:
Pastores, dicite quidnam <vidistis,
et annuntiate Christi nativitatem>.

Pastores:
95 Infantem vidimus pannis involutum,
    <et choros angelorum laudantes salvatorem>.

Angelus a long<in>quo:
Qui sunt <hi> q<uo>s stella ducit,
nos adeuntes,
inaudita ferentes?

Magi respondent:
100 Nos sumus, quos cernitis, reges
Tharsis et Arabum et Saba,

[87/8] habiti M
[88] dilienter] *sic* M
[93–6] *The completions are from Hartker's* Liber responsalis *(s. X): cf. Y II 21.*

The first answers:
I reign over Chaldaeans, governing them all as their King.

To the second:
You, say where you're from!

The second answers:
85 The region of Tharsis shines with the kingship of me, Zoroaster.

To the third:
You there, the third – where are you from?

The third answers:
The Arabians stand in awe of me: they obey me, utterly loyal.

The King, having taken counsel, says:
Go and find out carefully about the boy,
and when he is found, return and report to me,
90 so that I too may adore him.

X

The Magi, gazing at the star, shall sing:
Look, the star seen first in the Orient
will again precede us, radiant!

The Magi to the Shepherds:
Shepherds, tell us what you have seen,
and proclaim the birth of Christ.

The Shepherds:
95 We have seen the child wrapped in swaddling-clothes,
and choirs of angels praising the Saviour.

An Angel, from afar:
Who are these men whom a star is guiding,
approaching us,
bringing unheard-of things?

The Magi answer:
100 We whom you behold are Kings
of Tharsis and Arabia and Saba,

dona ferentes Christo nato domino,
quem stella duce adorare venimus.

XI

Obstetri\<ces\>:
Ecce p\<ue\>r adest quem queritis!
105 Iam properate et orate,
quia ipse est redempt\<io mundi\>.

Intrantes magi:
Salve, princeps seculorum!

Primus:
Suscipe, rex, aurum;

Secundus:
Tolle thus, tu vere deus;

Tercius:
110 Mirram, signum sepulture.

Angelus ad prostratos magos:
Impleta sunt omnia que prophetice dicta sunt.
Ite, viam remeantes aliam,
ne delatores tanti regis puniendi sitis.

Magi redeuntes, Antiphona:
O regem celi, \<cui talia
115 famulantur obsequia!
Stabulo ponitur qui continet mundum –
iacet in presepio, et in nubibus tonat\>.

XII

Internuntius:
Delusus es, domine: magi viam redierunt aliam!

Rex prosiliens:
Incendium meum ruina extinguam!

[113/14] Antiphona] ā M antiphonam Y
[118/19] ... probant. Rex prosiliens Y *There is nothing incomplete here: the word* Y *read as* probant *is more probably* probatam; *it is written superscript above* mucrone *(121), with an indication-mark that it belongs with line 121.*

bringing gifts to Christ the Lord who is born,
whom, with a star as our guide, we come to adore.

XI

The Midwives:
Look, here is the boy whom you are seeking!
105 Now make haste and pray,
for he is the redemption of the world.

The Magi, entering:
Hail, Prince of the ages!

The first:
Accept the gold, as King;

The second:
Take the frankincense, you who are truly God;

The third:
110 Take the myrrh – a token of burial.

The Angel, to the prostrate Magi:
All that was said prophetically has been fulfilled.
Go now, returning by another route,
lest you be punished as informers on so great a King.

As the Magi return, the antiphon is sung:
Oh King of heaven, whom such
115 homage attends!
He is set in a stable, he who compasses the world –
he lies in a manger, and thunders in the clouds.

XII

The Messenger:
You have been mocked, my Lord: the Magi went back by another route!

The King, leaping up:
I shall quench my blaze of rage by a cataclysm!

48 *Officium stelle*

Armiger econtra:
120 Decerne, domine, vindicare iram tuam
    exstricto mucrone probatam.
    Querere iube pueros: forte inter occisos
    et puer occidetur.

Rex, gladium versans, armigero redit, dicens:
    Armiger o prime,   pueros fac ense perire!

Vel:
125 Mas omnis <infans occidat!
    Scrutare nutricum sinus,
    fraus ne qua furtim subtrahat
    prolem virilis indolis>.

HOS VERSUS CANTENT PUERI IN <PRO>CESSIONE REGIS:

    Eia!
130 dicamus: regias <hic f>ert dies annua laudes!
    Hoc lux ista dedit   quod <men>s sperare nequivit,
    A<ttulit et> vere   votorum gaudia mille,
    Hoc regnum re<gi>,   pacem quoque reddidit orbi,
    N<obis di>vicias,   decus, odas, festa, choreas.
135 Hunc regna<re decet>, et reg<ni> sceptra tenere:
    Regis <nomen> amat,   nomen quia moribus or<nat>.

                       *

Expleto off<icio, pueri cant>ent:
Letabundus exu<lt>a<t fid>elis chorus angel<orum>.
Angelus con s<ilii natus est> de virgine, sol de stella.
Sicut sidus <rad>ium, pro<fert> virgo <filium, pari forma>.

[119/20] ... Armiger econtra Y – *but* M *has no space for any word before* Armiger.
[121] exstricto mucrone probatam] *sic* M *et* estricto mucrone querere Y
[123] occidetur et puer M – *but this is probably an incomplete hexameter: cf.* 121-2, 124.
[123/4] reddit (? redit) Y
[128/9] M *has this instruction in small capitals.*
[136/7] cantent... Y – *but no further letters or words in* M
[137-9] *The text of the widely diffused Christmas sequence,* Letabundus (*printed* Y II 450), *to which* M *is the earliest witness, makes the completions in these lines certain.* Letabundus *was later used in the* Carmina Burana *Christmas play (CB 227, vv. 106/1-12), though the text adapted there, like that in* M, *is incomplete. It is quite possible, however, that the* pueri *sang the whole sequence, which would here have served the same function of concluding the play in sacred chant, as the* Te deum *commonly served at the end of other plays (see below pp. 70, 142). As the words* Expleto officio (135/6) *indicate, the sequence falls outside the play as such; hence it is not given in full here.*

The Shieldbearer rejoins:
120 Determine, my Lord, to avenge your anger,
which is just, with a drawn sword.
Command to hunt down the boys: perhaps among the slain
that boy too will be found slain.

The King, brandishing his sword, returns to the Shieldbearer, saying:
Best of shieldbearers, let the boys perish by the sword!

And:
125 Let every male child die!
Search the bosoms of the nurses,
lest any, furtively, withhold
a child of manly kind.

LET THE BOYS IN THE KING'S PROCESSION SING THESE VERSES:

Let's sing
130 'hurrah!'—this yearly feast brings with it royal praises!
This day has given us what the mind could not have hoped:
it's truly brought a thousand joys in answer to our prayers,
restored this kingdom to its King, and peace too to the world,
to us it's brought wealth, beauty, singing, feasting, dancing.
135 It's good for him to reign and hold the kingdom's sceptre:
he loves the name of King, for he adorns that name with virtues.

*

The play now being over, let the boys sing:
Full of joy, the loyal choir of angels exults.
The Angel of counsel has been born of the maiden, the sun of the star.
As the star brings forth its ray, so does the maiden her son, in form like hers.

Explanatory notes

1   Though a rubric is lacking, the Chorus that sings at 11–12 and at various other moments in the play is likely to have sung this prologue (a solo expositor, however, cannot be ruled out). On the miming required here, see above p. 25.

2–3   The contrast is probably between the King's hearing the opinion of counsellors and his reflecting alone, before ordering the edict to be publicised. The change of tense, from subjunctive (2) to indicative (3), is unexpected, but no emendation is needed.

5–6   In its contents the edict ominously foreshadows Herod's vengeance at the close of the play.

7–10   The antiphons (based on Luke 2, 10–11 and 15), for which the cues only are given in M, can be completed from Y II 75, II 13. The translation of the second is problematic: *hoc verbum quod factum est* clearly alludes to the Incarnation, the Word made flesh; and yet the Word is, in the expression of the Nicene Creed, 'begotten, not made' (*genitum, non factum*), so that the literal meaning of *verbum....quod fecit dominus* can hardly be 'the Word.... that the Lord has made'. Thus the primary reference of *hoc verbum* would seem to be to the Angel's message rather than to the Incarnation itself.

11–12   Luke 2, 14.

17–18   Matthew 2, 11.

20   expectatio gentium] Genesis 49, 10.

21–3   Matthew 2, 2.

30–2   Adapted from Vergil, *Aen.* VIII 112–14 (see the introductory note).

33   Chaldei] While only the first Magus is of the Chaldean nation (cf. 83), all three of the Magi are *Chaldei* in the transferred wider sense of 'astrologers'.

36/7   Armiger] If, like Y, we assume *Armiger* and *Internuntius* to be distinct personages, *Armiger* must here simply be opening the scene with an expression of ritual acclaim (cf. *Danielis ludus* 21 and *passim, infra* p. 120), before the King addresses the Messenger (*Internuntius*). Yet one cannot wholly exclude the possibility that *Armiger* is only an alternative title for *Internuntius*: at 81, for instance, he addresses the Magi with the same command as *Internuntius* had used at 41.

39   I take the new element in the Messenger's report to be that the three strangers are kings. As this does not emerge from the first exchanges (30–6), these – unless some lines have gone missing at this point – will have been

accompanied or followed by a mime indicating the strangers' royal status. It is the word *reges* that makes Herod excitedly cut short the Messenger's speech.

59   sym*m*iste] Chr. Lat. *symmystae* ('fellow-initiates'): cf. Blaise, s.v. *symmystes*.

70–2   The antiphon, based on Matthew 2, 6 (and, for the words *ipse*.... *eorum*, on Matthew 1, 21), is essentially Matthew's free rendering of the prophecy in Micah 5, 2. It can be completed from Hesbert no. 1737.

74   vestris qui digni vatibus estis] Lit. 'you who are worthy of your prophets'.

80   While *tyrannus* does not always have a pejorative sense in classical or medieval Latin, the dramatist's choice of the word here is almost certainly another touch by which he characterises Herod's cast of mind: he cannot even imagine kings who are not *tyranni*.

88–90   Matthew 2, 8.

91–2   In a Magi play such as that of Compiègne (Y II 55), these verses are followed by five others that appear to be adapted from a sequence, *Quem non prevalent* (Y II 446). It is possible – though by no means necessary – that the couplet in M is a cue for this longer composition.

112   Cf. Matthew 2, 12.

113   The sense appears to be that God would punish the magi if they informed Herod where Christ was to be found. I do not know a source for this motif.

119   Sallust, *Catilina* XXXI (see introductory note).

121   exstricto mucrone] Cf. Prudentius, *Cath.* XII 110: *mucrone districto*.

124/5   Vel] Here used, as frequently, as a synonym for *et*: there is no need to suppose that 'Herod is provided with alternative utterances' (Y II 98).

125–8   I complete the strophe, like Y, from the hymn *Salvete, flores martyrum* (ed. A. S. Walpole, *Early Latin Hymns*, Cambridge 1922, no. 24), which was abridged for church use from Prudentius, *Cath.* XII.

129   Eia] The shout of joy falls outside the hexameter schema.

136/7   officio] In the eleventh century, *officium* comes to be used to mean 'mystery-play': John of Rouen mentions 'the play of the star' (*stellae officium*) at Epiphany (*Lexicon*, s.v., 12; cf. also *NG*, s.v., VI D 2).

138   Angelus consilii] Novatianus (*De trin.* 18) argued that *Angelus* was a name *competens ... Christo ... cum magni consilii Angelus factus sit*; Victorinus of Pettau (*in Apoc.* 10) identifies the *angelus fortis* of Apoc. 10, 1 with Christ: *angelum illum dicit, id est nuntium patris omnipotentis; vocatur enim 'magni consilii nuntius'* (Is. 9, 6, Vetus Latina).

III–IV *Tres filie*
Tres clerici
The Three Daughters, and *The Three Students*, from Hildesheim

It is not surprising that the earliest extant plays portraying the deeds and miracles of a saint (who does not feature in the Bible) should be a pair of plays about St Nicolas: his cult was ancient and immensely popular, first in the Byzantine, then also in the western Church.

Nothing we know about Nicolas seems secure as history. Tradition has it that he was born at Patara (on the Lycian coast, in present-day Turkey) *c.* 270, the only son of wealthy parents, that he was imprisoned for his faith under Diocletian, that he became Bishop of Myra, in Lycia, and (especially unlikely!) that he attended the Council of Nicaea in 325. His death is put on a December 6 – still the date of his feast-day – between 345 and 352. His cult was already intensive in Byzantium in the sixth century, when Justinian dedicated a church to him and St Priscus; from the seventh century on, pilgrimages to Myra are recorded. Two oratories were built for Nicolas in Rome in the reign of Pope Leo IV (847–55), two others in that of Pope Nicolas I (858–67), whose choice of papal name is likewise significant. But the apogee of his cult in the West comes in the twelfth century, soon after the dramatic 'translation' – i.e. theft – of his supposed bones from Myra in 1087, by sailors who brought them westward to Bari.

Before this act of piracy, however, the cult of Nicolas had given rise to keen literary activity. His life was twice written in Greek in the ninth century (and many times thereafter, in verse as well as prose), and it is on the second Byzantine life, by Methodius, that the earliest Latin one, by John, Deacon of Naples (*c.* 875), is based. In northern Europe, if we accept the arguments of C. W. Jones,[1] a secular clerk, Reginold of Eichstätt, drew on this *Vita* to compose a liturgy of St Nicolas shortly

---

[1] *The Saint Nicholas Liturgy and its Literary Relationships (Ninth to Twelfth Centuries)*, Berkeley–Los Angeles 1963. The fullest account of the sources for Nicolas' life and the development of his legends is that of G. Cioffari, *S. Nicola nella critica storica* (Bari 1987). Cioffari (p. 98) has discovered a tenth-century MS (Munich Clm 19162), from Tegernsee, of the liturgical 'Storia de Sancto Nicolao' that Jones attributes to Reginold.

before 966. From around the year 1000 onwards a vast number of Nicolas hymns and sequences survive; in 1020, the ferocious Fulk Nerra, Count of Anjou, built a church and abbey of St Nicolas at Angers. According to Jones, the Hildesheim Nicolas plays too were composed about this time, though in my view a date in the second half of the century is more probable.

Notwithstanding Jones's wide-ranging erudition concerning St Nicolas in the Middle Ages, I diverge from him radically in questions of poetic and dramatic judgement. It seems to me certain that the Hildesheim plays were intended from the outset for performance in a church – not, as Jones argues, in a classroom. I do not know any example of a purely scholastic play that ends with a *Te deum*, as *The Three Daughters* does (*infra*, after 90), or that includes the singing of a liturgical antiphon (*infra*, 166–9). So, too, on poetic grounds I would suggest that *The Three Daughters* and *The Three Students* were composed by the same author, in the same place and time, and were indeed conceived as a diptych:[2] the stylistic differences between the two plays, alleged by Jones, are in my view unconvincing.

While we know that the Bavarian Godehard, who had Nicolas as his patron saint, was Bishop of Hildesheim in the years 1022–38, this does not necessarily mean that the plays stem from the time of his episcopate. The dramatist was assuredly stimulated by a flourishing existing cult of the saint in Hildesheim; he was also stimulated in some aspects of his work by two of Hrotsvitha of Gandersheim's spoken plays (see above p. xx), which will have been accessible at the nearby foundation of Gandersheim at any time in the course of the eleventh century. Yet a number of scribal forms in the unique manuscript of these Nicolas plays suggest to me that its exemplar was written by someone of French, not German, origin (see below p. 59). That is, even if, as seems probable, the plays were composed in Hildesheim itself, their first copyist – who may be identical with their author – must have been a 'wandering scholar' from France rather than a German.

Finally, Jones – like Young before him – is lukewarm about the quality of the Hildesheim plays, stigmatising *The Three Daughters* in particular as 'mediocre verse in more than mere form' (*Liturgy* p. 103).

---

[2] This is also suggested by the fact that in the MS (L) the words *Hospes care* – the opening of *Tres clerici* – follow without any break after the words *Te deum*, that conclude *Tres filie*. My expression 'diptych' is not meant to exclude the possibility that the Hildesheim author also dramatised other Nicolas legends, such as the *Iconia* or *Filius Getronis*, that later became plays for instance at Fleury (cf. Y II 337–57) – but we have no positive testimonies pointing to lost Nicolas plays from Hildesheim.

54 Nine medieval Latin plays

To substantiate a different view, let us look more closely at these plays, their language and their structure. Their music, unfortunately, is not preserved.

Style, meaning and structure

As far as we know, the only narrative source available to the playwright for the *Three Daughters* story was the version in the saint's life by John the Deacon.[3] This is so far-reachingly different from the play in conception and detail that through a comparison of the two texts the power of original creation of the Hildesheim author becomes readily apparent.

It has often been noted that in John's *Vita* it is the father who, reduced to poverty, arranges for the prostitution of his daughters (*fornicari constituit*). The change in the play, however – where it is the first daughter who suggests to her father that whoring is the only remedy – is far more than an example of better 'taste' (thus Young). The girls in the *Vita* have a purely passive role: they say not a word and we are told nothing of their thoughts or feelings. The play opens with a father who is sympathetic, even if also pathetic in his helplessness. He is more troubled about the effect of penury on his daughters than on himself (11–14), and, reversing the roles of father and daughter as his audience knew and expected them, he asks his daughters' advice, instead of telling them what to do.

The eldest daughter's counsel – prostitution, with herself as the first, willing victim – is meant to console the father in his sorrow (16–17). He does not reject the advice out of hand: it simply makes him more miserable than before (31–5). Now we learn that his helplessness is bound up with the infirmity of old age. This motif too is the playwright's invention: he contradicts his source, where the father is still young and able-bodied. There the author himself has an imaginary dialogue with the father, and asks him why he won't go out to work with his hands, as the apostles did. He receives the reply, 'My noble birth stood in the way of my doing any work' (*Nobilitas, ait, mea renuebat aliquod opus facere*) – except, presumably, that of a pimp. Moreover, in the *Vita* the girls have already been sent to the brothel: the rumour of their disgrace had filled the city and reached the ears of Nicolas, who came from the same village as the father. In the playwright's new design, by contrast, the

---

[3] The passage is most conveniently accessible in Y II 488–90.

father is neither a monster nor a workshy snob. He is weak physically and psychologically, but still not wholly unappealing.

In the play, the proposal to embark on a life of prostitution is abandoned, because of the vigorous opposition to it by the second daughter (36–50), who warns her father against it on moral and religious grounds. Yet her advice remains negative: her father welcomes it, but still wavers, wondering if his elder daughter's drastic remedy might not be necessary after all (51–5).

The situation changes with the youngest daughter, who is differentiated from both her sisters. As in Hrotsvitha's plays it is always the youngest daughter – Hirena, or Karitas – who is the most determined, the most ready to challenge the ideas of the grown-up world,[4] so here the youngest tries to instil a godfearing love and trust in her weak-minded father.

In the *Vita* Nicolas makes three separate secret visits to help his fellow-villager, by throwing bags of gold through his window, so that each of the girls in turn can marry. (Presumably, though arrangements for their prostitution had been made, the daughters had not yet been deflowered, and their dowry of gold was held to outweigh any shame incurred.) The third time, in the source, the stealthy benefactor is caught redhanded and the father cries out after him – *Siste gradum!* – as in the play (71).

By simplifying, the dramatist has avoided monotony and achieved a *coup de théâtre*. At the very moment that the youngest daughter says 'Think of Job!' (again a motif not in the source), the mysterious gold is thrown in (70/1), and the old man tries to retain the thrower, who in the play is unknown to him. Here the generous deed, that became pedantically repetitive and predictable in the source, is hedged with enchantment. The moment of complete trust in God brings an instantaneous end to all woes. To this end any accountancy leading to three adequate dowries is irrelevant. Unlike John the Deacon, too, the playwright makes explicit the reason for Nicolas' secretive behaviour: Nicolas wants all the praise and thanksgiving to be rendered not to himself but to God (77–9). His affirmation of this leads to the joyful climactic speech of the father (which once more has no parallel in the *Vita*), culminating in the *Te deum*.

The playwright has essentialised his source, but also humanised it. Deftly he has individualised the three daughters, who had been mere ciphers before. He has removed the sordid element; instead, there are

---

[4] Cf. *Women Writers* pp. 77–9; *Sapientia* v 31–6.

flickers of gentle humour in his treatment of every character. He has replaced the clumsiness of the thrice-repeated visit, and the banalities of the marriage arrangements, by a single gesture, magnificent and startling, that shows the working of divine grace. This, the *peripeteia* of the play, has a religious meaning that leaves John the Deacon's crude rhetorical attempts at edification far behind.

For the complementary play, *The Three Students*, no written source or older version survives. The next earliest telling that is preserved comes in the Anglo-Norman verse of Wace's *Vie de Saint Nicolas* (c. 1150). Young, who cites Wace's version of the tale of the students, rightly underlines that 'We may be reasonably sure that the Hildesheim playwright did not invent it, however' (Y II 328). Attempts to find an origin for this story in a misinterpretation of Nicolas' iconography, or in confusion with another of his legends, where the saint saves three citizens of Myra and three army officers (*stratilates*) from being put to death, seem to me over-ingenious: there was such a wealth of Nicolas legends in circulation that it is hardly surprising that some circulated orally for centuries and were not gathered into a *Vita* in the earliest period. One of the oldest Nicolas sequences, *Perpes laus et honor*, which Schaller and Könsgen date to the beginning of the eleventh century,[5] amid a series of allusions to Nicolas' wondrous deeds, including his intervention on behalf of the three daughters, has the phrase *a morte iuvenes solvit* ('he released the young men from death'). While this could allude to the three *stratilates*, whose execution Nicolas prevented, the expression perhaps more naturally suggests the three students, whom he released from death by bringing them back (with divine help) to life.[6]

These students are wandering scholars, who have left their homes or native lands in order to study the *artes*: they endure exile for the sake of their literary education (92–3). All three ask the innkeeper for a night's lodging, but the third, trying to reassure him that they won't be any trouble, 'since we bring provisions with us' (103), unwittingly gives away that, unlike the typical *vagantes* of popular repute, he and his friends are not impoverished starvelings. The host replies (106–10) with a show of geniality and generosity that reveals itself not only false

---

[5] *AH* LIII 198; cf. D. Schaller, E. Könsgen, *Initia carminum Latinorum saeculo undecimo antiquiorum* (Göttingen 1977), no. 11918.
[6] The Nicolas hymn from Troyes, *Copiose caritatis*, cited by Jones (*Liturgy* p. 108), which has the unmistakable allusion *Suscitator clericorum*, is unfortunately not 'eleventh-century', as Jones claims, but stems from the later twelfth, as the form and rhymes clearly indicate. It was added to the Troyes MS in the twelfth century, as Dreves (*AH* XLVI 299) states.

but sinister in his very next speech (111–15). This cold-blooded killer is gentle of manner and spouts all the Christian platitudes.

Here, as in *Tres filie*, the stage-directions are extremely sparse. This does not necessarily mean, as most scholars suppose, that little in the way of gesture or action featured in the performance of these plays – rather that the writing down of detailed instructions was not considered vital. In *Tres filie*, the rubric (which I supply from the later, Fleury adaptation) is missing at the crucial moment of the throwing in of the bag of gold – perhaps because of scribal carelessness, or again because both director and actors knew perfectly well, without explicit instruction, what needed to be done at that point. This may be the case here too, at 110/11: for an ensemble familiar with the plot it was not necessary to make explicit that the host has, as he promised, made the students' bed, that they have gone to bed and fallen asleep, that when the host sees them sleeping he peers into their luggage and discovers how well off they are, and only then goes to his wife with his murderous plan (111–15).

She attempts to dissuade him (116–20), both on religious grounds and by stressing the widespread shame (*infamia*) they would incur if they were found out: the fear of being brought to justice does not seem to enter her thought. Her husband calms her anxiety and appeals to her greed (121–5), and she consents, even while still denouncing the deed as 'this so dangerous act of villainy' (128).

Again at the dénouement stage-directions have not been inserted, but it is not hard to imagine the enactment of the murder followed by a knocking at the door of the inn, as Nicolas asks admission. The mode of killing is not specified, but the remarkable later phrase, 'pouring death into the bodies of the students' (154–5), might well suggest a stratagem such as that used in Hamlet's 'Mousetrap', with the students writhing in a mimed death-agony as a poison, poured into their ears, penetrates their brains.

Nicolas arrives, claiming that he is poor and that he had been driven away from the inn (presumably because of his shabby look) earlier in the day. He entreats humbly for a night's lodging (131–5), and again the host in his reply oozes charitable concern. But suddenly the poor and meek stranger strikes a different note: once indoors, he asks for 'fresh meat' – as if he were a wealthy man who could afford the best. The host in turn claims to be too poor to have such luxuries (146–50), ruefully labouring his own neediness; but now the stranger has him cornered and denounces him (151–5). Again, as at the vital instant in *Tres filie*, there is a hint of mystery: it would seem that Nicolas had not witnessed the murders, but knows of them through miraculous clairvoyance.

After frightening the guilty innkeeper, Nicolas becomes gentle with him: he stresses, as Hrotsvitha had repeatedly done in her plays and her legends, that no sin, however terrible, is unredeemable.[7] As Hrotsvitha's Abraham joins his niece Mary in begging God's pardon for her life as a fallen woman, so here Nicolas beseeches 'to pardon us' – aligning himself with the host (and, it is implied, his wife) as if he too were one of the guilty. He prays to God on their behalf, as Abraham does on Mary's. The prayer is that the deed be cancelled visibly: not only within the souls of the guilty, but also by restoring the innocent to life. (This double annulment of guilt is another theme that Hrotsvitha had treated dramatically, in her *Drusiana and Calimachus*.)

At its conclusion, the play of the *Three Students* re-enters the world of liturgy: the choir sings an antiphon which, praising Christ's compassion, declares that the miraculous revival of the students is about to take place (166–9). During this time, Nicolas must be absorbed in silent prayer alongside the guilty couple: he is not himself the thaumaturge, but, as an Angel now reveals to him, it is through his prayers that the miracle has been accomplished.

A note on spelling[1]

Any serious attempt to determine the date and provenance of this pair of plays must in my view begin with some observations about the unusual spellings in the unique manuscript, L. The earlier editors, who normalised these play-texts extensively and without discussion, tended thereby to obscure the linguistic problems.

The twelfth-century inscription on fol. 1r of L, beginning *Lib sc̄i* (later altered to *ep̄i*) *Godehardi in hild̄*).,[2] suggests that L belonged to the Hildesheim convent that was founded in Bishop Godehard's memory in 1146, rather than to the Bishop in person: his episcopate (1022–38) is too early for the hands – of the late eleventh century – that copied the texts in L. The inscription, however, together with our knowledge of Nicolas' cult at Hildesheim from the time of Godehard onwards, and the accessibility there of Hrotsvitha's plays, which the dramatist appears to

---

[7] Cf. *Women Writers* p. 60.
[1] I am most grateful to Peter Rickard for some expert comments on this section.
[2] See G. R. Coffman, 'The Cult of St Nicholas at Hildesheim', in *The [J.M.] Manly Anniversary Studies in Language and Literature* (Chicago 1923), p. 274 n.1 (palaeographic notes by C. H. Beeson).

Eleventh-century plays   59

have known, all suggest that the Nicolas plays in L were composed at Hildesheim itself. At the same time, certain spellings in the play-texts seem to indicate that the L copyist's *exemplar* was written by a French, not German, hand.

In a whole series of instances, *sc* before *e* or *i* is written *s* or *ss*: 41 *simus* (= *scimus*), 97 *quiesere* (= *quiescere*), 104 *deposimus* (= *deposcimus*), 122 *siet* (= *sciet*), 146 *possis* (= *poscis*), 158 *depossite* (= *depossite*). These ways of writing appear to point to a French speaker. The only 'correct' use of *sc* in the two plays is at 67 *scimus*. Similarly, the examples of *o* for *u* – 101 *sommo* (= *summo*), 157 *tondite* (= *tundite*) – could reflect a French speaker's nasalisation.

Yet this is not the whole story, for the most bizarre spellings in these plays are seen when *sc* before *i* is written as *t*. Thus L has 13 *lativa* (= *lasciva*), 19 *sutipe* (= *suscipe*), 43 *depotimus* (= *deposcimus*), and 108 *sutipiam* (= *suscipiam*). In these examples I suspect we can glimpse two layers of transmission: the scribe of L, who retained a number of Gallicising spellings without thinking, probably found in his exemplar the spellings *laciva, sucipe, depocimus,* and *sucipiam*: for classical *sc* before *e* or *i*, that is, an eleventh-century French speaker could have written *c* (likewise pronounced *s* in such cases) as readily as *s* or *ss*. But as the *c* spelling may have been quite unfamiliar in northern Germany, and as the scribe of L was copying with little attention to sense, on these occasions it seems he misread his exemplar's *c* as *t*.

Other spellings in L are more difficult to analyse. At 112, *scensum* (= *censum*) may be an unfortunate attempt at hyper-correctness (of the 'abhominable' or 'posthumous' kind); at 14, *geiunia* (= *ieiunia*) may reflect a softened pronunciation of *g* by the scribe of the exemplar (cf. Old French spellings such as *gĕune, gĕuner* for the word for fasting). At 16, *lucere* (= *lugere*) may be one of a number of examples of simple carelessness. Other non-standard spellings – e.g. *t* for *c* at 23 *speties*, 91 *sotii*, 106 *conspitiam*, 109 *fatiam* – are relatively common everywhere and do not permit more specific inferences.

It seems clear, however, that the copyist of the Hildesheim manuscript, L, had before him an exemplar rich in Gallicising spellings, the most unfamiliar of which he misconstrued, whilst taking over others without a qualm. We may thus conjecture that his predecessor, the earlier copyist of the Hildesheim Nicolas plays – who may well have been the playwright himself – had come to Hildesheim from France.

Versification

This assumption is reinforced by the implications of the versification. The basic verse line in both plays, 4 + 6pp, is the one we have encountered in the Latin parts of the *Sponsus* (*supra*, 1) and shall encounter again in the Vic *Verses pascales* (*infra*, v). It is akin to the 4 + 6 vernacular line in the Provençal verses in the *Sponsus*, and to the verses in the eleventh-century northern French vernacular lyric *Quant li solleiz* (cf. Dronke 1984, pp. 225–32), which begin:

> Quant li solleiz   converset en Leon,
> en icel tens   qu'est ortus Pliadon,
>   per unt matin,
>
> Une pulcellet   odit molt gent plorer
> et son ami   dolcement regreter,
>   e jo lli dis:
>
> 'Gentilz pucellet,   molt t'ai odit plorer
> et tum ami   dolcement regreter –
>   et chi est illi?'

> When the sun dwells in the sign of Leo,
> in the time of the Pleiades' rising,
>   one morning,
>
> I heard a young girl weeping tenderly,
> sweetly lamenting her friend,
>   and I said to her:
>
> 'Gentle maiden, I've heard you weep so much,
> and heard your sweet lament about your friend –
>   who is he, then?'

It is noteworthy that in this lyric, as in the plays, the lines are built into a strophic form – here couplets, not quatrains – and that, as in the Nicolas plays, each strophe concludes with a four-syllabled line.

In the vernacular verses, Provençal and French, however, we do not find the strong proparoxytone final stress which is characteristic of all the Latin poems using this type of line. That there appears to be no *sustained* use of such a line in strophes outside France before the twelfth century is another indication that it was probably a scholar of French origin, wandering – perhaps like the Three Students! – to Hildesheim in the course of his studies, who there found inspiration for composing plays about St Nicolas. As none of the examples from France of the strophic use of 4 + 6pp lines can safely be dated to the *first* half of the

Eleventh-century plays 61

eleventh century, so early a date would also be difficult to propose for the Nicolas plays themselves.

Jones's attempt (*Liturgy* pp. 122–39) to link the 4 + 6pp lines of these plays with other kinds of decasyllabic lines that are attested earlier in the German language-area, and even with the hendecasyllabic lines of rhythmic Sapphic strophes (5p + 6p), does not take account of the position of the caesura, or of the proparoxytone principal stress, both of which are crucial to the Latin verse employed at Hildesheim.

For his rhymes, the playwright was often content with assonance of the last syllable only: e.g. in 11–14 *corpora* (13) fits only loosely into the *-ia* rhyme-pattern, or in 141–4 *tribuas* (142) does not quite match the *-eas* rhymes. There is no evidence that the author or his audience considered such lesser assonances a blemish. On the other hand, to accept Otto Schumann's procedure (*ZfrP* LVIII, 1938, 686–8; LXII, 1942, 386–90), of deleting the father's replies to his daughters (31–5 and 51–5 below), because they are too 'cleanly rhymed' (*sauber gereimt*) to belong to the original play, would be to allow a barbarous dramatic mutilation.

The manuscript

The manuscript, today Add. 22414 in the British Library, is a vellum palimpsest of the (later) eleventh century.[1] It consists of eight leaves. The first has the twelfth-century heading 'The book of St Godehard in Hildesheim' (*Liber sancti Godehardi in Hilde<ssemensi>*) which is signalled above. The word *sancti* was altered, 'much later, probably' (thus Beeson),[2] to *episcopi*. The next word, the interpretation of which defeated Coffman and Beeson, is *Will*; this is followed, in a darker ink, by *notulę de abaco*. I would conjecture that *Will* is short for *Willelmi*, and refers to the author of the abacus notes, which are included in fols. 4v–8v.

Fols. 1r–3r contain a group of medical prescriptions (inc. *Ad fistulas* ...). They are too brief to feature as separate items in Thorndike and Kibre's *Catalogue of Incipits of Mediaeval Scientific Writings in Latin* (2nd edn, London 1963). The thirteen medical hexameters on fol. 2r, however (inc. *Est etiam morbi species que dicitur ignis*), are ch. 40 of the *Liber medicinalis* of Serenus (c. 200 AD; cf. Schaller-Könsgen, cit. p. 56 n.5, no. 4584). Fols. 3v–4r are wholly taken up by the two Nicolas

---

[1] Cf. the brief description in the British Museum's *Catalogue of Additions 1854–60* (London 1875), p. 643.
[2] See above, p. 58 n.2.

plays. Fols. 4v–8v contain the mathematical *notulę* (inc. *Quid consideratur in Primis Analeticis* . . . expl. *restituetur prima figura*), followed, on the second half of 8v, by several brief medical prescriptions.

The pair of plays, that is, was copied amid scholastic, not liturgical, texts. Nonetheless, as I indicated, the *Te deum* and the Nicolas antiphon in the plays strongly suggest that they were intended for performance in a church.

< *Tres filie* >

<Pater:>

3v　Cara michi　　pignora, filie,
　　opes patris　　inopis hunice
　　et solamen　　mee miserie,
　　michi mesto　　tandem consulite!
5　　　*Me miserum!*

　　Olim dives　　et nunc pauperrimus,
　　luce feror　　et nocte anctius,
　　et – quam ferre　　non consuevi<mus> –
　　paupertatem　　graviter ferimus.
10　　　*Me miserum!*

　　Nec me mea　　tantum inopia
　　quantum vestra　　vexat penuria,
　　quarum olim　　laciva corpora
　　modo domant　　lo<n>ga geiunia –
15　　　*Me miserum!*

<Prima filia:>
　　Care pater,　　lugere desine
　　nec nos lugens　　lugendo promove,
　　et, quod tibi　　valeo dicere,
　　consilium　　hoc a me sucipe,
20　　　*Care pater!*

　　Unum nobis　　restat ausilium:
　　per dedecus　　et per obprobrium
　　ut nostrorum　　speties corporum

L: London, BL Add. 22414, fols. 3v – 4r
Y: K. Young, *The Drama of the Medieval Church* (2 vols., Oxford 1933), II 312–14, 325–7
(O. Schumann's attempted reconstruction of the 'original version' of *Tres filie*, on the basis of L and three later MSS – see above, p. 61 – does not contribute to establishing the text of L itself)
The copyist of L uses *e caudata* irregularly; it is noted below only where the *cauda* is used but *ae* is not appropriate (68, 162, 170).

Title: Tres filie, the traditional name for this legend, has no MS authority here.
[8]　con sueui L
[11]　me *superscript (same hand)* L
[13]　latiua L (*cf.* 19 *sutipe,* 43 *depotimus,* 108 *sutipiam, and above p.* 59)
[16]　lucere L (*em.* Y)
[19]　sutipe L
[23]　speties] *sic* L species Y

The Three Daughters

The Father:
Children, daughters, so dear to me,
only resource of a resourceless father
and consolation for my wretchedness,
advise me in my grief, as all else fails!
5   *How unhappy I am!*

Once I was rich and now am very poor,
I go about anxiously by day and night:
the burden that we were not used to bearing –
poverty – we now bear grievously.
10   *How unhappy I am!*

My own neediness does not trouble me
so much as does your penury,
you whose bodies, once full of game,
long times of fasting now make tame –
15   *How unhappy I am!*

The First Daughter:
Dear father, cease to mourn –
do not by mourning move us to mourn;
I can now tell you this:
take this advice from me,
20   *Dear father!*

Only one recourse is left us:
that by shame and by disgrace
the beauty of our bodies

victum nobis   lucretur puplicum,
25   *Care pater!*

Et me primam,   <pater>, si iubeas,
dedecori   submittet pietas,
ut sentiat   primam anctietas
quam contulit   primam nativitas,
30   *Care pater!*

<Pater:>
Consilium   hoc miserabile
michi prebet   cor lammentabile:
Corpus tuum,   tam venerabile,
meum frangit,   senio debile,
35   suspirando.

Secunda filia:
Noli, pater,   noli, carisime,
doloribus   dolores addere,
ne pro damno   velis inducere
periculum   irreparabile,
40   *Care pater!*

Simus quidem   quod fornicantibus
obstrusus est   celorum aditus.
Cave ergo,   te nos depocimus,
ne nos velis   addere talibus,
45   *Care <pater>!*

Ne<c> te velis   nec nos infamie
submittere,   pater, perpetue,
nec ab ista   labi pauperie
in eterne   lacu miserie,
50   *Care pater!*

Responsio:
Tuum, nata,   placet consilium
et exemplum   patet egregium;

---

[26] primam si L pater *suppl. from Orléans 201, p.178*
[41] Simus] *sic* L (*cf.* 97 quiesere, 104 deposimus, 122 siet, *and above p. 59*)
[43] Care, depotimus L
[47] perdetue L (*em.* Y)
[49] lacu] *sic* L lacu<m> Y
[52] palcet egreguum L placet egregium (*em.*) Y

should earn us a living openly,
Dear father!

And if you bid me, father, duty will make
me the first to submit to shame:
anxious as you are, you'll see I am the first,
I who was your firstborn,
    Dear father!

The Father:
This unhappy advice
makes my heart griefstricken:
your body, so worthy of reverence,
shatters mine, weakened by age,
    with sighing.

The Second Daughter:
Do not, father, dearest one, do not
heap sorrows upon sorrows:
do not, because of what we've lost, bring on
a danger that's irreparable,
    Dear father!

We know, in truth, that heaven's gate
is barred to those who fornicate.
Take care then, we implore you,
not to link us to such as those,
    Dear father!

Do not subject us or yourself,
father, to perpetual infamy –
don't let us slide from this our poverty
into the pit of endless misery,
    Dear father!

The Father's answer:
Your advice, daughter, pleases me,
and your fine example is well known;

68   *Tres filie*

    Set paupertas   augetur nimium
    que me gravat,   quem domat senium,
55   heu, frequenter!

    Tertia filia:
    Meum quoque,   pater per*opti*me,
    consilium   au*di*re sustine,
    Adque finem   breviter collige:
    deum, pater,   time et dilige,
60   Care <pater>!

    Nichil enim   deesse novimus,
    per scripturas,   deum timentibus,
    et omnia   ministrat omnibus
    omnipotens   se diligentibus,
65   Ca<re pater>!

    Neu desperes   propter inopiam,
    deo esse   quam scimus placidam:
    Iob respice,   pater, penuriam
    et deinde   secutam copiam,
70   Care pater!

    <*Proiecto auro, Pater:*>
    Siste gradum,   quisquis es, domine!
    siste gradum,   et qui sis exprime,
    qui dedecus   tolle<n>s infam*i*e
    onus quoque   levas inopie!
75   *Me beatum!* /

4r <*Nicolaus:*>
    Nicolaum   me vocant nomine;
    lauda deum   ex dato munere,
    et non velis   ulli ascribere
    largitatis   laudes dominice:
80   deum lauda!

---

    [56] perpetue L *(by confusion with 47)*
    [57] audice L *(em.* Y*)*
    [63] omnia] *followed by an erasure of 3 letters (probably* oīa*)* L
    [68] respicę L
    [70/1] Proiecto auro, Pater] *suppl. from Orléans 201, p. 178*
    [73] infamine L *(em.* Y*)*

yet our poverty becomes too great:
it weighs me down – me whom old age breaks –
55   alas, how often!

The Third Daughter:
My advice too, best of all fathers,
consent to hear
and, in brief, take up its goal:
father, fear and cherish God,
60   *Dear father!*

For we know, through Scripture,
that those who fear God lack nothing:
the Almighty ministers all things
to all that cherish him,
65   *Dear father!*

Don't despair because of poverty –
we know that it finds favour with God:
Father, think of Job's penury
and of the wealth that ensued from it,
70   *Dear father!*

The Father, when the gold has been thrown in:
Only wait, my Lord, whoever you are!
Only wait, and tell me who you are –
you who, lifting our shame of infamy,
also relieve our burden of poverty!
75   *How blessed I am!*

Nicolas:
Nicolas is the name they call me by;
give praise to God for the gift that has been given,
and do not seek to ascribe to any man
the praises due to the bounty of the Lord:
80   *God you shall praise!*

<Pater:>
Iam iam mecum   gaudete, filie,
paupertatis   elapso tempore:
ecce enim   in auri pondere
quod sufficit   nostre miser<i>e!
85   Me beatum!

Gratiarum   ergo p<r>e<conia
offeramus   et laudum munera
uni deo,   cui in secula
laus et honor,   virtus et gloria>,
90   o filie!

Te deum.

<*Tres clerici*>

<*Primus clericus:*>
Hospes care,   tres sumus sotii
litterarum   quos causa studii
cogit ferre   penas exilii –
nos sub tui   tectis hospitii
95   hospitare!

Secundus:
Fessi sumus   longo itinere:
tempus esset   iam nos quiesere.
Nobis velis   amoris federe
hospitium   noctu concedere
100   quo egemus.

---

[86] Grorum ergo pe L *Neither Y nor Schumann (see above, p. 61) recognised that these words in* L, *incomplete and slightly garbled, indicate as the conclusion of* Tres filie *the thanksgiving found in Orléans 201, p. 179* – Gratiarum ergo preconia ... – *which I complete from there. Between these words and* o filie *(90),* L *has two rhymed hexameters, the second incomplete, with an intervening instruction:*
        Hospes gaudeto   pacemque salutis habeto!
Responsio hospitis:
        Vobis letisiam   deus eximiam <...>
(letisiam: Cl. laetitiam – *cf. 21* ausilium)
This snatch of dialogue could well have belonged to a version of Tres clerici *in rhymed hexameters, of which we have a twelfth-century fragment from Einsiedeln (Y II 335–6).*
[90/1] *In* L *the words* Hospes care *follow* te deum *without a break.* Tres clerici, *the traditional name for the legend now to be dramatised, has no MS authority here.*
[92] litterarum] *corr. from* lott- L exul... *erased after* studii L

The Father:
Now, daughters, rejoice with me:
the time of poverty has slipped away –
for look, in that mass of gold there is
sufficient for our wretchedness!
85   *How blessed I am!*

So let us offer celebrations
of thanks and gifts of praises
to the one God, to whom forever be
praise and honour, power and glory,
90   oh my daughters!

Te deum.

The Three Students

The First Student:
Dear host, we are three friends
who for the sake of literary study
are compelled to bear the pains of exile –
under the roof of your inn
95   give us lodging!

The Second:
We are weary from a long journey:
now it would be time for us to rest.
Kindly, in the bond of friendship,
allow us the night-lodging
100   that we need.

Tertius:
Sommo <mane> cras, hospes, ibimus:
non de tuo vivere querimus,
quia victum nobiscum gerimus –
hospitium tantum deposimus,
105   causa dei.

Respondeat hospes:
Cum vos ita fessos conspitiam,
propter summam dei clementiam
vos hic intus noctu sucipiam –
vobis ignem cum lecto fatiam.
110   Ite sessum.

Uxor, audi meum consilium:
isti scensum gerunt eximium –
inpendamus eis exitium,
ut eorum tesauri pretium
115   habeamus!

<*Uxor:*>
Tantum nefas, coniux, si fiere<t>,
creatorem nimis offendere<t>,
et si quisquam forte percipere<t>,
nos per orbis spatium gere<ret>
120   infamia.

Respondeat <hospes>:
Frustra times. Bene celabitur,
nemo siet <quod> pertractabitur;
horum nobis morte para*b*itur
in manticis qui <magnus> clauditur
125   opum census.

[101] Sommo cras L *I adopt Y's completion.*
[106] Respondeat (R) *erased after* ita L
[108] sutipiam L
[109] fatiam] *sic* L faciam Y
[111] Voxor L (*cf. 101* Sommo, *130* Vuxor)
[116-19] *The necessary completions of the final words (as in Y) suggest that the Hildesheim scribe, working from an exemplar where a margin had been cut away, copied what was still visible without concern for grammar or sense.*
[122] siet pertractabitur L s<c>iet <si> p. Y
[123] parantur L (*em.* Y)
[124] qui clauditur L *I have supplied* magnus *for rhythm, but other completions are also possible.*

The Third:
At earliest dawn tomorrow, host, we'll be off:
we're not asking for any of your food,
since we bring provisions with us –
it's only lodging that we beg of you,
105   in God's name.

The Host shall answer:
Since I see you are so weary,
because of God's supreme mercy
I'll welcome you in here for the night –
I'll make you a fire and a bed.
110   Sit you down.

Wife, listen to my plan:
these fellows have uncommon riches with them –
let's put them to death,
so that we'll have the prize
115   of their treasure!

The Wife:
Husband, if such wickedness were done,
it would offend the Creator very greatly,
and if by chance anyone were to see it,
the whole world would get to know
120   our infamy.

The Host shall answer:
No need to fear. It'll be well concealed,
no one will know what will be carried out;
with their death it'll be there for us,
that great rich loot that's stowed away
125   in their hand-luggage.

74 *Tres clerici*

Uxor respondeat:
Fiat quod vis: ego consentiam,
que pro posse   tibi subveniam;
tam infeste   cladis nequitiam
caute tecum,   coniuns, incipiam,
130   uxor tua.

Verba sancti Nicol<a>i:
Ad te gradu   nocturno venio,
tuo pauper   amotus hostio –
hic exoro   frui hospitio:
fave michi,   pro dei filio,
135   precor, hospes!

<Respondeat hospes:>
Intra <cito   meum> hospitium,
ut per noctis   istius spatium
meum tibi   prosit auxilium:
quod exigis   habe remedium –
140   vade sessum.

Nicolaus:
Nove carnis   si quidquam habeas,
inde michi   parumper tribuas,
quam si michi   prebere valeas,
adiuro te   per deum, nequeas
145   <plus placere>.

Respondeat <hospes>:
Qua<m> tu possis,   hospes, non habeo,
nec hanc tibi   prebere valeo:
non sum dives   set pauper maneo –

---

[127] pro posse] *sic* L proposse Y
[130] Vuxor L
[131] Atte gradum L (*em.* Y)
[132] a<d>motus Y – *see explanatory note*
[135–6] precor hospes. Intra hospitium L Y *assumes a lacuna at 135, and reads 136 as* Precor, hospes, intra hospitium, *but the capital I of* Intra *precludes this: the lacuna must fall within* 136.
[144–5] Y *places a full stop after* nequeas, *but this yields no sense; nor does Dümmler's suggestion for 145,* care hospes, *reported by Y (II 326 n 6). My completion is only tentative, but any plausible suggestion for 145 must complete the sense following* nequeas.
[145/6] Responsio Y
[146] Qua L Que Y   possis] *sic* L (*cf.* 158 depossite, *and above p.* 59)

The Wife shall answer:
Do as you wish: I shall consent,
and shall help you as best I can;
this so dangerous act of villainy,
husband, I'll start off with you, cautiously,
130   I your wife.

The words of St Nicolas:
I've come to you, walking through the night,
a poor man who was driven from your gate –
I implore that I may have lodging here:
shelter me, in God's Son's name,
135   host, I beseech you!

The Host shall answer:
Quickly come into my inn,
so that for this night's space
my help may serve you:
take the comfort that you need –
140   sit you down.

Nicolas:
If you have any kind of fresh meat,
give me a little of it –
if you can offer me some,
I swear to you by God you couldn't
145   please me more.

The Host shall answer:
What you ask for, stranger, I do not have –
I cannot offer you this:
I am not rich, I've always been poor,

multis enim   semper indigeo
150   diutius.

Sanctus Nicolaus:
Falsum refers   adque mendatium!
Nuper enim   per infortunium
peregisti   opus nefarium,
clericorum   fundens exi<ti>um
155   per corpora;

ergo prece   mentis sollicite
nostro simul   pectora tondite,
et dominum   mecum depossite
indulgere   nobis illi<ci>te
160   crimen mortis!

Oratio sancti Nicolai:
Misere<re>   nostri, rex glorie,
nobis locum   concede venie
et clericis   peremtis impie
per virtutem   <tue> potentie
165   redde vitam!

<Chorus:>
O Christi pietas,
<omni laude prosequenda,
qui sui famuli Nicolai merita
longe lateque mirabiliter declarat!>

Angelus:
170 Nicolae,   vita fidelibus
reddita est   a deo tuis precibus!

---

[163] impię L *(with* redde uitam *erased after it)*
[164] uirtutem potentie L *I adopt Y's completion.*
[166–9] *This is a briefer version of the antiphon, Hesbert 4008, which Y used for the completion here. In Hesbert it continues: 'for from his tomb streams oil and it heals all who are sick'. But this is inappropriate in the present context, where Nicolas, addressed by the Angel, is not in his tomb but alive. The variant version above, printed by Jones (Liturgy p. 38) from Paris BN lat. 5277 (inc.* O Christi mira pietas*), finishes here, with the word* declarat*, and is followed by the antiphon* O per omnia laudabilem virum *(Hesbert 4052).*
[170] Nicolaę L *Three letters (*sta?*) erased after* uita
[171] tuis] *sic* L *uis or* ius Y *(II 327 n. 6)*
In the lower margin, below this verse: nobis in exilio proscripti *(see explanatory note)*

always been in want of many things,
150   a long long time.

St Nicolas:
What you say is false, it is a lie!
For, not long ago, calamitously,
you perpetrated an abominable deed,
pouring death into the bodies
155   of the students;

therefore, with the prayer of a troubled spirit,
beat your breasts now, as I shall mine,
and beseech the Lord, together with me,
to pardon us the crime of the unlawful
160   killing!

St Nicolas' prayer:
Have mercy on us, King of glory,
grant us the opportunity of pardon,
and to the students murdered impiously,
through the power of your might
165   give life again!

Choir:
Oh compassion of Christ,
that must be honoured by every praise –
Christ who declares his servant Nicolas' merits
by wonders far and wide!

An Angel:
170 Nicolas, God has given back
life to the faithful through your prayers!

Explanatory notes

2 hunice] Cl. unicae.
7 anctius] Cl. anxius.
13 laciva (lativa L)] For unfamiliar spellings involving c, s, and t, see the 'Note on Spelling', above p. 59.
14 geiunia] Cl. ieiunia.
21 ausilium] Cl. auxilium.
28 anctietas] Cl. anxietas.
28–9 Lit. 'so that anxiety may perceive her as the first whom birth brought forth as the first'.
38 (and 44, 46) The force of *velis* in each phrase adds to the imperative the sense of will or consent: 'Do not will to bring on a danger ... do not consent to link us to such ... Do not willingly subject us ...'.
41 simus] Cl. Scimus.
49 in... lacu miserie] Y emends to the Cl. *in ... lacum*, but cf. Hofmann-Szantyr p. 277. The phrase *lacu miserie* is from Psalm 39, 3.
56 peroptime] Chr. Lat.: cf. Blaise, s.v. *peroptimus*.
59–62 Cf. Ecclesiasticus 2, 8–10; 2, 18–19; 1, 11–15; Psalm 33, 10.
68–9 Cf. Job 42, 10–15.
71–2 Siste gradum] Lit. 'Stay your step'.
92–3 Lit. 'whom the cause of literary study compels to bear the pains of exile' – i.e. in order to pursue their studies, the three have had to leave home or leave their native lands.
95 hospitare] Infinitive as imperative: cf. Hofmann-Szantyr p. 366.
101 Sommo] Cl. Summo.
110/11 At this point, we must assume, the students go to bed and fall asleep; the Host, after peering into their *mantice* (portmanteaux), goes to another part of the playing-space to address his wife.
119–20 Lit. 'infamy would carry us through the space of the world'.
122 siet] Cl. sciet.
130/1 Before St Nicolas speaks, the Host and his wife must mime the killing of the sleeping students – possibly, like Claudius with King Hamlet, by pouring poison into their ears (cf. 154–5 *fundens exitium per corpora*).
132 Y's emendation of *amotus* to *admotus* ('led to your gate') is unnecessary: Nicolas appears to be saying that, because he was poor, he had been driven away from the Host's gate in the daylight; he has nonetheless returned at night to beg for lodging.

157   tondite] Cl. tundite.

165/6   After 165, as the Choir sings the antiphon, Nicolas must continue to kneel absorbed in silent prayer, while the three murdered students arise from their bed.

170   fidelibus] The reference must be, in the first place, to the three students, yet the Angel's words carry a wider implication for all the 'faithful', all who have watched the play: they can be delivered from the death of sin by Nicolas' prayers, just as the students are delivered from physical death at his intercession.

171   Despite the two extra syllables, on grounds of sense I hesitate to delete *tuis* (which can, *pace* Young, be read completely).

After 171   nobis in exilio proscripti] If these words belong with the play, they may represent a fragmentary concluding invocation of Nicolas by the Choir:

> <Ora pro> nobis in exilio proscripti<s> ...
> Pray for us, outlawed in our exile...

(Then this figurative *exilium*, earthly existence, might echo the *exilium* for the sake of study evoked in 93.) But the words could also be a scribal addendum unrelated to the play-text.

Twelfth-century plays

V–VI *Verses pascales de tres Maries*
Versus de pelegrino
Easter Verses of the Three Maries,
and *Verses about the Stranger*,
from Vic

Style, meaning and structure

The opening of the *Verses pascales* takes its cue from the first words in Mark 16, which tell how Mary Magdalen, Mary Jacobi, and Salome (called Mary Salome in later Easter-plays) bought spices in order to anoint Jesus' body. As far as the written records can show, the Vic dramatist, composing in the earlier twelfth century (see below, p. 89), was the first to transform these words into a scene, adding the character of a Merchant and creating dialogue between him and the three Maries: the phrasing and conception of this scene, like so much else in his play, would seem to be his individual creative contribution. Two strophes of lament (3–10) are followed by one of resolution (11–14) and another in which the Merchant is addressed (15–18).

Though the MS has no rubric before the Merchant's answer (18/19), the way these four strophes are used in a later play, at Tours (Y I 439 f.), makes it likely that Mary Magdalen sang the first, Mary Jacobi the second, Mary Salome the third, and that all three then addressed the Merchant in chorus. He answers in strophes of the same form as theirs, though without their grieving refrain; at the same time, he has a refrainlike echo (23), repeating a verse that they had sung.

The point of the exchanges is that the Maries are intent upon a kind of physical immortality for their beloved hero: they want to buy an ointment potent enough to keep him forever beautiful and undecaying. Its cost is immaterial to them. They see the one they want among the merchant's wares. He realises that they have recognised the uniquely valuable one, and names a very high price for it: they must want it keenly to pay so much (25–7). Mary Magdalen answers him, handing over the sum without demur (28–31). Her loving extravagance in the buying of ointment echoes that of the unnamed woman, who in the western Church was traditionally identified with the Magdalen, who anointed Christ with precious spikenard in the house of Simon the leper: 'she has anointed my body beforehand for its burial' (cf. especially Mark 14, 3–8). Mary now leads her companions, her 'sisters', to the body of Christ, in a beautiful, though in several places enigmatic, song (32–66), which is the next among this dramatist's notable creations.

The rubric '.a.', which features four times here (43, 52, 57, 62) and which baffled earlier scholars, in my view indicates that at these moments an Angel (A<ngelus>) intervenes in Mary's song. It is this Angel who stresses the inner meaning of the tears and the anointing (43–5), and who promises that a heavenly power will move the stone (52). In the fourth strophe (53–9), it would seem that the stone has indeed been rolled away and that the Angel is now seen in his awesome radiance: Mary summons her companions to joy, not fear, and the Angel sounds the first note of the Resurrection. Mary asks her sisters to echo this, and the Angel bids the women to seek out the sorrowing disciples and tell them the message of triumph (60–6).

When this lyric, with its moments of dialogue, is over, however, we are back with the reality of the still unrisen Christ. Mary Magdalen and her sisters are grieving; they resolve to make their way to the tomb, 'so that we may be able to have joy' (73), but they have not yet reached either tomb or joy (67–87). There is no simple solution to this dramatic contradiction. It would be possible to interpret the whole of the elaborate preceding lyric (32–66) as a kind of dream-scene, an oneiric anticipation of the discovery at the tomb, or again to see the lament (67–84) that leads to the encounter with the Angel at the tomb (85–90) as a 'flashback'. Yet such suggestions are probably over-ingenious. It is more likely that the Vic playwright, working with materials of diverse provenance, was not over-concerned to establish a naturalistic narrative sequence. It may well be, for instance, that he found the three quatrains of lament (67–78), whose rhythm is less steady than that of the long lyrical composition, ready to hand, and decided to integrate them rather than reject them. The contradictions among the evangelists' accounts of the visit to the sepulchre are often so palpable – with one Angel appearing to two women in Matthew and to three in Mark, two Angels to Mary Magdalen alone in John, or again, with the women running to tell the disciples the Angel's message in Matthew, but too fearful to say anything to anyone in Mark – that a presentation coherent in every detail would have been well-nigh impossible to achieve. What mattered more to the dramatist was to make vivid the oscillations between grief and joyful hope before the climax, the anagnorisis.

The six-line strophe of prayer (79–84), that follows the quatrains in which lamentation dominates, leads to Mary Magdalen's outcry (85–7) and to the celebrated question and answer of the archaic Easter trope, *Quem queritis* (88–9). Here, most unusually, the rubric says that it is she, and not the three women together, who answers the Angel's question. This establishes a certain continuity with Mary's earlier lyrical exchanges with the Angel, yet the scene once more changes course, with material of different origin. The urgent, affirming Angel of the lyric becomes the questioning Angel of the ancient Easter dialogue. In this guise, too, he then proclaims the Resurrection (90–1), and this time his affirmation is completed by Mary's joyous 'Alleluia', her acceptance of his message (93), and by the *Te deum*, the fourth-century hymn of praise and thanksgiving. After more than eighty lines rich in original invention, the 'Easter verses' close with traditional components.

But for the Vic dramatist this was not, after all, the close. Having made Mary Magdalen the protagonist of his 'Easter verses of the three Maries', he also wanted to portray the moment in John 20, where she, alone, encounters the risen Christ. To do this, he created another group of lyrical verses (95–100, 102–3). These are quite without parallel in the extant Easter plays, though they were soon adapted to an Easter sequence, *Epitalamica*, that retained certain quasi-dramatic features, and that was probably composed in the later twelfth century by one of the sisters at the Paraclete, the convent Abelard had founded for Heloise and her community.[1]

Mary Magdalen's two quatrains (see p. 88) are dense with allusions to the Song of Songs: she re-enacts the rôle of the bride who longs for her divine lover and suddenly finds that he has disappeared. The verses in the Canticle 3, 1–4, where she goes out into the night searching for him, is confronted by the town guards, and only then, having slipped past them, finds her beloved – the model of the second quatrain here – were given the rubric, in the Vetus Latina and in one group of MSS of the Vulgate, 'the voice of Mary Magdalen speaking to the Church' (*Vox Mariae Magdalenae ad Ecclesiam*).[2] The Vic dramatist availed himself of this ancient identification of the Song of Songs bride with the Magdalen in order freshly to create the scene of her recognition of the risen Christ, whom at first she supposes to be the gardener (*ortolanus* – cf. John 20, 15). The guards from the Canticle are transformed into John's two

---

[1] For a text and discussion of this sequence, and of its relation to the Vic play, see Dronke 1993.
[2] D. De Bruyne, 'Les anciennes versions latines du Cantique des Cantiques', *Revue Bénédictine* XXXVIII (1926) 97–122, at pp. 100, 105.

Angels. Yet the dramatist's choice of verse-form here (95 ff.) indicates that he also availed himself of a profane song, one that showed eery parallels to John's gospel narrative: his form – a rare one – is that of a lyrical ballad, *Foebus abierat*, composed in northern Italy *c*. 1000, which in the eleventh century had made its way to Ripoll, the Benedictine abbey close to Vic. In this ballad, a girl who has lost her beloved sees his image (*imago fidelis*) standing before her in the night, but as, full of ardour, she stretches out her arms to press her body to his, he vanishes again, she is left holding nothing; streams of tears flow over her cheeks, till the next day her weeping does not cease:

> Extensis brachiis   corpus applicui...
> evanuit enim!   nichil retinui!...
> Fluxerunt per genas   ploratus rivuli –
> donec in crastinum   nunquam abstinui.[3]

For the Vic dramatist, however, the bride's blissful moment of finding and recognising her beloved, from the third chapter of the Song of Songs, remains predominant. His strophes are a joyous counter to the tragic ballad: what he is saying is that the risen Christ was more than a phantom image. That, I suspect, is why he chose not to dwell on the moment in John 20, 17 – 'Do not touch me!' – which is closest to the ballad's climax. For the moment of recognition (107–8) he uses only the preceding gospel words – 'Maria!' 'Raboni!' – intensifying them by repetition and variation (John's gloss, *Magister*). Then, like a number of his thirteenth-century successors, for the encounter between Mary Magdalen and the disciples he borrows verses (110–23) from the early eleventh-century sequence *Victimae paschali*. Perhaps he was the first to do this, perhaps he was preceded by a decade or two by a Sicilian playwright (Y I 479); it is also possible that both lit upon the idea of adapting this sequence independently. In it the disciples, after the exchange with Mary, brood on her answer. Matthew's gospel tells that the Jews had conspired to lie about Christ's rising, bribing the guards to say the body had been stolen. The poet of the sequence traces the disciples' train of thought, overcoming doubt: one truthful witness outweighs a host of deceitful ones. Their final words in the sequence, which turn into a prayer to the risen Christ, offer an apt close to the scene.

In this scene, Christ had appeared to Mary as the Stranger, unrecognised. Now, in the last part of the play (124 ff.), he is the Stranger

---

[3] A critical text of the ballad, with translation and commentary, is given in Dronke 1968, II 334–41.

between the two disciples on the way to Emmaus. This part is not enacted but takes the form of a concluding series of antiphons based on words in Luke 24 and interspersed with Alleluias. The MS does not give the full range of these antiphons – perhaps because the series used was too well known in Vic to need complete recording. But we may suppose that those written in the MS, drawn from Luke 24, 17–19, were continued by others from later in the chapter (the episode concludes at 24, 35), before the final Doxology. Where the *Verses pascales*, like so many contemporary plays, conclude with a *Te deum*, the complementary *Versus de pelegrino*, equally fecund in poetic and dramatic innovation, likewise conclude in a way that anchors the play in sacred chant at the last.

Versification[1]

After a brief prelude (twice 8pp + 8pp), the dialogue between the Maries and the Merchant (3–31) is in a strophic form – three times 4 + 6pp – to which the Maries add a 9-syllabled refrain. This strophic form is closely analogous to that of the Latin strophes in the *Sponsus* (I) and that of the Hildesheim plays (III–IV), which consists of four 4 + 6pp lines followed by a refrain (see discussion above, pp. 10, 60 f.).

The form of the five strophes 32–66 is a virtuoso invention. Each strophe has seven 8pp lines, and each is monorhymed. In the first all rhymes are on *a*, in the second on *e*, in the third on *i*, in the fourth on *o*, in the last on *u*. This masterpiece of vowel-play, unique in its time, made its way to Austria before the end of the century, where the great Minnesinger Walther von der Vogelweide set himself the challenge of copying the form exactly in a comic vernacular lament over the passing of summer (*Diu welt was gelf, rôt unde blâ*),[2] and where Walther's disciple Marner imitated his master's feat in a Latin lament, *Iam dudum estivalia*,[3] in which winter comes to mean the growing cold of love. This path of transmission, which scholars have not observed hitherto, is one of the rare instances where we can chart the precise relations among lyrics on internal evidence alone: the form is too unusual to have been invented spontaneously a second time in the German-speaking world. The passage of the form from Vic to Austria also helps to explain the presence of some of the Vic lyrical exchanges, between the Maries and

---

[1] On Norberg's notation for medieval Latin verses, which is used here, see the General Introduction, p. xxxiv n. 32.
[2] Walther von der Vogelweide, *Die Gedichte* (ed. Lachmann-Kraus-Kuhn), 75, 25.
[3] *Carmina Burana* (ed. Hilka-Schumann-Bischoff), no. 3*.

the Merchant, in the *Carmina Burana* play of the Resurrection,[4] and, in another context, in the Passion play (see below, p. 208); the Codex Buranus, according to the most recent research, stems from the Tyrol region (see below, p. 195).

The verses 67–84 continue with 8–syllabled lines, alternating between 8p and 8pp. The three quatrains, 67–78, have an identical musical structure; that of the six-line strophe, 79–84, is distinct.

In the *Versus de pelegrino*, Mary Magdalen's song (95–100, 102–3) consists of two quatrains in rhythmic asclepiads (6pp + 6pp). Both the rhyme-scheme and the melody show that the verses 99–100, 102–3 (interrupted by the Angels' question at 101) constitute a second quatrain, identical in form with the first (95–8). The group of lyrics, from c. 1000 to the later twelfth century, that use rhythmic asclepiads in strophic form, is discussed more fully in Dronke 1993. The strophes are always monorhymed, but their length varies from one lyric to another (*Foebus abierat* is in 5-line strophes) and can vary within a lyric.

The disciples' verses 116–23, from *Victimae paschali*, show the syllabic parallelism of a classical sequence – each half-strophe is built 8p, 6p, 5p, 5p; in the preceding dialogue (110–15) the sequence verses, likewise heavily stressed on the paroxytone, are not syllabically symmetrical: the parallelism is 'made good' by the music.

The manuscript

The 85 leaves of the present codex 105 (CXI) in the Episcopal Museum at Vic consist of eleven gatherings spanning from the later eleventh to the thirteenth century. The whole is a Catalan manuscript chiefly of tropes and sequences, almost certainly copied in the Vic scriptorium in the course of this period:[1] new compositions, and compositions for new feasts, were added from time to time. The beginning of the oldest part (preceding the extant gatherings I–VI) is missing. At the close of gathering VIII the two dramatic compositions, *Verses pascales de tres Maries* and *Versus de pelegrino*, were added in the twelfth century on pages that had been left blank. Music – Aquitanian notation on ruled lines – was provided for the first piece, except for lines 43–84. While the seven-line strophes (32–66) will all have been sung to the same melody,

---

[4] Ibid., no. 15*, vv. 80–3, 88–91 (*Uxor apothecarii*).
[1] In all the older scholarly literature, and some of the new, it was assumed that this codex stemmed from the nearby Benedictine abbey of Ripoll; the first scholar to rectify this was Heinrich Husmann, *Tropen- und Sequenzhandschriften* (Répertoire International des Sources Musicales V 1, Munich-Duisburg 1964), pp. 97 f.

Anglès[2] assumed that this melody was also used for lines 67–84, which on metrical grounds seems to me questionable. Music for the second piece goes only as far as line 106 (i.e. to the foot of fol. 60v) and is missing for the rest, though the pages had been ruled in preparation for it.

The nature of the copyist's errors (e.g. the intrusive *dicxit angelus* after 5, *perfudia* 37, *augemus* 38, *cumuli* 50, *sudarum* 115, *quomodo* 118) makes clear that the text of the plays cannot be an autograph. If the pair of plays was copied *c*. 1160/70, they had already become garbled by the time of copying. The plays themselves were probably composed a good generation earlier, *c*. 1130.

---

[2] Anglès 1935: the musical transcription of the two pieces is on pp. 276–8 and 281; a brief description of the MS on p. 146. The fullest description is now that of Eva Castro Caridad, in her *Tropos y troparios hispánicos* (Santiago de Compostela 1991), pp. 61–79, to whose discussion the brief note above is particularly indebted.

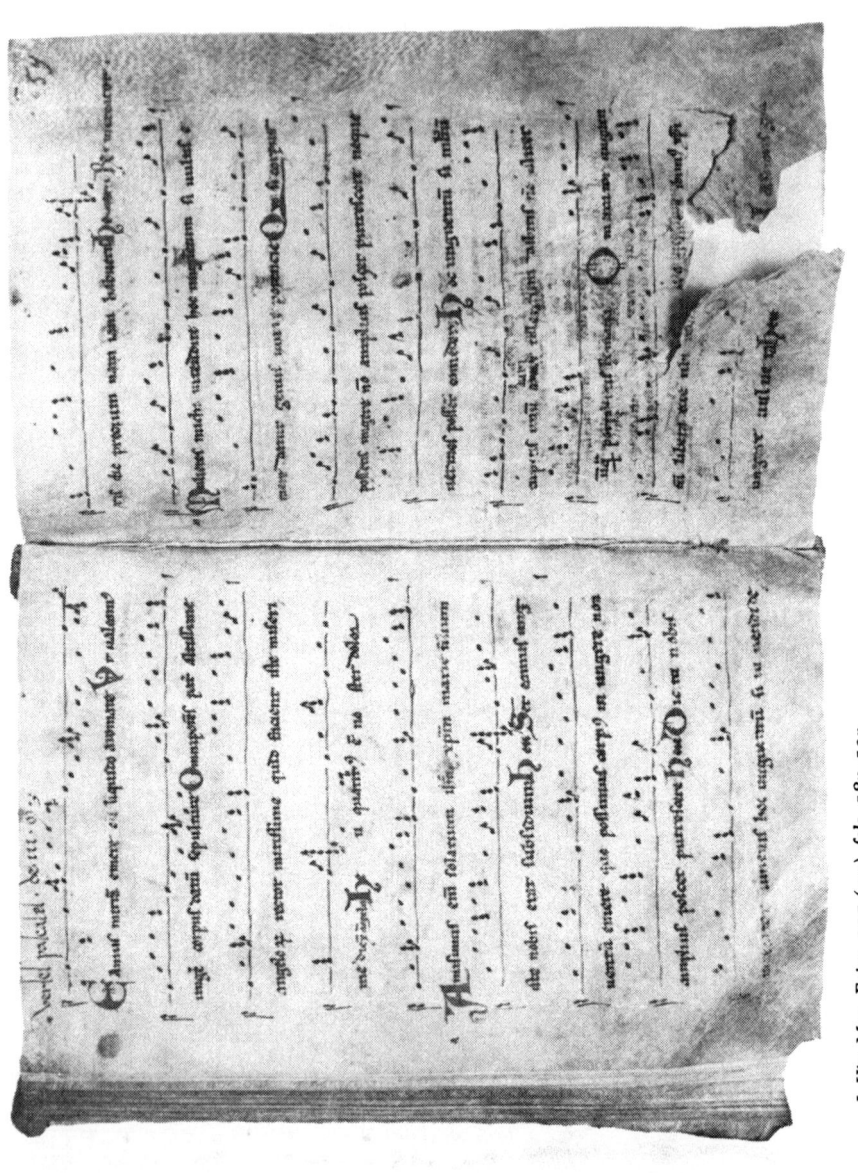

I Vic, Mus. Episc. 105 (cxi), fols. 58v–59r
(Verses pascales, 1–32)

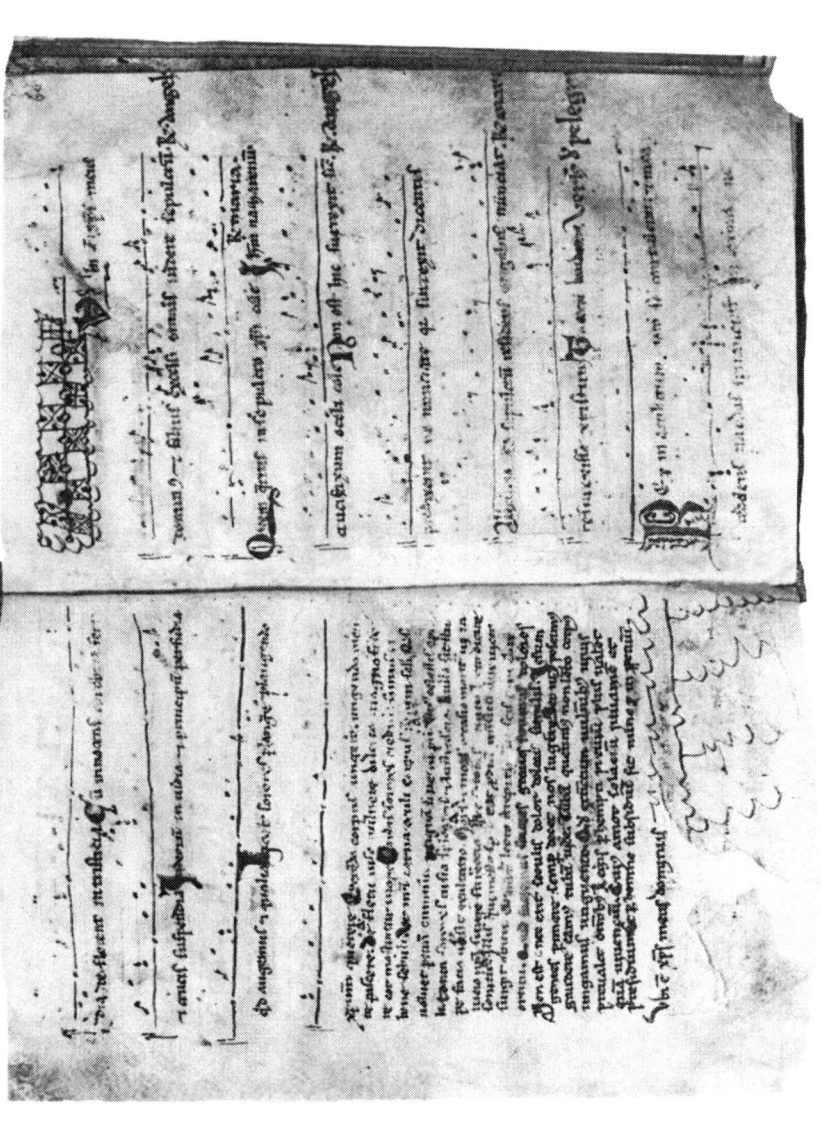

II Vic. Mus. Episc. 105 (cxi), fols. 59v–60r (Verses pascales, 32–97)

58v *Verses pascales de tres Maries*

<Maries:>
Eamus mirram emere   cum liquido aromate,
Ut valeamus ungere   corpus datum sepúlture.

Omnipotens   pater altissime,
angelorum   rector mitissime,
5 quid facient   iste miserime?
   Heu quantus est noster dolor!

Amisimus   enim solatium,
Ihesum Christum,   Marie filium:
iste nobis   erat subsidium.
10   *Heu <quantus est noster dolor!>*

Set eamus   unguentum emere
quo possimus   corpus inungere:
non amplius   poscet putrescere.
   Heu <quantus est noster dolor!>

15 Dic tu nobis,   mercator iuvenis,
59r hoc unguentum   si tu vendide/ris:

v: Vic, Mus. Episc. 105 (CXI), fols. 58v–61v
y: K. Young, *The Drama of the Medieval Church* (2 vols., Oxford 1933) I 678–81
a: H. Anglès, *La música a Catalunya fins al segle XIII* (Barcelona 1935), pp. 275–81
d: R. B. Donovan, *The Liturgical Drama in Medieval Spain* (Toronto 1958), pp. 78–81, 85
l: W. Lipphardt, *Lateinische Osterfeiern und Osterspiele*, Teil v (Berlin–New York 1976), pp. 1663–8
Many of the minor divergences between these four texts and mine are not noted below, nor are the normalisations of spelling intermittently introduced by the earlier editors.

Title: Verses pascales de .III. M.s (*rubric added by another hand*) v de III Mariis (*or* Mulieribus) edd. But the Catalan form Verses suggests that .III. and M.s should also be given a Catalan resolution (*cf. the later mention of* Les tres Maries *at Gerona,* Y II 504).
⁵ *after* miserime] dicxit angelus add.(*another hand*) v (Dicunt y). D *assumes that the angel sings 3–5,* L *that he sings 3–18. Yet in the Tours Easter play (s. XIII, cf.* Y I 439), *the strophes 3–6, 7–10, 11–14 are sung respectively by* Maria Magdalene, Maria Iacobi, *and* Maria Salome, *and in the Narbonne play (of uncertain date, cf.* Y I 285) *these strophes are sung by the three Maries 'together' (*insimul*). The Tours solution seems logically and dramatically best, that of Narbonne entails the slight awkwardness that the Maries refer to themselves in the third person. It may have been precisely a sense of this awkwardness that prompted a scribe to insert 'said the angel' after the first strophe. Yet the verses 6 ff. are so clearly sung by the Maries that it is dramatically more plausible to suppose either Mary Magdalen singing the opening (3–5), referring to her two wretched companions, as in Tours, or the three Maries referring to themselves as 'these most wretched women', as in Narbonne, than to introduce the angel singing at this stage.*
¹³ poscet putrescere] *sic* v putrescire YA
¹⁵ Dic tu] *corr. from* Dicitu v

Easter verses of the three Maries

Maries:
Let us go to buy myrrh   with liquid spices,
so that we may anoint   the body due for burial.

Almighty Father, highest one,
gentlest ruler of the angels,
5 what shall these most wretched women do?
    Alas, how great is our grief!

For we have lost our solace,
Jesus Christ, the son of Mary:
he was our support –
10   *Alas, how great is our grief!*

But let us go to buy the ointment
with which we may anoint his body:
after that, it cannot decay.
    Alas, how great is our grief!

15 Tell us, young merchant,
if you'll sell us this ointment –

dic precium,   nam iam habueris.
    Heu <quantus est noster dolor!>

Respondet mercator:
Mulieres,   michi intendite:
20 hoc unguentum   si vultis emere,
datur genus   mirre potencie;

Quo si corpus   possetis ungere,
non amplius   poscet putrescere,
neque vermes   possent comedere.

25 Hoc unguentum   si multum cupitis,
unum auri   talentum dabitis,
non aliter   unquam portabitis.

Respondet Maria:
O mercator,   unguentum libera:
ecce tibi   tradimus munera –
30 ibimus Christi   ungere vulnera.
    Heu <quantus est noster dolor!>

59v Tanta, sorores, gau/dia
deflorent in tristicia,
Cum innocens obrobria
35 fert et crucis suspendia
Iudeorum invidia
et principum perfidia.
Quid angemus, et qualia!

Licet, sorores, plangere,
40 plangendo Christum querere,
Querendo corpus ungere,
ungendo mente pascere.
A<ngelus>:
De fletu, viso vulnere,

[27] non] *sic* v nec YADL   i *erased before* unquam v
[29] tradimus] *sic* v dabimus YADL
[32] Tanta] Tta v Cuncta YAD
[37] perfudia v
[38] augemus v angemus YADL
[39] Licet] L *corr. from* C v. *For the melody of 39–45, see also Rankin 1990, p. 334.*
[43] (*and* 52, 57, 62) *Over these verses a red superscript* .a., *not mentioned by Anglès and regarded as inexplicable by Young, Donovan and Lipphardt, probably indicates* Angelus: *i.e. that in sts. 2–5 of Mary Magdalen's lyric the Angel intervenes and sings in alternation with her.*

tell us the price, for you shall have it now.
   Alas, how great is our grief!

The merchant answers:
Women, mark my words:
20 if you want to buy *this* ointment,
it is endowed with the nature of myrrh's power:

If you can use this to anoint a body,
after that, it cannot decay –
the worms will not be able to consume it.

25 If you want this ointment very much,
you must pay one talent of gold,
otherwise you'll never take it with you.

Mary answers:
Merchant, do release the ointment:
look, we're handing you the money –
30 we shall go to anoint Christ's wounds.
   Alas, how great is our grief!

Sisters, such great joys
shed their blossoms in sorrow,
when the innocent one endures
35 scorn and the gibbet of the cross
through the envy of the Jews
and the chief priests' perfidy.
What cause of anguish we shall have!

Sisters, it is right to mourn,
40 mourning to look for Christ,
looking to anoint his body,
anointing to feed on it with the mind.
Angel:
In weeping as you see the wound,

dilecto magno federe
45 cor mostratur in opere.

<Maria:>
Cordis, sorores, creduli
simus et bene seduli,
Ut nostri cerna<nt> oculi
corpus, precium seculi.
50 Quis volvet petram tumuli
magnam sine vi plurimi?
A<ngelus>:
Virtus celestis ep<u>li.

<Maria:>
Tanta, sorores, visio
sple<n>doris et lustrascio
55 Nulla sit stupefatio:
vobis sit exultatio.
A<ngelus>:
Mors et mor<t>is occasio
moritur vi<c>to vicio:
nostra, surge, surreccio!

<Maria:>
60 Hoc, sorores, <cir>cuitu
lecto dicite sonitu.
A<ngelus>:
Illis qui mesto spiritu
ea<n>t pro domni transitu,
dux victo surgit obitu.

---

[45] mostratur] *'Possibly the s is expunged' (Y); the dot, however, is to the left of the s.*
[48] cerna v (*without space for nt, but a stroke after* cerna *could have been intended as an insertion-sign*).
[49] corpus precium] *sic* v corpus Christi vim YADL
[50] cumuli v
[51] sine ui pł v sive vim populi YADL *But at* 131 *the copyist writes* ppł *for* populo, *and* plurimi *fits the sense better than* populi *here.*
[57] moris (*corr. from* mors) v
[58] ui..a v vita YADL
[63] eat pro dñi v et prodium YDL Et pro Domini A YDL *emend to* et proditio, *which contravenes both grammar and rhythm.*
[64] Lux A

to the loved one, in a great love-bond,
45 by your action, your heart is shown.

Mary:
Sisters, let us be of trusting
and eagerly attentive heart,
so that our eyes may contemplate
the body, treasure of the world.
50 But who will roll away the tombstone,
huge, without the strength of many a man?
Angel:
The power of the heavenly feast.

Mary:
Sisters, let so great a sight
and the gleam of splendour
55 not make you dazed:
let it bring you exultation.
Angel:
Death and the cause of death
are dying, vice being overcome:
arise, our resurrection!

Mary:
60 Sisters, sing this with the fairest
melody as you walk.
Angel:
For those who go about with mournful spirit,
because of their master's passing,
the Prince rises, with death conquered.

65 Querantur leto strepitu:
nunc scis\<citur\> dux ortitu!

\<*Maria:*\>
Quid faciemus, sorores? –
graves ferimus dolores.
Non est, nec erit seculis,
70 dolor dolori similis.

Iesum gentes perimere:
semper decet nos lugere.
Set ut poscimus gaudere,
eamus tu\<m\>bam videre.

75 Tumbam querimus non lento –
corpus ungamus ungento,
Quod extinctum vulneribus
vivis prevalet omnibus:

Regis perhempti previum
80 plus valet quam vivencium,
Cuius amor solacium,
iuvamen et presidium
Et per homne subsidium
sit nunc et in perpetuum.

85 Ubi est Christus, meus dominus /
60r et filius excelsi?
Eamus videre sepulcrum.

Respondet Angelus:
Quem queritis in sepulcro, christicole?

Respondet Maria:
Ihesum Nazarenum crucifixum, o celicole.

⁶⁵ lecto v *edd.*
⁶⁶ …scis…dux ortitu YD Nunc sanctis iam lux oritur AL *After* scis, *and a space for 2–3 letters, V probably has* ur, *or just possibly* m, *before* dux.
⁷⁰ dolori] *sic* v (s *erased*) doloris YADL
⁷⁹ preuium] *sic* v premium (*em.*) YADL
⁸³ per homne] *sic* v perenne (*em.*) YADL
⁸⁵/⁶ *The words* Ubi … dominus *(written as cue on* 59v*) recur with music on* 60r.
⁸⁸/⁹ R Maria v YADL *correct without discussion to* Respondent Mariae; *similarly at* 91/2, *where the margin in* v *is cut away and only* R Mari *can be read. This would bring the play in line with other versions of* Quem queritis. *Yet it is a play with so many unusual features that I hesitate to force conformity here. Especially if 3–5 above were sung by Mary Magdalen, referring*

65 Let those be sought with shouts of joy:
   now in his rising is the Prince made known!

   Mary:
   Sisters, what shall we do? –
   We endure grievous sorrows.
   There is not, nor in ages shall there be
70 a sorrow like our sorrow.

   The nations have slain Jesus:
   it is right for us to mourn unceasingly.
   Yet, that we may be able to rejoice,
   let us go to see the tomb.

75 Not slowly shall we seek the tomb –
   with the unguent let us anoint the body
   which, destroyed by wounds,
   prevails over all the living:

   What remains of the slain king
80 is worth more than the life of the living;
   may his love be solace,
   help and protection
   and support in everything,
   now and in perpetuity.

85 Where is Christ my Lord,
   the son of the one on high?
   Let us go to see the sepulchre.

   The Angel answers:
   Whom are you looking for in the sepulchre, friends of Christ?

   Mary answers:
   The crucified Jesus of Nazareth, friend of heaven.

---

to her two companions as iste miserime *– and the fact that she alone sings these verses in the Tours play makes this likely – then it is possible that here too she acts as coryphée and answers the Angel on behalf of her companions.*

Respondet Angelus:
90 Non est hic: surrexit sicut predixerat.
Ite, nunciate quia surrexit, dicentes –

Respondet Mari<a>:
Alleluia!
Ad sepulcrum residens angelus nunciat resurexisse Christum!

Te, deum, laudamus < . . .>

Versus de pelegri<no>

<Maria:>
95 Rex in acubitum   iam se contulerat
    et mea redolens   nardus spiraverat;
60v In ortum ve/neram   in quem descenderat,
    at ille transiens   iam declinaverat.

    Per noctem igitur   hunc querens exeo,
100 huc illuc transiens   nusquam reperio.

Angeli:
Mulier, quid ploras? Q<u>em queris?

Maria:
Occurrunt vigiles   ardenti studio,
quos cum transierim,   sponsum invenio!

Ortolanus:
Mulier, quid ploras? <Q>uem queris?

Maria:
105 Tulerunt dominum meum et nescio ubi posuerunt eum.

61r Si tu / sustulisti eum, dicito michi et eum tollam!

Ortolanus:
Maria, Maria, Maria!

Item responde Maria:
Raboni, Raboni, Magister!

---

[94] Versus de pelegri (*in hand of main rubricator of this page, margin cut away*) v pelegri<nis> YAL pelegri<no> D – *see explanatory note ad loc.*
[97] ortum v hortum YADL   [101] Qem v
[107/8] *A substantially later hand has deleted* Item responde *and added* R *superscript. In 108 this hand has deleted* magister *and added* rabōi *superscript. These alterations do not, in my view, have sufficient authority to be incorporated in the text (as they are in YADL).*

The Angel answers:
90 He is not here: he has risen as he foretold.
Go, proclaim that he has risen, saying –

Mary answers:
Alleluia!
The Angel sitting at the sepulchre proclaims that Christ has risen!

Te, deum, laudamus . . .

Verses about the Stranger

Mary:
95 The King had already gone to his place of rest
and my scent of spikenard filled the air;
I entered the garden where he had come down,
but already he had left and turned away.

So I go out looking for him, through the night,
100 turning now here now there, I find him nowhere.

Angels:
Woman, why are you weeping? Whom are you looking for?

Mary:
The guards, full of ardent zeal, are running towards me –
when I have passed them I shall find my bridegroom!

Gardener:
Woman, why are you weeping? Whom are you looking for?

Mary:
105 They have taken my Lord away and I don't know where they have put him.
If you have taken him away, tell me and I'll remove him.

Gardener:
Mary, Mary, Mary!

Mary, answer again:
Raboni, Raboni, Master!

Mar\<ia\> rediens dicit:
Dic, impie zabule, quid valet nunc fraus tua?

Discipuli:
110 Dic nobis, Maria,
quid vidisti in via?

Maria:
Sepulcrum Christi viventis
et gloriam vidi resurgentis,

Angelicos testes,
115 sudarium et vestes.

Discipuli:
61v Credendum est magis / soli
    Marie veraci
    quam Iudeorum
    turbe fallaci.
120 Scimus Christum surexisse
    a mortuis vere:
    tu nobis, Christe
    rex, miserere.

    *

\<*Chorus:*\>
Qui sunt hii sermones quos confertis ad invicem ambulantes
125 et estis tristes? alleluia.
Respondens unus, cui nomen erat Cleophas, dixit ei:
tu solus peregrinus es in Iherussalem
et non cognovisti que facta sunt in illa his diebus? alleluia.
Quibus ille dixit: Que?
130 Et dixerunt: De Ihesu Nazareno, qui fuit vir propheta,

108/9 Mar v *There is space for* ia; *a later hand has added superscript* i.
111 iuid v quid YADL
115 sudarum v sudarium YADL
115/6 Angli Non est hic surexit sicut predixerat ub v *(repetition of 90)*
118 quomodo v quam A
126 *The later hand of* 107/8 *has written* respodent du *(sic) superscript and deleted* ei.
127 Iherussalem] *sic* V
129 *The later hand has added* res *superscript over* Quibus.
130 *The later hand has added* resp. du *superscript over* dixerunt.

Returning, Mary says:
Tell me, impious fiend, what force has your guile now?

Disciples:
110 Tell us, Mary,
what did you see on the way?

Mary:
The sepulchre of Christ, the living,
and I saw the glory of his rising,

the angel-witnesses,
115 the head-shroud and the grave-cloths.

Disciples:
We should sooner believe Mary
    alone – she is truthful –
than the whole deceitful
multitude of Jews.
120 We know that Christ has truly
    risen from the dead:
    have mercy on us,
    Christ our King!

*

Choir:
What are these things you are discussing as you walk along
125 and are sad (alleluia)?
One, called Cleophas, answered him saying:
you must be the only stranger in Jerusalem
not to know what has been happening there in these last days (alleluia).
He said to them: What?
130 And they said: About Jesus of Nazareth, who was a man, a prophet,

potens in opere et sermone coram deo et omni populo, alleluia.
. . .
Gloria <patri et filio et spiritui sancto,
sicut erat in principio, et nunc et semper,
et in secula> seculorum, amen.

131/2 *No gap* v
132 G *(i.e. Gloria)* v *om.* YADL

mighty in deed and word before God and all the people (alleluia).
. . .
Glory be to the Father and to the Son and to the Holy Ghost,
as it was in the beginning, is now, and ever shall be,
world without end, amen.

Explanatory notes

1–2   The wording echoes Mark 16, 1: *Maria Magdalene et Maria Iacobi et Salome* **emerunt aromata ut... ungerent** *Iesum*; myrrh is mentioned in John 19, 39: *Nicodemus... ferens mixturam* **myrrhae** *et aloes*.
2   sepúlture] Rhythm and melody here imply a stress on the proparoxytone and shortening of the second *u*.
11   Cf. 1–2 n.
13   (*also* 23) poscet] Cl. posset.
15   mercator iuvenis] In the Tours Easter play (Y I 440), a young merchant (*mercator iuvenis*, 41) is distinguished from another merchant (*Alius Mercator*, 52/3), with whom the bargaining is concluded. It seems likely that the Tours dramatist developed this notion by taking a hint from the word *iuvenis* in this strophe, which almost certainly originated at Vic. The alternative, that the Vic text once included dialogue for an older merchant, which no longer survives, cannot be ruled out. The expression *iuvenis* is hardly on its own a reason for postulating it; yet it may also be relevant that in the *Sponsus* (above, p. 18), the merchants approached by the Foolish Virgins consist of a *mercator* and his colleague (*sotius*, 59).
16   (*also* 20, 25) hoc unguentum] The Maries, and then the Merchant, point to a particular ointment, that they and he know to be the most precious in his stock. Their question implies that they are also aware of its scarcity-value – he may not wish to part with it, or with all of it – and in their eagerness they let slip that no price is too high for them. So the Merchant, after confirming the power and value of this ointment, suggests a price, a talent of gold, that is about a thousand pounds by present-day reckoning.
21   datur] i.e. *huic datur*.
mirre] The Tours adaptor of this strophe (Y I 440) has the more banal reading *mire potencie* ('of wondrous power').
22   The capital at *Quo* indicates that the Merchant, like the Maries, has been given three-line strophes (though his are not followed by a refrain): 19–24 are not a single six-line strophe, as they are printed in YDL.
27/8   Maria] I.e. Mary Magdalen. It is she who addresses the two other Maries, her *sorores*, in the extended lyrical composition that follows (32–66), in the course of which the Angel answers her. On the form of this song, see the introductory note above, p. 87.
46   Though there are no rubrics to indicate that Mary resumes her song, the four places where the Angel's intervention is indicated (43, 52, 57, 62)

50 Mark 16, 3-4: ***Quis revolvet*** nobis lapidem? ... Erat quippe **magnus valde**.

51 The verse has been misread in YADL as *magnam sive vim populi*; this does not yield grammar or sense.

52 The Angel's cryptic answer seems to mean that only a heavenly power can remove the stone. The poet's use of *epuli* here may be due chiefly to the demands of rhythm and rhyme.

53-5 Cf. Matthew 28, 3-5; Mark 16, 5-6.

54 lustrascio] Cl. lustratio (here = *illustratio*).

60-1 That is, Mary is asking her two companions to repeat in song the Angel's verse (59), *nostra, surge, surreccio!*

63 While v's *dñi* can be resolved as *domini* or *domni*, the second is preferable rhythmically.

65-6 The Angel is telling the Maries to seek out all those who are grief-stricken at Christ's death (*qui mesto spiritu eant pro domni transitu*, 63 f.), and joyously to proclaim the Resurrection to them. My interpretation of these problematic verses depends on: (1) correcting v's *lecto* (65) to *leto* – it is less likely to be a variant spelling of *leto* than a scribal error, under the influence of *lecto* in 61; (2) taking *ortitu* to be the poet's own coined variant for *ortu* – he needed the extra syllable for the sake of his complex pattern of rhythm and rhyme. While one might also speculate whether a diminutive of *hortus* was intended here – cf. especially *ortilus, Novum Glossarium*, s.v. – the fact that none appears to exist in a fourth declension form makes this unlikely.

69-70 Cf. Jeremiah, Thren. 1, 12.

73 poscimus] Cl. possimus (cf. 13 n.).

75 I take the present *querimus* to have future force, though an emendation to *queramus* would be attractive and cannot be excluded on rhythmic grounds: the music for 75 is identical with that for 67 – *Quid faciémus, sorores?* – and hence can accommodate a stressed fourth syllable without difficulty.

79-80 Lit. 'The former state of the slain king is worth more than (that) of the living'; the emendation of *previum* to *premium* (sic YADL) seems unnecessary.

83 per homne] Cl. per omne (cf. 79 perhempti). I construe this phrase as qualifying *subsidium*; the emendation to *perenne* (sic YADL) seems unnecessary.

94 The *Te deum* indicated here, which was doubtless sung chorally, serves to demarcate the *Verses pascales* from the *Versus de pelegrino*. While I have adopted a continuous line-numbering, this is primarily for convenience: we have no evidence from twelfth-century Vic, to my knowledge, about whether the sequel was performed soon after the *Verses pascales*, or at a later hour the same day, or on Easter Monday. This was the commonest occasion for performing a *Peregrinus* play; on the other hand, the first part of these *Versus de Pelegrino* – unparalleled in the other examples of the genre – is intimately linked with the Easter Sunday *hortulanus* episode of John 20, 11-18, and must be seen at least

to some extent as the complement to the 'Easter verses of the three Maries'.

94/5   Versus de pelegri<no>] D gave this completion (as against that of YAL, *pelegrinis*). D's is preferable, in that the *pelegrinus* central to the action is the still unrecognised risen Christ. The connotations of the word – the spelling with *l* shows vernacular influence – are here probably those of 'stranger' rather than 'pilgrim'. In thirteenth-century plays (Rouen, Fleury, Padua) Cleophas and his companion are designated *peregrini*, and both they and Christ are dressed as pilgrims, but I know no earlier example of this. The heading may refer more especially to the closing antiphons (124–31), yet it is also possible that the dramatist saw Christ's encounter with Mary as another exemplification of his *peregrinus* rôle.

95–6   Song of Songs 1, 11: *Dum esset* **rex in accubitu** *suo,* **nardus mea** *dedit odorem suum.*

97   Song 6, 1: *Dilectus meus* **descendit in hortum** *suum.*

98   Song 5, 6: *at ille declinaverat atque* **transierat.**

99 f.   Cf. Song 3, 1–2.

101   John 20, 13. The *Quem queris?* has been added in order to make the Angels' question identical with that of the Gardener (104).

102–3   Song, 3, 3–4: *Invenerunt me* **vigiles...** *Paululum* **cum pertransissem eos, inveni** *quem diligit anima mea.*

104–8   John 20, 15–16.

108–9   Rediens] Mary returns from the sepulchre to the disciples: cf. John 20, 18.

109   zabule] Cl. diabole.

110–23   This is from the second half of the Easter sequence *Victime paschali*, attributed to the imperial chaplain Wipo (c. 1010). Because of their vivid element of dialogue, the verses were integrated in a number of Easter plays. There are only two other twelfth-century examples of this integration: in a *Peregrinus* play from Sicily (Y 1 476–80), which is in an older MS than that of Vic, and which includes the complete text of the sequence, and in one from St Lambrecht in Austria (Y 1 363–5), towards 1200.

115   sudarium et vestes] The *sudarium* is the cloth that covers the head of the dead person (cf. John 20, 7); the *vestes* are the *linteamina* mentioned in the same verse of John – linen cloths that cover the rest of the body.

115/16   The erroneous insertion of *Angeli Non est hic surexit sicut predixerat vobis* here may suggest that line 90 stood at the corresponding place on the lefthand page in v's exemplar. It is possible that the next verses of *Victime paschali – Surrexit Christus spes mea, / precedet suos in Galilea* – should have been copied here instead, but as the dramatist in any case does not use the complete sequence-text, I hesitate to insert these verses in the edition.

118–19   The allusion is to Matthew 28, 11–15, where the Jewish chief priests and elders bribe the guards of the tomb to say that Christ's body had been stolen while they slept.

124–31   The play concludes as a ceremony, with office antiphons based on Luke 24, 17–19. It is unlikely that these ended at 131, in the middle of the journey to Emmaus. Young (I 688–9) prints a group of antiphons that include those used here but that continue the Emmaus narrative in further ones, based on Luke 24, 26–32. Some of these will doubtless also have been used at Vic, before the final Doxology (132–4), for which a traditional English translation is here given. (For its use at the close of a dramatic ceremony, compare for instance the Padua 'Purification', Y II 254.)

VII *Danielis ludus*
The Play of Daniel, from Beauvais

Style, meaning and structure

The most vivacious and many-sided of the surviving Latin plays on an Old Testament theme, the Beauvais *Play of Daniel*, is not confined to its Old Testament theme. Like the Freising *Play of the Star* (II), this play forms part of the joyous celebrations of a cathedral school between Christmas and Twelfth Night, and was presented in the context of a Feast of Fools. The theme of Christmas here suffuses the Old Testament narrative. Daniel is the Daniel of the Bible story, the sage who serves but also stands up to the monarchs Belshazzar and Darius; yet he is equally the prophet of Christ and the *figura* of Christ. It is especially by adding the dimension of *figura* that this playwright enriches and surpasses the work of his predecessor, Hilarius of Orléans, who had composed an impressive 'Story of Daniel for Performance' (*Historia de Daniel representanda*) perhaps only a decade earlier.[1] Just as, in the Freising *Play of the Star*, the boys who sing at the close belong both to Herod's court in the past and to the Feast of Fools celebration – of the true King – in the present (see above, p. 29), so here the scholars of Beauvais belong fictively to the Babylonian realm, in which they function as actors and chorus, but they too belong to a present, in which they recall that Old Testament realm and the New which it prefigured, and bring both into a realm of play, in the heady festivities of their Christmas season.

The brief prologue (1–2) may have been sung by a precentor, and thus have been set off against the first choral piece, which follows. The 'inventors' of the play, it tells, are 'the young', *iuventus* – a term whose

---

[1] The plays are edited together in Bulst 1989 and Y II 276–306. It is possible that both pieces were written collaboratively: that of Hilarius, preserved among his collected *Versus et ludi*, has in the margins not only his own name but the names Iordanus, Simon and Hugo; the prologue of the Beauvais play alludes (2) to a collective effort by the *iuventus* of the cathedral school. Yet it would be hard to doubt that one exceptionally eloquent and imaginative writer was the controlling intelligence behind the Beauvais text, and in what follows I shall speak of 'the dramatist', rather than of 'the Beauvais drama committee'. That this dramatist included some verses composed by colleagues is at least possible; that he worked in close conjunction with one or more composers, a director, and the actor-singers seems highly probable.

extension could vary, but in the twelfth century tended to begin at 21 and not end before 50. The play is presented as a tribute to Christ: by giving us a Daniel who is *figura Christi*, the playwright makes this true in a more than formal sense.

The Beauvais play, like that of Orléans, is in two parts, which correspond to the biblical demarcation of the narrative. The prophet's encounter with Nebuchadnezzar (Daniel 1–4) is recalled only by allusions; it is principally his dealings with Belshazzar (Daniel 5), and then with Belshazzar's conqueror Darius (Daniel 6), that shape the two 'acts' of the drama. Like his predecessor Hilarius, this dramatist uses a series of choral lyrics as acclamations and processional songs (*conductus*) to accompany the entrances and exits of the protagonists, thus lending ceremonious princely splendour to his scenes. Here the first of these lyrics is the sequence (*prosa*: see p. 116 below) sung by Belshazzar's nobles at his entry (3–20). These nobles, or satraps, of the Babylonian court are deliberately revealed also as scholars – men and boys – of Beauvais. They sing their strophes (in alternating half-choirs) from a vantage from which they already know all that happens: as they celebrate Daniel's victorious emergence from his various tests, they recall in detail the story that is about to be unfolded. The past/present tension which underlines this chorus results in one anomaly: as nobles acclaiming Belshazzar, the singers cannot yet 'know' of their King's murder by Darius; so the instigator of the lions' den ordeal (15 ff.) is left obscure: to one unfamiliar with the story, it would indeed sound as though Belshazzar, not Darius, was the culprit.

The satraps conclude with the acclamation 'King, live for ever!' (21), that runs as a refrain through both the biblical narrative and the play. A second sequence of lyrical acclamation follows, with the fetching of the Jewish Temple vessels, recalling the victory of the King's father, Nebuchadnezzar, over the Jews (26–45). This song, by contrasting Jerusalem and Babylon – the divinely chosen city and the profane one – in the way familiar from Augustine's *City of God*, brings out the blasphemy implicit in the use of these sacred vessels for revelling, and prepares for the nemesis (46/7), the mysterious hand's writing on the wall. (Sadly, there is no contemporary documentation of how this effect was staged.)

The summoning of the diverse mages, and their failure to interpret the words (47–54), closely follow the biblical narrative (5, 7–8). But the *conductus* acclaiming the Queen at her entry (55–67) is freely invented.[2]

---

[2] The 'dress of cloth of gold' that the Queen wears (58) will, like the Temple vessels, have been borrowed for the performance from the Beauvais cathedral treasure – just as Geoffrey of St Albans borrowed rich vestments from the abbey for his 'play of St Catherine' (see above, p. xix).

The Babylonian nobles again become momentarily a chorus in the present. The transformation occurs within the song itself: after heralding the Queen's arrival (55–8), which is happening at that moment, they tell what has not yet happened but lies in the imminent future – the calling of Daniel and his grim reading of the inscription (59–60). Then swiftly the singers step back into their rôle as jubilant Babylonian courtiers (61–2).

The Queen's advice to send for Daniel (66–73) is followed by a bilingual scene (75–95) between the satraps and the prophet. The precise connotation of the vernacular snatches (which have no counterpart in the earlier Daniel play) is not easy to gauge. Here Latin and vernacular diction interpenetrate more fully than they do for instance in the *Sponsus* (I) or the *Passion Play* (IX): here, that is, we have passages of truly macaronic verse. The content does not suggest a comic effect: rather, perhaps, the bridging of the high, Latinate world of the court and the everyday, colloquial world outside it, from which Daniel is fetched. That everyday world, unlike the palace, is lowly, and three times Daniel calls himself 'poor and exiled' (88, 92, 96). Where in the Bible he had already been highly honoured by Belshazzar's father, who had made him principal court sage (Daniel 5, 11), the dramatist ignores this and shapes the scene more as in a *Märchen*: the stranger who has nothing and who comes to the court is not only the wisest but the handsomest and noblest man there (89–90).

Daniel's speech to the King (104–18) – explaining the cause of the downfall and dementia of his father, Nebuchadnezzar, warning the King himself of the same hubris with regard to the vessels, and at last interpreting the writing as Belshazzar's impending doom – is essentially biblical. What is new and unexpected is Belshazzar's repentance and decision to restore the vessels to the Jews (or to Daniel as their spokesman), and the two *conductus* that lead to carrying this out. The first (122–35) is the processional song accompanying the Queen's departure. Hilarius, too, had given the Queen a second *conductus*, couching both songs in the effusive *courtoisie* typical of his panegyric poems to young noblewomen and nuns:[3] she is 'the glory of all women ... the only one that has no flaw!'; 'giving solace, you surpass all ranks of women ... such beauty, modesty and wisdom scarcely exist elsewhere'. The Beauvais dramatist wanted something more specific: for him this Queen fulfils Solomon's evocation of the brave and virtuous woman (Proverbs 31, 10–11). And from Solomon, who like Daniel is *figura*

---

[3] Cf. Bulst 1989, nos. II, III, IV, V.

Christi, the chorus moves back into the joyful present, the Christmastide of the 'true Solomon', to echo this praise of the Queen: the last verse of the *conductus* (135) may even contain an allusion to the physical mode of this echo, inviting 'those from afar' – perhaps a small choir set in a gallery in another part of the cathedral – to harmonise their melody.

At once (136 ff.) the young scholars of Beauvais slip back into their rôle as satraps, returning the vessels, the booty of long ago. Yet what they sing is an acclaim of Daniel that by its wording again shows how they reach beyond their part at this particular moment. They praise Daniel not only for deciphering the writing, but also for his deliverance of the wronged Susannah – an episode that will occur only near the close of the biblical narrative. As is fully revealed in Daniel's last *conductus* (194–206), in his saving of Susannah (cf. Daniel 13) and his destroying of the dragon (cf. Daniel 14),[4] this prophet of Christ also foreshadows Christ, as saviour and as harrower of hell.

The second part of the play begins with the acclamation of King Darius advancing upon Babylon (153–68). The *conductus* mentions dancing (156, 165), the playing of drums or tambourines (167), the *cythariste* touching their stringed instruments, and the *organa* (perhaps portable organs, though possibly a more general word for harmonies) of other musicians (168). These are precious performance indications, which should clearly not be thought of as confined to this one *conductus* in the play. If the staging of the play in Beauvais at all matched the sophistication of its language, we can assume, for instance, that there was some riotous instrumental festive music, and a mimed feast, before the writing appeared on Belshazzar's wall (46/7), just as the instruments summoned to herald Darius in 167–9, at the close of his processional, will have continued to play during the mimed killing of Belshazzar and Darius' ascent of the Babylonian throne (169/70).

Once more Daniel is summoned to a King. The Bible simply tells (6, 2–4) that, after being one of Darius' three chief satraps, Daniel was given supreme command, and that this roused the other satraps to plot against him. Here this is elaborated with much by-play (170–210). Two men first secretly persuade Darius to have Daniel at court (170/1), then they do not send for him themselves, but instruct legates to seek him out (171–80). This time the embassy into the lower, non-royal world retains its pomp: the legates sing only in Latin (181–92). When Daniel answers them laconically in French (193) – his last vernacular words in

[4] In the Latin Bible, both Vetus Latina and Vulgate, these stories form part of the Book of Daniel; they are not (as in the Authorised Version) separated and reckoned with the Apocrypha.

the play – it is as if to show that, with all his fame, he has retained his candid simplicity – his native way of speaking.

As they bring Daniel to Darius, these legates by their song (194–206) re-enter the Christmas celebrations of the present, or better, they blithely conflate past and present in the play's most ambitious omnitemporal vision. The biblical text which made Daniel appear a prophet of Christ was an obscure passage (9, 24–6) about the destruction of Jerusalem, which in the Vetus Latina said that 'anointing will be destroyed' (*exterminabitur unctio*) when the 'holy one of holy ones' (*sanctus sanctorum* – cf. 273 in our play) will be anointed. It was these phrases which, adapted in the fifth-century polemical sermon of pseudo-Augustine 'Against Jews, Pagans and Arians' (cf. Y II 125 ff.), made their way from the eleventh century into versions of the 'Play of the Prophets' (*Ordo prophetarum*). Thus as the scholars – *alias* courtiers – exult in the Christmas festivities, they see Daniel as having proclaimed not only Christ but a new covenant, which supplants the *unctio* and sacral power of Judaism (196–200). From this they pass to the exploits by which Daniel prefigured Christ (201–5) – as saviour of the oppressed (Susannah), as slayer of the dragon, and as himself miraculously delivered from death. The parallels, which here remain implicit, began to be developed already in the oldest Christian commentary on Daniel, that of Hippolytus of Rome († 235).[5]

The intrigue of the envious courtiers must, as the rubric (210/1) suggests, begin with a mime of their plotting. Their mode of trapping the King into giving Daniel to the lions is as in the Bible, but with a change of emphasis: where the sacred text tells of a decree that for thirty days no one should 'address any petition to any God or man' other than Darius (Daniel 6,7), here the courtiers tempt Darius with the prospect of total idolatry (217): 'you shall be adored as God of all, oh King!' (*adoreris ut deum omnium, o Rex!*). Darius approves this proposed decree with a high-flown phrase – *Ego mando et remando* – that echoes Isaiah's caricature of false prophets (Isaiah 28, 10 and 13); yet his speech ends with an outright comic effect, as Darius utters the last vernacular expression in the play: *O hez!* (225). In sound this echoes the courtiers' ostensibly reverent *o Rex!* (217, 223) of the preceding strophes, but in fact it is the exclamation used to urge animals forward. It is a 'low' usage (not unlike the 'gee-up!' shouted by children), and it was inserted for added mirth in various versions of the 'Prose of the Ass' (cf. Y I 551), to drive the ass through the church during Feast of Fools ceremonies.

---

[5] Hippolyte de Rome, *Commentaire sur Daniel* (Sources Chrétiennes 14, Paris 1947).

Darius' French exclamation thus provided a moment of farce. Perhaps its specific point lay in the linguistic contrast; the monarch from Persia, elated at the prospect of being 'adored as God of all' in his freshly won kingdom Babylon, decides momentarily to condescend to his new court by addressing it in its vernacular – but gets his 'Babylonian' badly wrong. (Further stage-business involving a pantomime-ass at this point cannot be excluded, but the rubrics give no indications.)

The dénouement of the plot is fully biblical: the envious courtiers catch Daniel praying to his God and insist against 'the King, wanting to set Daniel free' (232/3), that his own ratified decree cannot be waived. What is freshly created is the *planctus*, free-ranging in its verse-form and melody (238–45), in which Daniel laments his fate and appeals, almost without hope, to the King's mercy.

At this point in the plot both Hilarius of Orléans and the Beauvais dramatist chose to enrich the pit scene with the help of the doublet of this scene near the close of the Book of Daniel (14), where a later monarch, Cyrus, condemns Daniel for a second time to the lion-pit. It is only there that an angel arranges the air-lift of Habakkuk from Judaea to Babylon, to help Daniel with food, gripping the reluctant older prophet by his hair during the voyage. It must have been feasible to present the illusion of their flight, in a larger cathedral, by means of pulleys and cables worked from the upper galleries. In both plays – unlike either of the biblical episodes – two angels are required: one to threaten the lions in the pit (247/8), a second (*alius angelus*, 251/2) to cope with Habakkuk.

The meeting of the two prophets (256–61), and Habakkuk's return flight, are based closely on the Cyrus episode (14, 36–8). It is only then that the two dramatists return to the Darius story proper. Young argued (II 288, 301–2) that the Beauvais playwright's characterisation of Darius was 'quite the opposite of the irate personage invented by Hilarius', whose consoling of Daniel in the pit was merely 'ironical'. It seems to me likelier that the King in Hilarius' play was annoyed (*iratus*) because of the slanderers who had ensnared him, and that both playwrights took their cues about Darius' character from the biblical text. There he is 'very much saddened' (*satis contristatus*) that he cannot save Daniel (6, 14), he is unable to eat or sleep (6, 18) while the prophet is in the pit, and he visits Daniel at earliest dawn, addressing him 'with tearful voice' (*voce lacrimabili*, 6, 19 – cf. *lacrimabiliter* at 261/2 in the Beauvais play). A certain humane freedom vis-à-vis the biblical text can be seen rather in an omission that is common to both dramatists: the slanderers themselves are at last thrown to the lions, but not, as in the

Bible (6, 24), their children or their wives. One touching addition is the Beauvais dramatist's own: as the slanderers go to their death, they are stripped and left at the pit-edge, where, before dying, they admit their guilt and repent (268–70). The lions who devour them (270/1) will have been actors in lion-costumes. They may have had the 'fearsome-comic' aspect of the demons at the close of the *Sponsus* (see above, p. 9) – though quite possibly, as with Pyramus and Thisbe's lion in *A Midsummer Night's Dream*, the comic element predominated.

In both the Orléans and the Beauvais play the delivered Daniel takes on his prophetic mantle. In his prophecy Daniel's God, whom Darius now acknowledges and proclaims (271–2), is no longer the God of Judaism but the Messiah, 'the holy one who is coming' (273). The prophecy is instantly fulfilled: in both plays an angel sings a strophe (from a renowned older lyric, by Fulbert of Chartres) announcing that Christ is born in Bethlehem. Darius and his court respond by singing the *Te deum*.[6]

In Hilarius' piece, nothing in the earlier parts of the play had prepared for such a close; the Beauvais dramatist's achievement was to endow his theme with figural perspectives from start to finish. The close of his piece thus becomes the resolution of all its past/present tensions: the cruel world of the Persian monarch and his lions finally reveals itself as play, the envious courtiers dissolve for the last time into scholars who bask in the joy of all that Daniel's ordeals and triumphs had prefigured. These scholars who span past and present, who are and are not the kings and nobles of Babylon, are the Beauvais dramatist's most imaginative invention.

Versification

The Beauvais dramatist likewise shows great formal inventiveness. He outdoes Hilarius in rhythmic and metrical variety, and in matching verses with music in unusual ways. This has been discussed in great detail by Avalle (1984, 1987), but at least some brief indications – drawing to some extent on his analyses – may be helpful here.

The first two of the play's eight acclamations and processionals (3–20, 26–45) are entitled *prosa* ('sequence') in their rubrics. The structure of the first might seem to be purely strophic, and indeed the melody varies little from one strophe to the next. These strophes, however – each consisting of five 5p lines (the rhythmic equivalent of

---

[6] Hilarius suggests the *Magnificat* as an alternative, if his play is performed at Vespers and not at Matins.

classical 'adonics') – are structured and differentiated by their rhyme-scheme. Thus 1a-b (3–6) rhyme aabbc; 2a-b (7–10) rhyme *a**a; 3a–b (11–14) rhyme **a*a. So far so good. More problematic is the scheme of the last three strophes: though 4a (15–16) has weak rhymes (aabbb), I would see its counterpart (4b) in 19–20, where the rhymes (again aabbb) are strong. Lines 17–18, rhyming *a**a,[1] repeat the scheme of 2a–b: such irregular repetition of an earlier strophe is typical of the variant of sequence known as *lai lyrique*, but rare among classical sequences.

I print the second *prosa* (26–45) as ten couplets, varying between two forms: I – 2 x 8p + 6p; II – 7pp + 6p, 8p + 6p. While the alternations give the rhythmic structure:

        I II I II II I I II I

there are five melodies, and the melodic structure is:

        AAB CB B DEB C

The poetic–musical form, that is, while not shunning repetition, moves far from the systematic parallelism of classical sequences (AA BB CC ..) to the freer patterns sanctioned in *lais lyriques*.

The first *conductus*, for the advent of the Queen (55–67), consists of eight verses of the form 4p + 4p + 7pp. These could also be printed as four couplets; Avalle, however, has signalled the subtle counterpoint between the verses, with their internal rhymes (aab, ccb, dde, ffe ...), and the melody, in which each 7pp element returns to the same music, giving the whole the musical structure of a fourfold ABCB (where A and C correspond to the pairs of 4p components, and the unvarying B to the 7pp ones).

Of the two *conductus* for Daniel, one (85–96) has four strophes with the relatively simple form 2 x 7pp + 7pp (with internal rhymes), and the refrain 8p, 6pp + 6. More unusual formally is the other (136–52), with alternation between three- and four-line strophes of 4p + 4p lines, followed by a refrain 4p, 7pp + 4p. But the most freely built lyric is the acclamation of Darius (153–69): a pair of strophes 6pp + 7pp, 7pp (153–6) is followed (157–66) by a series of rhythmic variations on 5p, 6p, 6pp and 7pp elements, and at last (167–9) by a strophe (twice 4p + 4p + 7pp, then 4 + 6pp) in the form of the late-antique hymn on the day of judgement, *Apparebit repentina* (see above, p. 10). Another unusually built piece is Daniel's *planctus* (238–45): it can be seen as two widely divergent strophes:

    2 x 6p + 5p, 9p (238–41); 2 x 7p, 8p (242–5).

---

[1] Counting only the strong rhymes, not the assonance *illos/malignos*; for a slightly different picture of the overall form, see Avalle 1987, p. 29.

118 Nine medieval Latin plays

The principal remaining rhythmic patterns found in the play are:

1–2, 233:	8p + 8p	122–35:	3 + 7p
22–5:	10p	171–80:	6pp + 6pp
47–8, 50–2,		194–9,	
208–10,		201–6,	
230,		273–6:	8p + 7pp
252–5,		200:	3 x 7pp
267:	8pp + 8pp	224–5:	4p + 4p
64–73,		226–9,	
81–4,		231–2,	
120–1,		234–5:	4p + 4p + 7pp
181–92,		236–7,	
212–23,		246–7:	5p + 5pp
256–8,		248–51:	2 x 8p, 8p + 4pp
260–1:	4p + 6pp	268,	
75–80:	3 x 6p + 5, 6pp + 4	272:	7pp + 6pp
98–103:	11pp		

Finally, the dramatist uses classical hexameters at 262–3 and 265–6, and cites a classically built Sapphic strophe at 277–80.

Even so swift a summary will indicate that the polymetry in this play was a virtuoso feat. The architects of Beauvais cathedral, trying to build more daringly than their predecessors, overreached themselves; the dramatist, outdoing Hilarius and his predecessors in formal inventiveness, created a linguistic edifice that – unlike the cathedral – did not subside.

The manuscript, and the date of *Danielis ludus*

The codex which today bears the signature Egerton 2615 in the British Library was compiled in the scriptorium of Beauvais cathedral in the early thirteenth century.[1] It is generally agreed that the whole of the monodic part of this manuscript is a copy of an older exemplar, of c. 1160 (for the evidence, see esp. Arlt 1970, I 30).

The manuscript as we have it consists of three distinct parts. The first (fols. 1r–78r) contains the complete texts and monodic music of the liturgical ceremonies at Beauvais for the feast of the Circumcision, together with a range of polyphonic additions; the second (fols. 79r–94v) is devoted entirely to polyphony; the third (fols. 95r–110r),

---

[1] Arlt 1970, I 21–37, gives an excellent account of the MS; the brief notes below are much indebted to his discussion.

which has the same copyist and monodic musical notator as the first, contains the *Daniel* play (fols. 95r-108r), and two gospels with musical notation, for the Easter mass and the feast of Peter and Paul (fols. 108r-110r). The first and third parts of the manuscript were copied in the 1220s or 1230s, and were probably intended (like their lost exemplar) for use by the master of music, particularly for the cathedral's New Year celebrations.

It is not possible to assign a precise date of composition to the *Daniel* play preserved in this manuscript. It seems to me certain that the Beauvais play is directly related to the *Daniel* composed by Abelard's pupil, Hilarius of Orléans.[2] The question of priority is more delicate, and has divided medieval Latin specialists. While Meyer and most recently the Bulsts argued that the Beauvais play preceded that of Hilarius, in my view the correct judgement was reached by Young (Y II 304):

> It seems unlikely that if Hilarius had had the Beauvais version before him, he and his collaborators would have so generally renounced its superior dramatic and literary qualities.

I believe we can date Hilarius' play with reasonable accuracy to *c.* 1130. Hilarius is mentioned seventeen times in the cartulary of Le Ronceray at Angers from *c.* 1105 to 1122,[3] and the recipients of his lyrical poetry, insofar as they can still be identified, are likewise documented within those years. His famous lyric 'To Peter Abelard' (VI in the Bulst edition) was composed, as the text reveals, at the oratory of the Paraclete while Abelard was teaching there – that is, in the years 1123-7.[4] There is only one later reference to Hilarius, 'already an old man',[5] after 1145. It is likely that by 1127, when Abelard's school at the Paraclete closed, Hilarius had returned to Orléans to teach, and that he composed his plays for the cathedral school there soon afterwards: stylistically there are too many affinities between Hilarius' poems and his plays for a late dating of the plays to be plausible. If we assume a date *c.* 1130 for Hilarius' *Daniel*, then the relations of its forms and style to those of the Beauvais play strongly suggest that this will have been composed within a decade or so of its predecessor – probably *c.* 1140.

---

[2] This was shown, I think conclusively, by Wilhelm Meyer, *Fragmenta Burana* (Göttingen 1901), p. 57. It has not to my knowledge been disputed until very recently, in Fassler 1992, pp. 86f. Fassler asserts: 'Surely Young and others are wrong in claiming that the two plays must be directly related.' She does not attempt to substantiate this assertion; it is not even clear from her wording ('and others') whether she is aware of the evidence that Meyer offered.
[3] Bulst 1989, pp. 1-2.
[4] D. E. Luscombe, 'From Paris to the Paraclete', *Proceedings of the British Academy* 74 (1988) 247-83, at p. 261.
[5] Bulst 1989, p. 15.

95r **Incipit Danielis ludus**

Ad honorem tui, Christe,   Danielis ludus iste
in Belvaco est inventus,   et invenit hunc iuventus.

Dum venerit Rex Balthasar, principes sui cantabunt ante eum hanc prosam:

Astra tenenti,   cunctipotenti,
turba virilis   et puerilis   contio plaudit,

5 Nam Danielem   multa fidelem
et subiisse   atque tulisse   firmiter audit.

Convocat ad se   Rex sapientes,
gramata dextre   qui sibi dicant   enucleantes;

Que quia scribe   non potuere
10 solvere Regi,   ilico muti   conticuere.

95v Sed Dani/eli   scripta legenti   mox patuere
que prius illis   clausa fuere;

Quem quia vidit   Balthasar illis   prevaluisse,
fertur in aula   preposuisse.

15 Causa reperta,   non satis apta,
destinat illum   ore leonum   dilacerandum;

Sed, deus, illos   ante malignos
in Danielem   tunc voluisti   esse benignos.

Huic quoque panis,   ne sit inanis,
20 mittitur a te,   prepete vate   prandia dante.

Tunc ascendat Rex in solium, et Satrape ei applaudentes dicant:

Rex, in eternum vive!

Et Rex apperiet os suum dicens:

L: London, BL Egerton 2615, fols. 95r–108r
A: D'A.S. Avalle, *Helikon* XXII–XXVII (1982–7) 5–20
B: W. Bulst, M.L. Bulst-Thiele, *Hilarii Aurelianensis Versus et Ludi, Epistolae, Ludus Danielis Belouacensis* (Leiden 1989), pp. 99–114

[13] prevaluisse Balthasar illis LB *(em. A, to preserve rhyme-scheme)*

120

Here begins the play of Daniel

In your honour, Christ, this play of Daniel
was composed in Beauvais – it was the young who composed it.

While King Belshazzar is making his entry, his nobles shall sing this sequence in his presence:

For him who rules the stars, all-powerful,
the crowd of men and throng of boys are dancing with joy,

5 Because they hear that Daniel the loyal
has endured many trials and borne them with steadfastness.

The King summons the wise men to him,
that they should tell him the explanation of the writing by a hand;

Because the doctors were unable to
10 solve this for the King, they at once, dumbly, lapsed into silence.

But to Daniel, as he read the writing, what had been hidden
there in advance was soon revealed,

And as Belshazzar saw him surpassing those sages,
he is said to have given him preferment in court.

15 A pretext that's found, a far from just one,
destines Daniel to be torn apart in the lion's jaws;

Yet you, God, wanted those who'd been hostile
before to Daniel then to become benign.

To him also bread (lest he be hungry)
20 was sent by you, the swift-flying prophet bringing him meals.

Then the King shall mount the throne, and his satraps, acclaiming him, shall say:

King, live for ever!

And the King shall open his mouth saying:

Vos qui pa/retis meis vocibus,
Afferte vasa meis usibus
Que templo pater meus abstulit
25 Iudeam graviter cum perculit.

Satrape, vasa deferentes, cantabunt hanc prosam ad laudem Regis:

Iubilemus Regi nostro   magno ac potenti!
Resonemus laude digna   voce competenti!

Resonet iocunda turba   sollempnibus odis!
Cytharizent, plaudant manus,   mille sonent modis!

30   Pater eius destruens   Iudeorum templa
Magna fecit, et hic regnat   eius per exempla.

Pater eius spoliavit   regnum Iu/deorum;
Hic exaltat sua festa   decore vasorum.

Hec sunt vasa regia   quibus spoliatur
35 Iherusalem et regalis   Babylon ditatur.

Presentemus Balthasar   ista Regi nostro,
Qui sic suos perornavit   purpura et ostro.

Iste potens, iste fortis,   iste gloriosus!
Iste probus, curialis,   decens et formosus.

40 Iubilemus Regi tanto   vocibus canoris:
Resonemus omnes una   laudibus sonoris!

Ridens plaudit Babylon,   Iherusalem plorat;
Hec orbatur, hec triumphans   Balthasar ad/orat.

Omnes ergo exultemus   tante potestati,
45 Offerentes Regis vasa   sue maiestati.

Tunc principes dicant:

Ecce sunt ante faciem tuam!

Interim apparebit dextra in conspectu Regis scribens in pariete: Mane, Thechel, Phares. *Quam videns Rex stupefactus clamabit:*

Vocate mathematicos,   Caldeos et ariolos,
auruspices inquirite   et magos introducite!

46/7 Techel B

You who obey my words,
bring for my use the vessels
which my father snatched from the Temple
25 when grievously he beat Judaea down.

The satraps, bringing the vessels, shall sing this sequence in praise of the King:

Let us jubilate for our King,   the great and mighty one!
Let us proclaim the praise he merits,   with harmonious voice!

Let the joyous crowd proclaim it   in ceremonial songs!
Let their lutes play it, their hands clap it,   making it sound in a thousand ways!

30   His father, destroying   the temples of the Jews,
did great deeds, and the son reigns   following his example.

His father despoiled   the kingdom of the Jews;
the son adds lustre to his feasts   with the splendour of their vessels.

    These are the royal vessels   of which Jerusalem
35 has been despoiled and regal   Babylon enriched.

    Let us present them   to our King, Belshazzar,
who has so greatly graced his men   with purple and with scarlet.

He is mighty, he is brave,   he is glorious!
He is gallant, courtly,   seemly and handsome too.

40 Let us jubilate for so great a King   with tuneful voice –
let us make music all together   with resounding praise!

    Babylon leaps laughing,   Jerusalem weeps:
she is bereft; the other, triumphant,   pays Belshazzar homage.

Let us all exult then   at such mighty power,
45 offering the royal vessels   to his majesty.

Then the nobles shall say:

Behold, they are before your eyes!

Meanwhile, in full view of the King, a hand shall appear writing on the wall:
    Mane, Thechel, Phares. On seeing it the King, aghast, shall cry out:

Call the astrologers,   Chaldaeans and diviners,
seek out the haruspices,   and bring in the magicians!

124 *Danielis ludus*

Tunc adducentur magi, qui dicent Regi:

Rex, in eternum vive!   Adsumus ecce tibi.

Et Rex:

50   Qui scripturam hanc legerit   et sensum aperuerit,
97v   sub illius potentia   subdetur Baby/lonia,
      et insignitus purpura   torque fruetur aurea.

Illi vero, nescientes persolvere, dicent Regi:

Nescimus persolvere   nec dare consilium
que sit superscriptio,   nec manus inditium.

Conductus Regine venientis ad Regem:

55   Cum doctorum   et magorum   omnis adsit contio,
      secum volvit   neque solvit   que sit manus visio.
      Ecce prudens,   styrpe cluens,   dives cum potentia,
      in vestitu   deaurato   coniunx adest regia.
      Hec latentem   promet vatem   per cuius indicium

98r   Rex describi   suum ibi   no/verit exitium.
61   Letis ergo   hec virago   comitetur plausibus,
      cordis, oris-   que sonoris   personetur vocibus!

Tunc Regina veniens adorabit Regem dicens:

Rex, in eternum vive!
Ut scribentis   noscas ingenium,
65   Rex Balthasar,   audi consilium.

Rex audiens hec versus Reginam vertet faciem suam. Et Regina dicat:

Cum Iudee   captivis populis,
prophetie   doctum oraculis,
Danielem,   a sua patria
captivavit   patris victoria.
70   Hic, sub tuo   vivens imperio,
      ut mandetur   requirit racio.
98v   Ergo / manda   ne sit dilatio,
      nam docebit   quod celat visio.

Tunc dicat Rex principibus suis:

[54] indicium B

Then these mages shall be brought on and shall say to the King:

King, live for ever!   Look, we are here before you.

And the King:

50 Whoever shall read this writing   and make its meaning plain,
Babylon shall be made   subject to his power,
and he, robed in purple,   shall enjoy a golden torque.

But they, not knowing the solution, shall say to the King:

We don't know how to solve this   or how to give advice
on what the writing might be   or what the hand might mean.

The processional song of the Queen coming to the King:

55 Though a whole throng   of sages and mages   is present here,
they have pondered   but not resolved   the vision of the hand.
Look how the wise one,   of renowned race,   rich and mighty,
wearing a robe   of cloth of gold,   the royal spouse draws near.
She will bring out   a prophet from hiding,   through whose unfolding
60 the King will know   that his own death   is written there.
So let this mighty   Queen be accompanied   by joyful dancing –
in the heart's and voice's   vibrant music   she shall be proclaimed!

Then the Queen as she enters shall pay the King homage, saying:

King, live for ever!
That you may know   the writer's mind,
65 King Belshazzar,   hear my advice.

Hearing this, the King shall turn to the Queen, and she shall say:

Among the captive   people from Judaea
a man wise in   oracles of prophecy,
Daniel, was taken   away from his land,
a prisoner,   by your father's victory.
70 He now lives   under your authority –
reason demands   that you should send for him.
Command it then –   let there be no delay –
for he'll teach us   what the vision conceals.

Then the King shall say to his nobles:

126   *Danielis ludus*

Vos Danielem querite   et inventum adducite.

Tunc principes invento Daniele dicant ei:

75 Vir propheta dei,   Daniel, vien al Roi:
veni, desidérat   parler a toi.
Pavet et turbatur –   Daniel, vien al Roi –
vellet quod nos latet   savoir par toi.
Te ditabit donis –   Daniel, vien al Roi –
80 si scripta potérit   savoir par toi.

Et Daniel eis:
Multum miror   cuius consilio
me requirat   regalis iussio.
99r Ibo tamen,   et erit cogni/tum
per me gratis   quod est absconditum.

Conductus Danielis venientis ad Regem:

<Principes>
85 Hic verus dei famulus,   quem laudat omnis populus,
Cuius fama prudentie   est nota regis curie.
   Cestui manda li Rois par nos.
Daniel
Pauper et exulans   en vois al Roi par vos.

Principes
In iuventutis gloria,   plenus celesti gratia,
90 Satis excellit omnibus   virtute, vita, moribus.
   Cestui manda li Rois par nos.
Daniel
Pauper et exulans   en vois al Roi par vos.

Principes
99v Hic est / cuius auxilio   solvetur illa visio,
In qua scribente dextera   mota sunt Regis viscera.
95   *Cestui manda li Rois par nos.*
Daniel
Pauper et exulans   en vois al Roi par vos.

---

⁸⁵ <*Principes*>] *om.* LB (*suppl. A*)
⁸⁸ (*also* 92, 96) enuois LB

Go and search for Daniel,   and when you've found him, bring him
  here.

Then the nobles, having found Daniel, shall say to him:

75 You who are God's prophet,   Daniel, come to the King:
come, for he is longing   *to speak with you.*
The King's afraid and troubled –   Daniel, come to the King –
what's hidden from us he'd like   *to know through you.*
With gifts he will enrich you –   Daniel, come to the King –
80 if he can know the writing's   *meaning through you.*

And Daniel to them:
I very much wonder   at whose advice
the royal command   is seeking me out.
Yet I shall go,   and what is hidden
shall be revealed   freely by me.

The processional song for Daniel as he comes to the King:

85 <Nobles>
This is God's true servant,   whom each nation praises,
the fame of whose wisdom   is known to the King's court.
  The King has summoned this man through us.
Daniel
I, poor and exiled,   *am off to the King, through you.*

Nobles
In the glory of his youth,   full of heavenly grace,
90 he far surpasses everyone   in excellence, life, refinement.
  The King has summoned this man through us.
Daniel
I, poor and exiled,   *am off to the King, through you.*

Nobles
He is the man with whose help   that vision will be explained,
at which, as the hand was writing,   the King's heart was moved.
95   *The King has summoned this man through us.*
Daniel
I, poor and exiled,   *am off to the King, through you.*

Veniens Daniel ante Regem, dicat ei:

Rex, in eternum vive!

Et Rex Danieli:

Tune Daniel nomine diceris,
huc adductus cum Iudee miseris?
100 Dicunt te habere dei spiritum
et prescire quodlibet absconditum.
Si ergo potes scripturam solvere,
immensis muneribus ditabere.

Et Daniel Regi:

100r Rex, tua nolo / munera: gratis solvetur litera;
105 est autem hec solutio: instat tibi confusio.
Pater tuus, pre omnibus   potens olim potentibus,
turgens nimis superbia,   deiectus est a gloria.
Nam cum deo non ambulans,   sed sese deum simulans,
vasa templo diripuit,   que suo usu habuit.
110 Sed post multas insanias   tandem perdens divitias,
forma nudatus hominis,   pastum gustavit graminis.
Tu quoque, eius filius,   non ipso minus impius,
100v dum patris / actus sequeris,   vasis eisdem uteris!
Quod quia deo displicet,   instat tempus quo vindicet,
115 nam scripture indicium   minatur iam supplitium.
Et 'Mane', dicit dominus,   est tui regni terminus;
'Thechel' libram significat   que te minorem indicat;
'Phares', hoc est divisio,   regnum transportat alio.

Et Rex:

Qui sic solvit latentia   ornetur veste regia.

Sedente Daniele iuxta Regem, induto ornamentis regalibus, exclamabit Rex ad principem militie:

120 Tolle vasa,   princeps militie,
101r ne sint / michi   causa miserie.

Tunc, relicto palatio, referent vasa satrape. Et Regina discedet. Conductus Regine:

---

[115] supplicium B

As he comes before the King, Daniel shall say:

King, live for ever!

And the King to Daniel:

Are you the man named Daniel,
brought here with Judaea's wretched ones?
100 They say you have the spirit of God
and can foretell whatever's hidden.
So if you can unravel the writing,
you'll be enriched with boundless gifts.

And Daniel to the King:

King, I do not want your gifts: the writing will be unravelled free.
105 This, however, is the meaning: calamity looms over you.
Your father, who once was mighty   beyond all mighty ones,
swelling over-much with pride,   was cast down from glory.
For he, not walking with God   but pretending to be God,
looted the vessels from the Temple   and kept them for his use.
110 After many acts of madness,   losing his wealth at last,
stripped of human form,   his food became the grass.
But you too, his son,   no less impious than he,
following your father's deeds,   are using those same vessels!
Since this displeases God,   the time of his vengeance looms.
115 for the warning in the writing   threatens punishment now.
And 'Mane', says the Lord,   is your kingdom's end;
'Thechel' means the balance   on which you are found wanting;
'Phares', that is, division,   brings your kingdom to another.

And the King:

Let him who has thus solved the riddle   be graced with royal robes.

As Daniel sits beside the King, wearing royal ornaments, the King shall call out to the General:

120 General, take away the vessels,
lest they bring me to wretchedness.

Then, leaving the palace, the satraps shall take the vessels back, and the Queen shall depart. The Queen's processional song:

Solvitur   in libro Salomonis
digna laus   et congrua matronis.

Precium   est eius, si qua fortis,
125 procul et   de finibus remotis.
Fidens est   in ea cor mariti,
spoliis   divitibus potiti.

Mulier   hec illi comparetur,
cuius Rex   subsidium meretur.
130 Eius nam   facundia verborum
arguit   prudentiam doctorum.

Nos quibus   occasio ludendi
101v hac die   conce/ditur sollempni,
Demus huic   preconia devoti,
135 veniant   et concinent remoti!

Conductus referentium vasa ante Danielem:

Regis vasa   referentes
quem Iudee   tremunt gentes,
Danieli   applaudentes,   *gaudeamus:*
   laudes sibi debitas   referamus!

140 Regis cladem   prenotavit
cum scripturam   reseravit;
testes reos   comprobavit
et Susannam   liberavit –   *gaudeamus:*
   laudes <sibi debitas   referamus!>

145 Babylon hunc   exulavit
cum Iudeos   captivavit,
Balthasar quem   honoravit;   *gaudeamus:*
   <laudes sibi debitas   referamus!>

102r Est propheta   sanctus dei:
150 hunc honorant   et Caldei
et gentiles   et Iudei.
Iubilantes   ergo ei,   *gaudeamus, et cetera.*

---

[124] quam LA (*em.* B)
[152] ergo iubilantes LAB *I have reversed the words to restore formal symmetry.*

In Solomon's book a fine and fitting
praise of married women is unlocked.

Her excellence, if a wife is at all brave,
125 travels far, and from far-off lands.
Her husband's heart sets trust in her –
the rich prize he has won.

Let this woman be likened to such a one:
the King rightly relies on her support,
130 for the persuasiveness of what she said
confuted the wisdom of his learned men.

Since we have been given the chance to play
on this ceremonial day,
let us herald her devotedly
135 and let those from afar come sing with us!

The processional song of the men bringing the vessels back to Daniel:

Bringing back the vessels of the King
at whom Judaea's people tremble,
applauding Daniel,   *let us rejoice:*
let us proclaim the praises   that are his due!

140 He warned of the King's disaster
when he unlocked the writing;
he proved Susannah's accusers guilty
and he set her free –   *let us rejoice:*
let us proclaim the praises   that are his due!

145 Babylon made him an exile
when she brought the Jews into captivity –
this man whom Belshazzar honoured;   *let us rejoice:*
let us proclaim the praises   that are his due!

He is the holy prophet of God:
150 the Chaldeans honour him,
and the Gentiles and the Jews.
So, making jubilation for him,   *let us rejoice:*
let us proclaim the praises   that are his due!

132   *Danielis ludus*

Statim apparebit Darius Rex cum principibus suis, venientque ante eum cythariste et musici *sui, psallentes hec:*

    Ecce Rex Darius   venit cum principibus,
                          nobilis nobilibus,
155 Eius et curia   resonat leticia,
                          adsunt et tripudia!

      Hic est mirandus,   cunctis venerandus,
   illi imperia   sunt tributaria:

      Regem honorant   omnes et adorant,
160 illum Babylonia   metuit et patria.

102v Cum armato agmine   ruens / et cum turbine,
      sternit cohortes,   confregit et fortes.

      Illum honestas   colit et nobilitas,
   Hic est babylonius   nobilis Rex Darius!

165 Illi cum tripudio   gaudeat hec contio,
     laudet et cum gaudio   eius facta fortia   tam admirabilia!

    Simul omnes   gratulemur,   resonent et tympana,
    cythariste   tangant cordas,   musicorum organa
169   resonent ad   eius preconia!

Antequam perveniat Rex ad solium suum, duo precurrentes expellent Balthasar quasi interficientes eum. Tunc sedente Dario Rege in maiestate sua, Curia exclamabit:/

103r Rex, in eternum vive!

Tunc duo, flexis genibus, secreto dicent Regi ut faciat accersiri Danielem. Et Rex iubeat eum adduci. Illi autem, aliis precipientes, dicent hec:

   Audite, principes   regalis curie,
   qui leges regitis   tocius patrie:
   Est quidam sapiens   in Babylonia
   secreta reserans   deorum gratia.
175 Eius consilium   Regi complacuit,
   nam prius Balthasar   scriptum aperuit.

[152/3] principes LAB *It is unlikely that this rubric should mention* principes *twice; my emendation* musici *is suggested by 168.*
[155] letitia B (*similarly* 172 totius B, 180 tertius B – *as normalisations?*)
[162] confrrgit (? confugit) L

At once King Darius and his nobles shall appear, and his lutanists and musicians shall come before him, performing the following song:

    Look! King Darius   is coming with his lords,
              noble among his nobles,
155 and his court   resounds with joy,
              and there is dancing too!

        He is to be admired,   reverenced by all,
    to him empires   must render tribute:

        All honour him as King   and pay him homage;
160 Babylon fears him,   as does his native land.

    Swooping with an armed force,   with a whirlwind,
        he lays cohorts low   and has crushed the mighty.

        Honour and nobility   are his ornaments.
    This is noble Darius,   King of Babylon!

165 Let this gathering   show its joy in him with dancing,
    joyously let it praise   his mighty deeds,   so wonderful!

    Let us all rejoice together,   let the drums roll,
    let the lutanists pluck their strings   and the musicians' instruments
              ring out   to herald him!

Before the King reaches his throne, two men, running ahead, shall drive Belshazzar out, as if killing him. Then, as King Darius sits in majesty, the Court shall exclaim:

170 King, live for ever!

Then two men, kneeling, shall secretly tell the King to have Daniel summoned. And the King shall command that he be fetched. But those men, instructing others, shall say:

    Listen, nobles   of the royal court,
    you who control the laws of the whole land:
    there is a certain   sage in Babylon
    who unlocks secrets,   through the grace of the gods.
175 It has pleased our King   to have advice from him,
    for he explained Belshazzar's   writing before this.

134 *Danielis ludus*

      Ite velociter,   ne sit dilatio:
      nos uti volumus   eius consilio.
      Fiat, si venerit,   consiliarius
180 Regis, et fuerit   in regno tercius.

    Legati, invento Daniele, dicent hec ex parte Regis: /

103v Ex regali   venit imperio,
      serve dei,   nostra legatio.
      Tua Regi   laudatur probitas,
      te commendat   mira calliditas,
185 Per te solum   cum nobis patuit
      signum dextre,   quod omnes latuit.
      Te Rex vocat   ad suam curiam,
      ut agnoscat   tuam prudentiam.
      Eris supra,   ut dicit Darius,
190 principalis   consiliarius.
      Ergo veni: iam omnis curia
      preparatur   ad tua gaudia.

    Et Daniel:

G'en vois al Roi.

    Conductus Danielis:

104r Congaudentes celebremus   natalis sollemp/nia:
195 iam de morte nos redemit   dei Sapientia.
      Homo natus est in carne,   qui creavit omnia,
      nasciturum quem predixit   prophete facundia
      Danielis. Iam cessavit   unctionis copia,
      cessat regni Iudeorum   contumax potentia.
200 In hoc natalitio,   Daniel, cum gaudio   te laudat hec contio.
      Tu Susannam liberasti   de mortali crimine
      cum te deus inspiravit   suo sancto flamine:
      Testes falsos comprobasti   reos accusamine,
104v Bel draconem peremisti   coram ple/bis agmine,
205 Et te deus observavit   leonum voragine –
      ergo sit laus dei Verbo   genito de virgine!

---

[189] Eris, supra (*punct.*) AB
[193] Genuois LB
[202] fla-flamine L (*B reads* ad flamine)

Go swiftly, let there be no delay:
we ourselves want to use his advice.
If he will come, let him be made adviser
180 of the King, and he shall be third highest in the realm.

The legates, having found Daniel, shall say on the King's behalf:

Under royal authority,
servant of God, our mission comes.
Your uprightness is praised before the King,
your wonderful subtlety commends you,
185 since through you alone the portent of the hand,
hidden from all, became clear to us.
The King is bidding you to his court,
to give recognition to your wisdom.
Besides, as Darius says, you shall become
190 the principal giver of advice.
Come therefore: the whole court has now
been prepared, so as to do your pleasure.

And Daniel:

I'll go to the King.

Daniel's processional song:

Joyously let us celebrate the Christmas feast:
195 now God's Wisdom has redeemed us from death.
He is man, born in flesh, he who created all,
whom the eloquence of a prophet foretold would be born –
prophet Daniel. The means of anointing have now ceased,
ceased the contumacious power of the Jews.
200 At this birth, Daniel, this throng praises you with joy.

You rescued Susannah from a deadly charge
when God inspired you with his holy breath:
you proved the false witnesses guilty in their accusing,
you destroyed Bel's dragon before a host of people,
205 and God watched over you in the pit of lions –
praise be to God's Word, born of a maiden!

Et Daniel Regi:

Rex, in eternum vive!

Cui Rex:

Quia novi te callidum,   totius regni providum,
te, Daniel, constituo   et summum locum tribuo.

Et Daniel Regi:

210 Rex, michi si credideris,   per me nil mali feceris.

Tunc Rex faciet eum sedere iuxta se; et alii consiliarii, Danieli invidentes quia gratior erit Regi, aliis in consilium ductis ut Danielem interficiant, dicent Regi:

Rex, in eternum vive!

Item:

105r Decreverunt   in tua / curia
    principandi   quibus est gloria
    Ut ad tui   rigorem nominis,
215 omni spreto   vigore numinis,
    Per triginta   dierum spatium
    adoreris   ut deus omnium,   *o Rex!*

    Si quis ausu   tam temerario
    renuerit   tuo consilio,
220 Ut preter te   colatur deitas,
    iudicii   sit talis firmitas:
    In leonum   tradatur foveam –
    sic dicatur   per totam regiam,   *o Rex!*

Et Rex dicat:

    Ego mando   et remando
225 ne sit spretum   hoc decretum.   *O hez!*

105v *Daniel, hoc audiens, ibit in domum suam / et adorabit deum suum; quem emuli videntes, accurrent et dicent Regi:*

    Nunquid, Dari,   observari   statuisti omnibus
    qui orare   vel rogare   quicquam a *n*uminibus

---

[226] Numquid AB
[227] muminibus L

And Daniel to the King:

King, live for ever!

The King to him:

Since I know you are subtle,   and care for all the realm,
I appoint you, Daniel,   and give you highest place.

And Daniel to the King:

210 King, if you trust in me,   through me you will do no ill.

Then the King shall make Daniel sit beside him; and other counsellors, envying Daniel because he is too much favoured by the King, having intrigued with others in order to kill Daniel, shall say to the King:

King, live for ever!

And then:

In your court   those who have the honour
of governing   have made the decree
that, for the authority   of your name,
215 supplanting all   divine validity,
for the space   of thirty days
you shall be adored   as God of all,   *oh King!*

If anyone show   such foolhardy daring
as to resist   this scheme of yours,
220 so that a deity   other than you is worshipped,
let this be   the unswerving judgment:
he shall be put   in the lions' den –
so be it declared   throughout the capital,   *oh King!*

And the King shall say:

I command it   and command again
225 that this decree   shall not be scorned.   *On with it!*

Daniel, on hearing this, shall go into his house and adore his God; his enemies, seeing him, shall run up to the King and say:

Surely, Darius   you ordered it   to be noted by all
who want to pray   or to request   anything from a God

ni te deum,   illum reum   daremus leonibus?
Hoc edictum   sic indictum   fuit a principibus.

Et Rex, nesciens quare hoc dicerent, respondet:

230 Vere iussi me omnibus   adorari a gentibus.

Tunc illi, adducentes Danielem, dicent Regi:

Hunc Iudeum   suum deum   Danielem vidimus
adorantem   et precantem,   tuis spretis legibus.

Rex, volens liberare Danielem, dicet:

Nunquam vobis con/cedatur   quod vir sanctus sic perdatur.

Satrape, hoc audientes, ostendent ei legem, dicentes:

Lex Parthorum   et Medorum   iubet in annalibus
235 ut qui sprevit   que decrevit   Rex, detur leonibus.

Rex, hoc audiens, velit nolit dicet:

Si sprevit legem   quam statueram,
det penas ipse   quas decreveram.

Tunc satrape rapient Danielem, et ille, respiciens Regem, dicet:

Heu, heu, heu! quo casu sortis
venit hec dampnatio mortis?
240 Heu, heu, heu! – scelus infandum! –
cur me dabit ad lacerandum

hec fera turba feris?
Sic me, Rex, perdere queris?/
Heu, qua morte mori
245 me cogis? Parce furori!

Et Rex, non valens eum liberare, dicet ei:

Deus quem colis   tam fideliter
te liberabit   mirabiliter.

Tunc proicient Danielem in lacum, statimque angelus, tenens gladium, comminabitur leonibus ne tangant eum. Et Daniel, intrans lacum, dicet:

Huius rei non sum reus:
miserere mei, deus –   *eleyson!*

other than you, that we would give such culprits to the lions?
This was the edict, this the writ that the nobles announced.

And the King, not knowing why they were saying this, answers:

230 Indeed I ordered I should be adored by everyone.

Then, bringing Daniel before him, they shall say to the King:

This Jew, Daniel, we have seen adoring
and praying to his own God, scorning your laws.

The King, wanting to set Daniel free, shall say:

You shall never be allowed thus to destroy a holy man.

The satraps, on hearing this, shall show him the Law, saying:

The Law of the Persians and the Medes, in its records, demands
235 that whoever scorns what the King decrees be given to the
lions.

The King, hearing this, shall – willy-nilly – say:

If he has scorned the law that I laid down,
he shall pay the penalty that I decreed.

Then the satraps shall seize Daniel and he, looking at the King, shall say:

Alas, alas, alas! Through what mischance of fate
has this death-sentence come about?
240 Alas, alas, alas! The monstrous crime!
Why will this savage crowd give me to be torn
by the savage beasts?
Is it thus, King, that you seek to destroy me?
Alas, what kind of death do you compel me
245 to die? Relent your rage!

And the King, powerless to set him free, shall say to him:

The God whom you worship so loyally
will set you free miraculously.

Then they shall throw Daniel into the pit, and at once an angel, holding a sword, shall threaten the lions in case they touch him. And Daniel, entering the pit, shall say:

I am not guilty in this case:
have mercy on me, God – *eleyson!*

250 Mitte, deus, huc patronum
    qui refrenet vim leonum –   *eleyson!*

Interea alius angelus admonebit Abacuc prophetam ut deferat prandium quod portabat messoribus suis Danieli in lacum leonum, dicens:

    Abacuc, tu senex pie,   ad lacum Babylonie
107r Danieli fer prandium: mandat ti/bi Rex omnium.

Cui Abacuc:

    Novit dei cognitio   quod Babylonem nescio,
255 neque lacus est cognitus   quo Daniel est positus.

Tunc angelus, apprehendens eum capillo capitis sui, ducet ad lacum. Et Abacuc, Danieli offerens prandium, dicet:

    Surge, frater,   ut cibum capias;
    tuas deus   vidit angustias;
    deus misit –   da deo gratias
    qui te fecit.

Et Daniel, cibum accipiens, dicet:

260 Recordatus   es mei, domine!
    Accipiam   in tuo nomine –   *alleluia!*

His transactis, angelus reducet Abacuc in locum suum. Tunc Rex, descendens de solio suo, veniet ad lacum, dicens lacrimabiliter:

107r Tene, putas, Daniel, / salvabit ut eripiaris
    a nece proposita, quem tu colis et veneraris?

Et Daniel Regi:

Rex, in eternum vive!

Item:

265 Angelicum solita misit pietate patronum,
    quo deus ad tempus conpescuit ora leonum.

Tunc Rex gaudens exclamabit:

Danielem educite   et emulos immittite!

---

²⁵⁰ partronum L

250 God, send a protector here
    who can curb the lions' strength –   *eleyson!*

Meanwhile another angel shall bid the prophet Habakkuk to take the meal that
    he was bringing to his harvesters to Daniel in the lion-pit, saying:

Habakkuk, merciful old man,   to the pit in Babylon
carry the meal to Daniel: you're bidden by the King of all.

To whom Habakkuk:

God in his knowledge knows   I'm ignorant of Babylon
255 and I don't know the pit   where Daniel has been set.

Then the angel, seizing him by the hair of his head, shall bring him to the pit.
    And Habakkuk, offering Daniel the meal, shall say:

Rise, brother,   to take your food;
God has seen your   anxiety;
God has sent this: give thanks to God
who made you.

And Daniel, accepting the food, shall say:

260 Lord, you have   remembered me!
I shall accept   it in your name –   *alleluia!*

When this is over, the angel shall bring Habakkuk back to his own place. Then
    the King, descending from his throne, shall come to the pit, saying tearfully:

Do you think he'll save you, Daniel, snatching you
from the death decreed, he whom you worship and revere?

And Daniel to the King:

King, live for ever!

And then:

265 In his unfailing mercy God has sent an angelic protector,
through whom for the time he has quelled the jaws of the lions.

Then the King shall call out joyfully:

Take Daniel out   and put his enemies in!

Cum expoliati fuerint et venerint ante lacum, clamabunt:

    Merito hec patimur,   quia peccavimus:
    in sanctum dei   iniuste egimus,
270 iniquitatem fecimus!

Illi, proiecti in lacum, statim consumentur a leonibus. Et Rex, videns hoc, dicet:

108r Deum Danielis   qui regnat / in seculis
    adorari iubeo   a cunctis populis!

Daniel, in pristinum gradum receptus, prophetabit:

    Ecce venit sanctus ille,   sanctorum sanctissimus,
    quem rex iste iubet coli   potens et fortissimus.
275 Cessant phana, cesset regnum,   cessabit et unctio:
    instat regni Iudeorum   finis et oppressio.

Tunc angelus ex inproviso exclamabit:

    Nuntium vobis fero de supernis:
    natus est Christus, dominator orbis,
    in Bethleem Iude – sic enim propheta
280 dixerat ante.

His auditis, cantores incipient Te deum laudamus.

Finit Daniel.

When they have been stripped and have come to the pit-edge, they shall cry out:

We suffer this deservedly,   for we have sinned:
we acted unjustly   towards God's holy one,
270 we did a shameful deed!

Thrown into the pit, they shall at once be devoured by the lions. And the King, seeing this, shall say:

The God of Daniel, who   reigns perpetually,
I command shall be adored   by every nation!

Daniel, restored to his former rank, shall prophesy:

See, the holy one is coming,   holiest of holy ones,
whom this King, most brave and mighty,   commands to be adored.
275 Temples shall cease, the kingdom cease,   anointing too shall cease:
the end and overthrow of the kingdom   of the Jews is near.

Then, from an unexpected place, an angel shall call out:

I bring to you a message from on high:
Christ is born, the ruler of the world,
in Bethlehem of Judah – thus of old the
280 prophet predicted.

On hearing this, the singers shall begin Te deum laudamus.

Here Daniel *ends.*

Explanatory notes

4   plaudit] *Plaudere* can, according to context, suggest applause, clapping, stamping of feet, or dancing; the use of the specific term for dancing (*tripudia* 156, *tripudio* 165) during the entry of Darius suggests that Belshazzar's entry too will have been accompanied by dance as well as music.

17–18   The forward reference could be not only to Darius (cf. 267), but also to the change of heart in Daniel's slanderers (cf. 268–70).

20   prepete vate prandia dante] Habakkuk (Daniel 14, 32ff.) 'flies' to Babylon in the Angel's grip; the biblical text speaks of one 'meal' (*prandium*) only – the plural *prandia* may have been improvised on account of the six days that, in the version in Daniel 14, the prophet spent in the lions' pit.

20/1   Satrape] Used synonymously with *Principes* throughout the play.

21   Rex, in eternum, vive!] Cf. Daniel 3, 9; 5, 10; 6, 6; 6, 21 (in sempiternum 2, 4).

22–5   Cf. Daniel 5, 2–3.

29   Cytharizent] Cf. Apocalypse 14, 2 (*vocem citharedorum citharizantium in citharis suis*). The *cithara* referred to here and later in the play is the stringed instrument often alluded to in Roman poetry, closer to the zither than to the Hispanoarabic or Renaissance European lute.

39   probus, curialis ...] In the acclamations, the protagonists are praised for their specifically courtly excellence. Thus Daniel (89f.) *in iuventutis gloria ... satis excellit omnibus virtute, vita, moribus*, and Darius (163) is celebrated for *honestas* and *nobilitas*.

47   Caldeos et ariolos] As the Chaldaeans were famed for astrology, *Caldeus* is often almost synonymous with 'astrologer'; *arioli* are mentioned at Daniel 2, 10.

52   Cf. Daniel 5,7.

54/5   Here and several times below, directions are abrupt, and presuppose further stage-business which is not indicated. The *conductus* must have been preceded by a mime, for instance of a messenger coming to the Queen with the terrible news.

62   cordis] Possibly for *chordis*: 'with strings, and with the sonorous sounds of human lips'; but the pairing of heart and lips is also common, esp. in lyrical poetry.

87   (and 91, 95) manda] On the use of a past definite with the force of a perfect, to indicate a very recent action, cf. L. Foulet, *Petite syntaxe de l'ancien français*, sect. 333.

89–90   See note on 39 above.
98–100 Cf. Daniel 5, 13–14.
102–4   Cf. Daniel 5, 16–17.
112   Cf. Daniel 5, 22 (the remainder of Daniel's speech has fewer literal correspondences).
124–7   Cf. Proverbs 31, 10–11.
132 ff.   Note the swift transition from Belshazzar's feast to the feast at Beauvais.
142–3   Cf. Daniel 13, and above p. 112.
152/3   cythariste] See note on 29 above.
163   See note on 39 above.
167–8   tympana ... organa] Where the context does not point to a particular rendering, such terms remain problematic: *tympana* could be drums or tambourines, *musicorum organa* could be portable organs or – less specifically – instruments, or songs.
180   in regno tercius] At Daniel 5, 16 Belshazzar promises this, and fulfils the promise at 5, 29 (presumably the meaning is, Daniel's power came next to that of the King and Queen). The phrase does not recur in the Darius episode.
194 ff. On the significance of this *conductus*, in which the legates return from Babylon to Beauvais, see above p. 113.
200   This verse may well have been repeated as a refrain after 206.
203   accusamine] *Accusamen* (for *accusatio*) would seem to be the playwright's coinage, for the sake of his rhyme-scheme.
210/11 Here the directions, less laconic than usual, indicate a mime for the conspirators before the next episode.
215   spreto] Variants of *spernere* recur at 225, 232, 235, 236; they epitomise the authoritarian nature of Darius and the counsellors. Here at its first occurrence the term could well be ambiguous or ironic: the counsellors, trying to suppress all divine power save that of the King, are 'spurning' the power of the true *numen*.
224   Cf. Isaiah 28, 10 and 13.
225   O hez!] In Old French the exclamation *hez!* is used to urge animals forward: see Tobler-Lommatzsch IV 1095 f. It is addressed *to* an animal (thus also at Beauvais, in the *conductus* of the ass, Arlt 1970, II 4); there is no instance where it represents the sound made by an animal. The assertions that Darius' words are 'the ass's bray' (Smoldon 1980, p. 225), and that 'King Darius brays like an ass at one highly dramatic moment' (Fassler 1992, pp. 81, 92), are based on a misunderstanding.
226–30 Cf. Daniel 6, 13.
246–7   Cf. Daniel 6, 16.
248   (and 251) *eleyson!*] 'Have mercy!', as in the liturgical invocations *Kyrie, eleyson! ... Christe, eleyson!* that precede the *Gloria* in the Roman Mass.
251/2   Cf. Daniel 14, 32–38, and above pp. 114f. The wording in 252–60 remains close to the biblical text.
252   Abacuc, tu senex píe] This half-verse is one of the very rare rhyth-

mically anomalous ones in the play; a classicising pronunciation, stressing the long syllable (*senéx pie*) cannot be ruled out. Cf. also 261 (*Accipíam?*).

262–6   Cf. Daniel 6, 20–2.

271   Cf. Daniel 6, 26. The playwright has chosen the expression *qui regnat in seculis* with the recurrent *Rex, in eternum vive!* (last heard at 264) in mind: through Daniel, Darius now perceives the King who in truth lives for ever.

273–6   On Daniel's prophecy, see above, p. 113.

275   Cessant phana] Cf. Ezekiel 6, 6. The sequence of tenses – *Cessant ... cesset ... cessabit* – is disconcerting, but the pres. indic. and subj. probably have future force here.

277–80   The angel sings 'from an unexpected place' – perhaps from one of the cathedral's upper galleries, to create an effect of surprise and awe – the opening strophe (or perhaps the whole) of the early eleventh-century hymn by Fulbert of Chartres, in classical Sapphic stanzas (cf. Y II 433), which is also used in some twelfth-century plays of the Magi (cf. Y II 62), as well as by Hilarius to conclude his play of Daniel (Y II 286).

VIII *Ordo Virtutum*
The Play of the Virtues,
by Hildegard of Bingen

Style, meaning and structure

The *Ordo Virtutum* is in essential ways unlike any of the other plays in this volume; it is also the only play in the volume that is not anonymous. We have come to know much about the composer of its words and music, Hildegard of Bingen (1098–1179), prolific as mystic, lyrical poet, and scientist, and as the impassioned epistolary adviser of the luminaries of Church and State in her time.[1] We can, moreover, make well-grounded conjectures about the circumstances and date of this play's composition and first public performance (see pp. 152–5 below).

The *Ordo Virtutum* stands apart, above all, by the range of its characters and its language. The characters are personifications: there is the heroine, Anima, and her companion Souls, there is the villain, Diabolus, and sixteen *Virtutes* – Virtues conceived not only as qualities within the human being but as creative forces in the cosmos, forces that fight on Anima's behalf. Such deploying of an almost wholly allegorical cast is familiar, from the fourteenth century onwards, in the 'morality-plays', that reach a high point with *Everyman*; it is unique in Hildegard's own age. Her language draws subtly upon the imagery of the Song of Songs, Isaiah, and the Apocalypse, but achieves a poetic density and originality, and at times a soaring lyricism, that is unique not only among twelfth-century plays but in the whole of medieval drama.

The division of the play into a Prologue, four scenes and a Finale is editorial – there are no corresponding indications in the two extant manuscripts. It is intended purely as an aid to perceiving the dramatic articulation of the whole.

The Prologue (1–8), whose concentrated language establishes the

---

[1] For an account of Hildegard's career and writings see esp. my *Women Writers* ch. 6 (pp. 144–201, texts pp. 231–64, notes pp. 306–15); there is a more detailed study of her achievements as poet and dramatist, together with an edn of the *Ordo Virtutum* and of some of her melodies, in Dronke 1986, pp. xxxiii–xlii, 150–92, 209–31 (melodies ed. I. Bent).

co-ordinates for the play that follows, opens with a choir of Patriarchs and Prophets singing a phrase – 'Who are these, who are like clouds?' – from Isaiah 60, a chapter that evokes the building of the heavenly Jerusalem. The imagery of this chapter (including Isaiah's images of sailing and growth) is vividly present in later scenes.

The choir of Virtues, who 'dwell in the heights' (67) – in the staging probably on a raised dais within the sanctuary – answer, developing and varying Isaiah's image. They, like clouds, are irradiated by the sunlight of the Logos (3–4) – through them that light is mediated to the world; but they are also the boughs and fruits of a tree whose roots are formed by those same Patriarchs and Prophets (6–7). Where in Isaiah's heavenly city God calls the just 'the shoot of my planting' (*germen plantationis meae*, 60, 21), here the Virtues, 'building the limbs of the beautiful body' of the Logos, are seen as 'fruits of the living eye' (*fructus viventis oculi*). *Oculus*, which means both 'eye' and 'bud', unifies the imagery of light and growth: the divine sunlight ripens these fruits, that are the culmination of the tree of the Word, whose divine buds burgeon on earth. The Patriarchs and Prophets, from the world of the Old Testament, are the shadow (*umbra*, 8), or foreshadowing, of this process of light-giving and growth, which was made possible, in the world of the New, by the incarnation.

The scene changes (9 ff.). We are shown a different *umbra* (12), a dark shadow of sins existing in the present. A group of Souls lament their flawed, embodied condition: they have fallen from their paradisal state as 'daughters of the King' (11) into a shadow from which they beg the 'living Sun' to deliver them – though they also know that deliverance implies a battle. Hildegard here combines the tradition of a 'play of the Prophets' (*Ordo Prophetarum*), in which Old Testament figures are summoned to reveal the *umbra* of the New, with that of the battle of virtues and vices in and for the human soul, in the fifth-century poetic allegory, the *Psychomachia*, of Prudentius.[2]

Among the lamenting Souls, only one – the play's heroine, Anima – is happy (16–19). To her the restoration to heavenly life is already so real that she longs for the 'radiant robe' of her glorified body. The Virtues (20–2) commend her for 'loving much' (echoing Christ's words of the woman who anointed his feet); but when they remind Anima of the battle against sin, against Diabolus, that must precede the paradisal bliss, she grows depressed (*gravata*, 25/6, *infelix*, 35/6), and laments too,

---

[2] For versions of the *Ordo Prophetarum*, see Y II 125–71; for Prudentius' *Psychomachia*, see Prudentius, ed. and tr. H. J. Thomson (Loeb Classics, 1949), I 274–343.

more fiercely than the other Souls. What she is wearing is not yet her shining heavenly robe, but an earthly dress, a destiny that has to be 'completed' in this world (38). Despairing, Anima casts this dress off (40); like the guilty Adam and Eve, she hides from the Creator (43); defiantly she declares that she'll enjoy the world – after all, God created it for use (45–7).

This outburst of Anima's prompts the first intervention of Diabolus (48–9), who encourages her desire to 'look to the world'. Diabolus, who 'hath no music in himself... Is fit for treasons, stratagems, and spoils': he is differentiated from the rest of the cast in an original way – he never sings, only speaks, and his speech is *strepitus*, a violent shouting. After his words, Anima leaves the Virtues' fellowship: she makes her way out of their playing-space in the sanctuary, perhaps also, through the audience, out of the chapel itself.

The Virtues grieve over Anima's loss, and summon Innocentia, one of their number, to mourn. Diabolus intervenes once more, asserting his own power, pretending (as in his temptation of Christ in the desert) that he can give everything to one who follows him. Addressing Humilitas, who is the 'glorious queen' of the Virtues (cf. 72), he mocks her powerlessness to give anything to *her* followers, and mocks all the Virtues for their ignorance of their own natures (59–62) – this is how Diabolus construes their total conformity with the divine will. Humilitas retorts that she knows *his* nature: he was Lucifer, the dragon who was flung into the abyss (63–6). The scene concludes in the stark contrast of depth and height.

Then follows a long episode of the Virtues alone (68–158). It is predominantly lyrical, and hardly carries the plot forward, but unfolds and celebrates the natures of the Virtues in richly textured imagery, and in a choreography that is implied by the text itself. In the course of the scene five Virtues – Humilitas, Karitas, Obedientia, Fides, and Contemptus Mundi – invite the others, 'Come to me!', and each of these invitations must be followed by the chorus's moving swiftly towards the summoner (cf. 79). The scene consists entirely of alternations between the individual Virtues as soloists and the assembled company – except for one sardonic interjection by Diabolus. (This, and some of the detailed aspects of the language, are elucidated in the explanatory notes below.)

At the opening (70), an image drawn from the parables of repentance (the lost sheep and the lost drachma) in Luke 15 offers a glimmer of hope that the errant Anima may be found again. Then the images turn especially to those of the love-union in the Song of Songs, to growth, flowering and light, but also at times to combat. To the Canticle's range belong the royal wedding-chamber (75, 104), the kiss of the King (90), burning in the King's embraces (105), the flower in the meadow (109), the embraces of the princess (125, 129), the royal nuptials (131), and the rocky cavern (*caverna petre*, 154) – though the bride who hides there is not called 'dove', as in the Song, but 'glorious warrior'.

Hildegard has a special gift for fusing and compressing images. Thus Karitas promises to lead the other Virtues *in candidam lucem floris virge* – 'into the radiant light of the flower of the rod' (78). Aaron's rod (*virga*) that bursts into flower (cf. Numbers 17) is the traditional figura of Mary (*virgo*) bringing forth the flower that is Christ – thus the complex metaphor, with its double genitive, is a promise to lead the Virtues into the luminous realm of the incarnation. With similarly penetrating conflations, Fides (93–7) is a mirror (*speculum*) who, by her mirroring (*speculata*), can lead the other Virtues to the leaping fountain (cf. John 4, 14); the never-failing flower praised by Castitas, the flower through which the Sun blazes without parching it, dwells in the symphonies of heavenly habitants (106–11). Again, there is a compelling fusion of images to characterise the Virtue Victoria (143–5). It begins with Old Testament figurae: she fights *in lapide* (like David), she treads the serpent underfoot (like Mary, fulfilling the prophecy of Genesis 3, 15); she enters 'the scorching fountain that swallowed up the voracious wolf': Victoria's combat, that is, takes place in a river of fire (the antithesis of the 'leaping fountain'), in which the Satanic wolf has been engulfed in his own burning greed, so that she can, by enduring that blaze, fight and win as the 'gentlest of warriors'. In the final image of the scene, Humilitas reminds the Virtues of the world-tree, the body of the Logos on which they were raised, in images that bring together the Song of Songs (8, 5) – 'I raised you from beneath the apple-tree' – and Isaiah (60, 21) – 'the shoot of my planting'.

Yet Humilitas' call to joy, which closes this scene (158), is at once contradicted by the Virtues' mourning for Anima, which opens the next. Anima returns, griefstricken, ailing and battered on account of her sojourn outside the Virtues' realm. The Virtues, seeing her as the lost sheep of the parable (160, 169), repeatedly call her back to themselves, unaware that she is still too weak to approach unaided. The pervasive imagery of Anima's wounds and sickness (171, 177, 187, 190) is suffused by that of Christ's sacrificial wounds (182, 190), and of healing: Humilitas is a 'true medicine' (185), Christ is 'the great surgeon', who 'has suffered harsh and bitter wounds' for Anima's sake (196–7). Humilitas bids the Virtues lift Anima and carry her back to their dwelling – but as they do so, singing an exultant thanksgiving (198–208), Diabolus irrupts on their cortège and claims Anima for himself (209 f.).

She is now strong enough to defy Diabolus: 'now, you trickster, I'll fight you face to face' (213). The imagery of combat, while not absent from the previous scene (cf. 178–9, 184), emerges with full force in these climactic moments in which, at Humilitas' command, the Virtues, led by Victoria, attack Diabolus and succeed in chaining him (227: cf. Apocalypse 20, 2). Then comes an unexpected dramatic twist: as Castitas, echoing Victoria's phrase in the second scene (143), boasts that she too trod on the serpent's head, in Mary's miraculous virgin birth, Diabolus rejoins savagely: the virgin birth is merely a transgression of the 'sweet act of love' that God enjoined upon mankind, the 'debt that the husband shall pay the wife, and the wife the husband' (1 Corinthians 7, 3): virginity is an emblem of human ignorance, not of divine privilege (235–7). Castitas answers by defending the incarnation not as a human birth, but as the start of the reintegration in God of the human race (*genus humanum ad se congregat*, 240–1).

The play concludes with two resplendent choruses. The first, in which the Virtues give praise and thanks for the 'great counsel', the schema of salvation, takes up the image of the 'scorching fountain' in which the wolf was swallowed (144–5, and again 220–1), transforming it into a fountain that flows from the Father in fiery love (*ex te fluit fons in igneo amore*, 248); then the fountain-image changes into that of Isaiah's sea, on which the ships of souls sail towards the heavenly Jerusalem.

In the second, final chorus (252 ff.), the Virtues are (I believe) joined by the chorus of Souls who had lamented at the opening of the first scene. They recollect how, with the Fall, creation had lost its 'greenness' (*viriditas*, 254), its paradisal fertility and beauty. Within this recollection, they evoke Christ, the 'champion' of humanity, recalling his redemptive suffering to the Father. His wounded body is *plenum gemmarum* (264): the phrase means at once 'full of gems' and 'full of buds'. As in the Prologue the 'living eye' was also the bud on a twig of the world-tree, so here at the close the body *plenum gemmarum* is that same tree blossoming; yet it is equally the heavenly Jerusalem, the city 'full of gems', and Jerusalem the bride, the heavenly ideal to which Anima aspires. Here poetic concentration and suggestiveness together are stretched to the limit.

Date of composition and performance

In a study, 'Problemata Hildegardiana', first published in 1981, I set out evidence indicating that the *Ordo Virtutum* must have been completed latest in 1151. This is the year when Hildegard, on her own testimony, finished her first visionary prose work, *Scivias*, in the final vision of which she includes some passages that are closely similar to ones in the *Ordo Virtutum*. Textual comparisons showed that the play-version of these passages was the earlier: they were adapted to *Scivias*, not the other way round.[1]

With this early dating in mind, I suggested, in 1986, first that Hildegard's music for the *Ordo* 'itself indicates that hers was no "closet drama", but was planned for an audience from the start'; then, that the major festive event for her and her community which took place soon after 1151, the solemn consecration of her Rupertsberg convent on 1 May 1152, would also have been the perfect occasion for the presentation of the *Ordo*.[2] That day the Archbishop of Mainz and other prelates from Mainz cathedral must have been at the convent, as well as members of the aristocratic families from whom Hildegard had assembled her sisterhood – in particular the illustrious von Stade family, to which Richardis, Hildegard's best loved disciple, belonged, the family that had helped Hildegard to obtain her independent foundation on the Rupertsberg.

In 1991, however, without cognisance of my discussion, Eckehard Simon introduced a volume, *The Theatre of Medieval Europe. New Research in Early Drama*, with the surprising assertion that Hildegard's play had *not* been performed:

> By the thirteenth century, to be sure, liturgical plays were sung by nuns in some convents, and fifteenth-century civic records occasionally mention women in minor parts. But from the Winchester Easter play of *c.* 975 to Shakespeare and beyond, theatre was the province of men ... [Hildegard's] so-called *Ordo Virtutum* – involving vices, virtues and the devil – may in fact be the first morality. But it is poor sociology to claim, as music performance groups like *Sequentia* do, that Hildegard and the nuns of Bingen would have staged the *Ordo* in the convent cloister.[3]

It is true that evidence for the performance of the *Ordo Virtutum* is circumstantial and not direct – that is, we do not have an eye-witness account, nor is there a medieval equivalent of the Elizabethan

---

[1] 'Problemata Hildegardiana', *Mittellateinisches Jahrbuch* XVI 97–131, repr. (with some revisions) in Dronke 1992, pp. 143–91, esp. pp. 148–56.
[2] Dronke 1986, pp. xxxv–xxxvi.   [3] Simon 1991, p. xiii.

Stationer's Register. Yet a number of considerations are relevant to this question. It may be as well to set these out here and to remove certain historical misconceptions.

If it was unusual for medieval religious women to perform plays, Hildegard was far-reachingly unusual.[4] She did many things that were otherwise held to be 'the province of men': she undertook preaching journeys, addressing sermons to bishops, clergy and monks as well as laity; she was asked to exorcise, and on one notable occasion (1167) composed a mimetic scenario for this purpose that was close to drama in form;[5] because Pope Eugene in 1147 had publicly accredited her work, the greatest temporal rulers, as well as high-ranking clergy, asked her advice, and she instructed, at times even commanded, them in their decisions and actions.

At the Rupertsberg, under Hildegard's guidance, there was an intense cultivation of vocal and instrumental music, which she recalls in her long letter (1178) to the prelates of Mainz.[6] She also instituted in her convent a custom that aroused both amazement and criticism among her contemporaries: she and her nuns celebrated major Church feasts by dressing up in white veils, rings, and elaborately designed tiaras, enacting – as Hildegard makes clear in her defence of this innovation – the rôles of the brides of Christ.[7] In the light of such a practice, as well as of the musical life in Hildegard's foundation, is it at all plausible to claim that in Hildegard's day the *Ordo Virtutum* was not performed?

By his phrase 'so-called *Ordo Virtutum*', Simon presumably wishes to suggest that this was not Hildegard's own choice of name: that these words – which, applied to a work in dialogue, can only mean 'The *Play* of the Virtues' – must be a misnomer due to someone who wrongly took this to be genuine drama. However, the play is headed *Incipit Ordo Virtutum* by the scribe of the text itself in the main manuscript (the '*Riesenkodex*'), which was copied on the Rupertsberg in the last years of Hildegard's life – that is, still under her supervision (see pp. 156–7 below). There can be no doubt: the title *Ordo Virtutum* is Hildegard's own, and she conceived her composition as a play.

The play-text is preserved not only with complete, carefully written music, but with some guiding phrases that would seem to have been

---

[4] For documentation of the details that follow, see esp. *Women Writers* ch. 6.
[5] First published in 'Problemata' (= Dronke 1992, text pp. 185–8, tr. and discussion pp. 173–8). We have a testimony that this piece had at least one performance (see p. 178).
[6] Cf. *Women Writers* pp. 196–9, 313–15; there is now a complete edn of the letter in *Hildegardis Bingensis Epistolarium* I, ed. L. Van Acker (CC CM 91, 1991), no. xxiii.
[7] Cf. *Women Writers*, pp. 165–9.

intended for performers rather than simply for readers. Such expressions in the rubrics as *felix* (15/16, 22/3), *gravata* (25/6), *infelix* (35/6), *Querela penitentis* (161/2), and *penitens* (175/6, 211/12), are hardly needed by the readers, for whom the mood and tone emerge in the words immediately following: are they not rather directions to the singer of the rôle of Anima to convey these emotions by her voice and bearing? Similarly, *strepitus* (47/8) is best seen as an indication to the performing Diabolus how to speak his lines.

With a number of points, inevitably, we cannot pass beyond informed conjecture about what is historically most probable. Is it a pure coincidence, for example, that the number of rôles in the play accords so well with the 'twenty noble girls of wealthy parentage'[8] that Hildegard brought with her to found the Rupertsberg convent? The play has seventeen solo parts for women – for Anima and sixteen Virtues – as well as requiring a group of lamenting Anime (for which three further nuns would have been to hand). It seems likely, that is, that Hildegard composed expressly with her twenty available women performers in mind. There is only one male solo part, that of Diabolus. As I suggested in 1986, there was just one man who was constantly present in the convent – Hildegard's loved secretary and provost, Volmar; as only he could have rehearsed regularly with the nuns, it may well be he who took the Diabolus part. (The brief use of a chorus of Patriarchs and Prophets in the Prologue would not have required any lengthy presence of other clergy, e.g. from Mainz cathedral, at the convent for rehearsing.)

Was the *Ordo* first performed somewhat in the manner of an oratorio, or more in that of a drama? There are certain indications (apart from the choreography implied by the words in scene 2) in favour of the second alternative. Why, for instance, does Hildegard in *Scivias* describe the *costumes* of the Virtues with a richness of detail unique in the tradition of such allegorical descriptions? Why did the illuminated *Scivias* manuscript, prepared under Hildegard's direction c. 1170, render the often outlandish costumes of these Virtues in meticulous detail in its miniatures? The 'shadowy' dress of Timor Dei, on which many closed eyes are painted in silver (she is irradiated by the divine light, but afraid of being dazzled if she looks at it), affords a striking example. Can there really have been no connection between the keenly visualised and depicted Virtues in the prose work and the mode of their presentation in the play?

I do not know of any other medieval play which survives with its

---

[8] The phrase (*cum viginti puellis nobilibus et de divitibus parentibus natis*) occurs in Hildegard's autobiographic notes, ed. *Women Writers*, p. 233.

complete music where scholars have doubted that the play was performed. Such a singular prejudice in the case of Hildegard's *Ordo* can only be a lingering remnant of the older prejudice, the notion that medieval women were themselves incapable of writing or composing – that such things were always done for them by men. The range of evidence suggesting that the *Ordo Virtutum* was performed is probably the strongest we have for any of the plays in this volume. The 'sociology' of leading performers today, such as *Sequentia*, cannot be faulted; it is the scholars, not the performers, who at times tend to imitate the action of the ... ostrich.

Versification

Hildegard composed words and music together. Her poetry consists for the most part of what today would be called 'free verse': its movements and rhythms are adjusted to the melody, but are otherwise autonomous. While in the *Ordo* there are many instances of syllabic and syntactic parallelism, and some of rhyme, neither device is used systematically or in order to determine verse structure. Only in some of the lyrical pieces in the *Symphonia* are there traces of more elaborate symmetries, though they do not include fully regular strophic forms.

In the *Ordo* there is a clear differentiation between the five speeches of Diabolus, which move in a jagged staccato fashion, and the flowing cadences, lyrical and even incantatory in rhythm, which the Virtues deploy. Anima, when she is in harmony with the Virtues, does likewise, but at the moment she defies them, her words take on something of Diabolus' jaggedness:

> Deus creavit mundum:
> non facio illi iniuriam,
> sed volo uti illo! (45–7)

The decision to introduce line-divisions for all speeches except those of Diabolus is, of course, editorial. They are intended to help to show some of the rhythmic movement and to correspond as far as possible to the articulation of the melodies.

156 Nine medieval Latin plays

The manuscript

The main source for the *Ordo Virtutum*[1] is the 'giant codex' (*Riesenkodex*, = R), or 'codex with the chain', that today is MS 2 in the Hessische Landesbibliothek, Wiesbaden. It is a 'collected edition' of Hildegard's works, with the principal exception of her medical and scientific writings (known today as *Causae et curae*, *Physica*, and the 'Berlin fragment'). In a fundamental study of 1956,[2] Marianna Schrader and Adelgundis Führkötter demonstrated that the *Riesenkodex* was copied in Hildegard's own scriptorium, in her convent on the Rupertsberg, and that it was preserved there from the outset. While they believed that the codex was compiled in 1180–90, the decade following Hildegard's death, two recent scholars and editors of Hildegard, Albert Derolez and Lieven Van Acker, have been able to show that this dating is too late. To cite Derolez: 'as the two texts [in R] composed after Hildegard's death have clearly been interpolated into the *Riesenkodex*, it is reasonable to assume that the codex was in fact composed during Hildegard's lifetime'.[3] Derolez and Van Acker both suggest that the compilation of the codex will have been done under the direction of Guibert of Gembloux, Hildegard's last secretary, who stayed at the Rupertsberg from 1177 till 1180.

The codex, consisting of 481 vellum leaves, written in double columns, begins with Hildegard's visionary trilogy (fols. 1v–308r) – *Scivias* ('Know the Ways'), *Liber vite meritorum* ('The Book of Life's Merits'), and *Liber divinorum operum* ('The Book of Divine Handiworks') – and also includes a large group of her letters (fols. 328r–434r). It contains her lyrical compositions (*Symphonia*) and her play in the two final gatherings (fols. 466r–481v).[4] The lyrics and play are carefully

---

[1] On the text of the *Ordo Virtutum* in London BL Add. 15102, fols. 207r–221r, which was written in 1487 for Johannes Trithemius, and which may be based wholly on the copy in the *Riesenkodex*, see Dronke 1986, pp. 180, 192. It is likely that there was a further text of the *Ordo* in the MS Dendermonde 9, in a gathering that is missing today: see my discussion, 'The Composition of Hildegard of Bingen's *Symphonia*', *Sacris Erudiri* XIX (1969–70) 381–93.

[2] *Die Echtheit des Schrifttums der heiligen Hildegard von Bingen* (Cologne–Graz 1956), esp. pp. 154–79.

[3] Cf. *Guiberti Gemblacensis Epistolae* I ed. A. Derolez (CC CM 66, 1988), pp. xxx–xxxi; *Hildegardis Bingensis Epistolarium* I, ed.L. Van Acker (CC CM 91, 1991), pp. xxvii–xxix.

[4] For a succinct bibliographic guide to Hildegard's writings, see *Women Writers*, ch. 6 and pp. 326–7. The text printed below is essentially that of my critical edition in *Poetic Individuality in the Middle Ages* (Oxford 1970, 2nd edn London 1986), pp. 180–92, though with some changes of punctuation. The translation, first published in extracts *ibid.* pp. 170–8, and then complete in the libretto of the recording of *Ordo Virtutum* by Sequentia

written by 'hand 2', who likewise wrote a brief section of *Scivias* earlier in R. The words *Incipit Ordo Virtutum* occur at the foot of fol. 478va; the play itself extends from the next column, 478vb, to fol. 481vb, concluding the vast codex.

(Harmonia Mundi 1982), has been revised in many points of detail. The Introduction and notes have been written expressly for this volume.

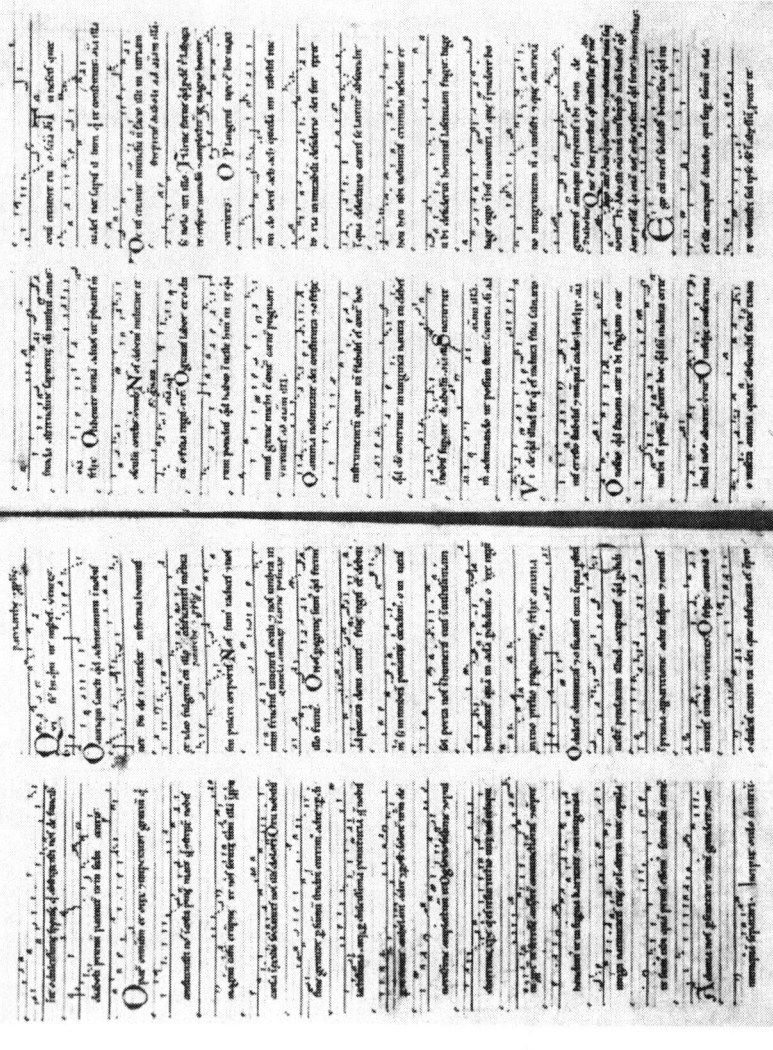

III Wiesbaden, Hess. Landesbibl. 2, fols. 478v–479r (Ordo Virtutum, 1–66)

IV Wiesbaden, Hess. Landesbibl. 2, fols. 479r–480r (Ordo Virtutum, 67–144)

Incipit Ordo Virtutum

Patriarche et Prophete:
Qui sunt hi, qui ut nubes?

Virtutes:
O antiqui sancti, quid admiramini in nobis?
Verbum dei clarescit in forma hominis,
et ideo fulgemus cum illo,
5 edificantes membra sui pulcri corporis.

Patriarche et Prophete:
Nos sumus radices et vos rami,
fructus viventis oculi,
et nos umbra in illo fuimus.

Querela Animarum in carne positarum:
O nos peregrine sumus.
10 Quid fecimus, ad peccata deviantes?
Filie regis esse debuimus,
sed in umbram peccatorum cecidimus.
O vivens sol, porta nos in humeris tuis
in iustissimam hereditatem quam in Adam perdidimus!
15 O rex regum, in tuo prelio pugnamus.

Felix Anima:
O dulcis divinitas, et o suavis vita,
in qua perferam vestem preclaram,
illud accipiens quod perdidi in prima apparitione,
ad te suspiro, et omnes Virtutes invoco.

Virtutes:
20 O felix Anima, et o dulcis creatura dei,
que edificata es in pro/funda altitudine sapientie dei,
multum amas.

R: '*Riesenkodex*', Wiesbaden, Hessische Landesbibliothek 2 (1177–80), fols. 478va–481vb (For the readings in London BL Add. 15102, and a discussion of their significance, see Dronke 1986, pp. 180–92)

Here begins the Play of the Virtues

Prologue

Patriarchs and Prophets:
Who are these, who are like clouds?

Virtues:
You holy ones of old, why do you marvel at us?
The Word of God grows bright in the shape of man,
and thus we shine with him,
5 building up the limbs of his beautiful body.

Patriarchs and Prophets:
We are the roots, and you, the boughs,
fruits of the living eye,
and in that eye we were the shadow.

Scene 1

The lament of (a chorus of) embodied Souls:
Oh, we are strangers here!
10 What have we done, straying to realms of sin?
We should have been daughters of the King,
but we have fallen into the shadow of sins.
Oh living Sun, carry us on your shoulders
back to that most just heritage we lost in Adam!
15 King of kings, we are fighting in your battle.

Anima (happily):
Oh sweet divinity, oh gentle life,
in which I shall wear a radiant robe,
receiving that which I lost in my first manifestation –
I sigh for you, and invoke all the Virtues.

Virtues:
20 You happy Soul, sweet and divine creation,
fashioned in the deep height of the wisdom of God,
you show great love.

Felix Anima:
O libenter veniam ad vos,
ut prebeatis michi osculum cordis.

Virtutes:
25 Nos debemus militare tecum, o filia regis.

Sed, gravata, Anima conqueritur:
O gravis labor, et o durum pondus
quod habeo in veste huius vite,
quia nimis grave michi est contra carnem pugnare.

Virtutes ad Animam illam:
O Anima, voluntate dei constituta,
30 et o felix instrumentum, quare tam flebilis es
contra hoc quod deus contrivit in virginea natura?
Tu debes in nobis superare diabolum.

Anima illa:
Succurrite michi, adiuvando, ut possim stare!

Scientia Dei ad Animam illam:
Vide quid illud sit quo es induta, filia salvationis,
35 et esto stabilis, et numquam cades.

Infelix, Anima:
O nescio quid faciam,
aut ubi fugiam!
O ve michi, non possum perficere
hoc quod sum induta.
40 Certe illud volo abicere!

Virtutes:
O infelix conscientia,
o misera Anima,
quare abscondis faciem tuam / coram creatore tuo?

Scientia Dei:
Tu nescis, nec vides, nec sapis illum qui te constituit.

Anima illa:
45 Deus creavit mundum:
non facio illi iniuriam,
sed volo uti illo!

[44] quec R

Anima (happily):
Oh let me come to you joyfully,
that you may give me the kiss of your heart!

Virtues:
25 We must fight together with you, royal daughter.

Anima, depressed, laments:
Oh grievous toil, oh harsh weight
that I bear in the dress of this life:
it is too grievous for me to fight against my body.

Virtues (to Anima):
Anima, you that were given your place by the will of God,
30 you instrument of bliss, why are you so tearful
in the face of the evil God crushed in a maidenly being?
You must overcome the devil in our midst.

Anima:
Support me, help me to stay firm!

Knowledge of God (to Anima):
Look at the dress you are wearing, daughter of salvation:
35 be steadfast, and you'll never fall.

Anima (unhappily)
I don't know what to do
or where to flee.
Woe is me, I cannot complete
this dress I have put on.
40 Indeed I want to cast it off!

Virtues:
Unhappy state of mind,
oh poor Anima,
why do you hide your face in the presence of your Creator?

Knowledge of God:
You do not know or see or taste the One who has set you here.

Anima:
45 God created the world:
I'm doing him no injury –
I only want to enjoy it!

Strepitus Diaboli ad Animam illam:
Fatue, fatue quid prodest tibi laborare? Respice mundum, et amplectetur te magno honore.

Virtutes:
50 O plangens vox est hec maximi doloris!
Ach, ach, quedam mirabilis victoria
in mirabili desiderio dei surrexit,
in qua delectatio carnis se latenter abscondit,
heu, heu, ubi voluntas crimina nescivit
55 et ubi desiderium hominis lasciviam fugit.
Luge, luge ergo in his, Innocentia,
que in pudore bono integritatem non amisisti,
et que avariciam gutturis antiqui serpentis ibi non devorasti.

Diabolus:
Que est hec potestas, quod nullus sit preter deum? Ego autem dico, qui
60 voluerit me et voluntatem meam sequi, dabo illi omnia. Tu vero, tuis
sequacibus nichil habes quod dare possis, quia etiam vos omnes nescitis
quid sitis.

Humilitas:
Ego cum meis sodalibus bene scio
quod tu es ille antiquus dracho
65 qui super summum volare voluisti –
sed ipse deus in abyssum proiecit te./

Virtutes:
Nos autem omnes in excelsis habitamus.

Humilitas:
Ego, Humilitas, regina Virtutum, dico:
venite ad me, Virtutes, et enutriam vos
70 ad requirendam perditam dragmam
et ad coronandum in perseverantia felicem.

Virtutes:
O gloriosa regina, et o suavissima mediatrix,
libenter venimus.

---

[59] preter deum] *corr. from* preter me *by the same hand in* R

Devil (shouting to Anima):
What use to you is toiling foolishly, foolishly? Look to the world: it will embrace you with great honour.

Virtues:
50 Is this not a plangent voice, of utmost sorrow?
Ah, a certain wondrous victory already
rose in that Soul, in her wondrous longing for God,
in which a sensual delight was secretly hidden,
alas, where previously the will had known no guilt
55 and the desire fled man's wantonness.
Mourn for this, mourn, Innocence,
you who lost no perfection in your fair modesty,
who did not devour greedily, with the gullet of the serpent of old.

Devil:
What is this power – as if there were no one but God? I say, whoever
60 wants to follow me and do my will, I'll give him everything. As for you,
Humility, you have nothing that you can give your followers: none of
you even know what you are!

Humility:
My comrades and I know very well
that you are the dragon of old
65 who craved to fly higher than the highest one:
but God himself hurled you in the abyss.

Virtues:
As for us, we dwell in the heights.

Scene 2

Humility:
I, Humility, queen of the Virtues, say:
come to me, you Virtues, and I'll give you the skill
70 to seek and find the drachma that is lost
and to crown her who perseveres blissfully.

Virtues:
Oh glorious queen, gentlest mediatrix,
gladly we come.

Humilitas:
Ideo, dilectissime filie,
75 teneo vos in regali talamo.

Karitas:
Ego Karitas, flos amabilis –
venite ad me, Virtutes, et perducam vos
in candidam lucem floris virge.

Virtutes:
O dilectissime flos, ardenti desiderio currimus ad te.

Timor Dei:
80 Ego, Timor Dei, vos felicissimas filias preparo
ut inspiciatis in deum vivum et non pereatis.

Virtutes:
O Timor, valde utilis es nobis:
habemus enim perfectum studium numquam a te separari.

Diabolus:
Euge! euge! quis est tantus timor? et quis est tantus amor? Ubi est
85 pugnator, et ubi est remunerator? Vos nescitis quid colitis.

Virtutes:
Tu autem exterritus es per summum iudicem,
479vb quia, inflatus superbia, mer/sus es in gehennam.

Obedientia:
Ego lucida Obedientia –
venite ad me, pulcherrime filie, et reducam vos
90 ad patriam et ad osculum regis.

Virtutes:
O dulcissima vocatrix,
nos decet in magno studio pervenire ad te.

Fides:
Ego Fides, speculum vite:
venerabiles filie, venite ad me
95 et ostendo vobis fontem salientem.

Virtutes:
O serena, speculata, habemus fiduciam
pervenire ad verum fontem per te.

Humility:
Because of this, beloved daughters,
75 I'll keep your place in the royal wedding-chamber.

Charity:
I am Charity, the flower of love –
come to me, Virtues, and I'll lead you
into the radiant light of the flower of the rod.

Virtues:
Dearest flower, with ardent longing we run to you.

Fear of God:
80 I, Fear of God, can prepare you, blissful daughters,
to gaze upon the living God and not die of it.

Virtues:
Fear, you can help us greatly:
we are filled with the longing never to part from you.

Devil:
Bravo! Bravo! What is this great fear, and this great love? Where is the champion? Where the prize-giver? You don't even know what you are
85 worshipping!

Virtues:
But you, you were terrified at the supreme Judge,
for, swollen with pride, you were plunged into Gehenna.

Obedience:
I am Obedience, the shining one –
come to me, lovely daughters, and I'll lead you
90 to your homeland and to the kiss of the King.

Virtues:
Sweetest summoner,
it is right for us to come, most eagerly, to you.

Faith:
I am Faith, the mirror of life:
precious daughters, come to me
95 and I shall show you the leaping fountain.

Virtues:
Serene one, mirror-like, we trust in you:
we shall arrive at that fountain through you.

Spes:
Ego sum dulcis conspectrix viventis oculi,
quam fallax torpor non decipit –
100 unde vos, o tenebre, non potestis me obnubilare.

Virtutes:
O vivens vita, et o suavis consolatrix,
tu mortifera mortis vincis
et vidente oculo clausuram celi aperis.

Castitas:
O Virginitas, in regali thalamo stas.
105 O quam dulciter ardes in amplexibus regis,
cum te sol perfulget
ita quod nobilis flos tuus numquam cadet./
48ora O virgo nobilis, te numquam inveniet umbra in cadente flore!

Virtutes:
Flos campi cadit vento, pluvia spargit eum.
110 O Virginitas, tu permanes in symphoniis supernorum civium:
unde es suavis flos qui numquam aresces.

Innocentia:
Fugite, oves, spurcicias Diaboli!

Virtutes:
Has te succurrente fugiemus.

Contemptus Mundi:
Ego, Contemptus Mundi, sum candor vite.
115 O misera terre peregrinatio
in multis laboribus – te dimitto.
O Virtutes, venite ad me
et ascendamus ad fontem vite!

Virtutes:
O gloriosa domina, tu semper habes certamina Christi,
120 o magna virtus, que mundum conculcas,
unde etiam victoriose in celo habitas.

Amor Celestis:
Ego aurea porta in celo fixa sum:
qui per me transit
numquam amaram petulantiam in mente sua gustabit.

[110] uirginintas R

Hope:
I am the sweet beholder of the living eye,
I whom no dissembling torpor can deceive.
100 Darkness, you cannot cloud my gaze!

Virtues:
Living life, gentle, consoling one,
you overcome the deadly shafts of death
and with your seeing eye lay heaven's gate open.

Chastity:
Maidenhood, you remain within the royal chamber.
105 How sweetly you burn in the King's embraces,
when the Sun blazes through you,
never letting your noble flower fall.
Gentle maiden, you will never know the shadow over the falling flower!

Virtues:
The flower in the meadow falls in the wind, the rain splashes it,
110 But you, Maidenhood, remain in the symphonies of heavenly habitants:
you are the tender flower that will never grow dry.

Innocence:
My flock, flee from the Devil's taints!

Virtues:
We shall flee them, if you give us aid.

World-rejection:
I, World-rejection, am the blaze of life.
115 Oh wretched, exiled state on earth,
with all your toils – I let you go.
Come to me, you Virtues,
and we'll climb up to the fountain of life!

Virtues:
Glorious lady, you that always fight Christ's battles,
120 great power that tread the world under your feet,
you thereby dwell in heaven, victoriously.

Heavenly Love:
I am the golden gate that's fixed in heaven:
whoever passes through me
will never taste bitter rebelliousness in her mind.

Virtutes:
125 O filia regis, tu semper es in amplexi/bus quos mundus fugit,
480rb O quam suavis est tua dilectio in summo deo!

<Disciplina>:
Ego sum amatrix simplicium morum qui turpia opera nesciunt;
sed semper in regum regem aspicio
et amplector eum in honore altissimo.

Virtutes:
130 O tu angelica socia, tu es valde ornata
in regalibus nuptiis.

Verecundia:
Ego obtenebro et fugo atque conculco
omnes spurcicias Diaboli.

Virtutes:
Tu es in edificatione celestis Ierusalem,
135 florens in candidis liliis.

Misericordia:
O quam amara est illa duricia que non cedit in mentibus,
misericorditer dolori succurrens!
Ego autem omnibus dolentibus manum porrigere volo.

Virtutes:
O laudabilis mater peregrinorum,
140 tu semper erigis illos,
atque ungis pauperes et debiles.

Victoria:
Ego Victoria velox et fortis pugnatrix sum –
in lapide pugno, serpentem antiquum conculco.

Virtutes:
480va O dulcissima / bellatrix, in torrente fonte
145 qui absorbuit lupum rapacem –
o gloriosa coronata, nos libenter
militamus tecum contra illusorem hunc.

Discretio:
Ego Discretio sum lux et dispensatrix omnium creaturarum,
indifferentia dei, quam Adam a se fugavit per lasciviam morum.

---
[127] <Disciplina>] *speaker's name erased in* R
[143] pugna R
[149] in differentia (*probably as two words*) R

Virtues:
125 Royal daughter, you are held fast in the embraces the world shuns:
how tender is your love in the highest God!

Discipline:
I am one who loves innocent ways that know nothing ignoble;
I always gaze upon the King of kings
and, as my highest honour, I embrace him.

Virtues:
130 Angelic comrade, how comely you are
in the royal nuptials!

Shamefastness:
I cover over, drive away or tread down
all the filths of the Devil.

Virtues:
Yours is a part in the building of heavenly Jerusalem,
135 flowering among shining lilies.

Mercy:
How bitter in human minds is the harshness that does not soften
and mercifully ease pain!
I want to reach out my hand to all who suffer.

Virtues:
Matchless mother of exiles,
140 you are always raising them up
and anointing the poor and the weak.

Victory:
I am Victory, the swift, brave champion:
I fight with a stone, I tread the age-old serpent down.

Virtues:
Oh gentlest warrior, in the scorching fountain
145 that swallowed up the voracious wolf –
glorious, crowned one, how gladly
we'll fight against that trickster, at your side!

Discretion:
I am Discretion, light and moderator of all creatures –
the impartiality of God, that Adam drove away by acting wantonly.

Virtutes:
150 O pulcherrima mater, quam dulcis et quam suavis es,
quia nemo confunditur in te.

Pacientia:
Ego sum columpna que molliri non potest,
quia fundamentum meum in deo est.

Virtutes:
O firma que stas in caverna petre,
155 et o gloriosa bellatrix que suffers omnia!

Humilitas:
O filie Israhel, sub arbore suscitavit vos deus,
unde in hoc tempore recordamini plantationis sue.
Gaudete ergo, filie Syon!

Virtutes:
Heu, heu, nos Virtutes plangamus et lugeamus,
160 quia ovis domini fugit vitam!

Querela Anime penitentis et Virtutes invocantis:
O vos regales Virtutes, quam speciose
et quam fulgentes estis in summo sole,
et quam dulcis est vestra mansio –
48ovb et ideo, o ve / michi, quia a vobis fugi!

Virtutes:
165 O fugitive, veni, veni ad nos, et deus suscipiet te.

Anima illa:
Ach! ach! fervens dulcedo absorbuit me in peccatis,
et ideo non ausa sum intrare.

Virtutes:
Noli timere nec fugere,
quia pastor bonus querit in te perditam ovem suam.

Anima illa:
170 Nunc est michi necesse ut suscipiatis me,
quoniam in vulneribus feteo
quibus antiquus serpens me contaminavit.

---

[171] qūo (*i.e.* quomodo) R

Virtues:
150 Fairest mother, how sweet you are, how gentle –
in you no one can be confounded.

Patience:
I am the pillar that can never be made to yield,
as my foundation is in God.

Virtues:
You that stay firm in the rocky cavern,
155 you are the glorious warrior who endures all.

Humility:
Daughters of Israel, God raised you from beneath the tree,
so now remember how it was planted.
Therefore rejoice, daughters of Jerusalem.

Scene 3

Virtues:
Alas, alas, let us lament and mourn,
160 because our master's sheep has fled from life!

Anima (laments, penitent and calling upon the Virtues):
You royal Virtues, how graceful,
how flashing-bright you look in the highest Sun,
and how delectable is your home,
and so, what woe is mine that I fled from you!

Virtues:
165 You who escaped, come, come to us, and God will take you back.

Anima:
Ah, but a burning sweetness swallowed me up in sins,
so I did not dare come in.

Virtues:
Don't be afraid or run away:
the good Shepherd is searching for his lost sheep – it is you.

Anima:
170 Now I need your help to gather me up –
I stink of the wounds
that the age-old serpent has made gangrenous.

Virtutes:
Curre ad nos, et sequere vestigia illa
in quibus numquam cades in societate nostra,
175 et deus curabit te.

Penitens Anima ad Virtutes:
Ego peccator qui fugi vitam:
plenus ulceribus veniam ad vos,
ut prebeatis michi scutum redemptionis.
O tu omnis milicia regine,
180 et o vos, candida lilia ipsius, cum rosea purpura,
inclinate vos ad me, quia peregrina a vobis exulavi,
et adiuvate me, ut in sanguine filii dei possim surgere.

Virtutes:
481ra O Anima fu/gitiva, esto robusta,
et indue te arma lucis.

Anima illa:
185 Et o vera medicina, Humilitas, prebe michi auxilium,
quia superbia in multis viciis fregit me,
multas cicatrices michi imponens.
Nunc fugio ad te, et ideo suscipe me.

Humilitas:
O omnes Virtutes, suscipite lugentem peccatorem,
190 in suis cicatricibus, propter vulnera Christi,
et perducite eum ad me.

Virtutes:
Volumus te reducere et nolumus te deserere,
et omnis celestis milicia gaudet super te –
ergo decet nos in symphonia sonare.

Humilitas:
195 O misera filia, volo te amplecti,
quia magnus medicus dura et amara vulnera
propter te passus est.

Virtutes:
O vivens fons, quam magna est suavitas tua,
qui faciem istorum in te non amisisti,

Virtues:
Run back to us, retrace those steps
where you'll never falter, in our company:
175 God will heal you.

Anima (penitently, to the Virtues):
I am the sinner who fled from life:
riddled with sores I'll come to you –
you can offer me redemption's shield.
All of you, warriors of Queen Humility,
180 her white lilies and her crimson roses,
stoop to me, who exiled myself from you like a stranger,
and help me, that in the blood of the Son of God I may arise.

Virtues:
Fugitive Anima, now be strong:
put on the armour of light.

Anima:
185 And you, true medicine, Humility, grant me your help,
for pride has broken me in many vices,
inflicting many scars on me.
Now I'm escaping to you – so take me up!

Humility:
All you Virtues, lift up this mournful sinner,
190 with all her scars, for the sake of Christ's wounds,
and bring her to me.

Virtues:
We want to bring you back – we shan't desert you,
the whole of heaven's host will have joy in you:
thus it is right for us now to play our symphony.

Humility:
195 Oh unhappy daughter, I want to embrace you:
the great surgeon has suffered harsh and bitter wounds
for your sake.

Virtues:
Living fountain, how great is your sweetness:
you did not reject the gaze of these upon you –

200 sed acute previdisti
　　quomodo eos de angelico casu abstraheres
　　qui se estimabant illud habere
481rb　quod non licet sic / stare;
　　unde gaude, filia Syon,
205 quia deus tibi multos reddit
　　quos serpens de te abscidere voluit,
　　qui nunc in maiori luce fulgent
　　quam prius illorum causa fuisset.

Diabolus:
Que es, aut unde venis? Tu amplexata es me, et ego foras eduxi te. Sed
210 nunc in reversione tua confundis me – ego autem pugna mea deiciam te!

Penitens Anima:
Ego omnes vias meas malas esse cognovi, et ideo fugi a te.
Modo autem, o illusor, pugno contra te.
Inde tu, o regina Humilitas, tuo medicamine adiuva me!

Humilitas ad Victoriam:
215 O Victoria, que istum in celo superasti,
　　curre cum militibus tuis
　　et omnes ligate Diabolum hunc!

Victoria ad Virtutes:
O fortissimi et gloriosissimi milites, venite,
et adiuvate me istum fallacem vincere.

Virtutes:
220 O dulcissima bellatrix, in torrente fonte
　　qui absorbuit lupum rapacem –
　　o gloriosa coronata, nos libenter
　　militamus tecum contra illusorem hunc.

Humilitas:
Ligate ergo istum, o Virtutes preclare!

213/14　anima illa (*between* contra te. *and* Inde) R

200 no, acutely you foresaw
how you could avert them from the fall the angels fell,
they who thought they possessed a power
which no law allows to be like that.
Rejoice then, daughter Jerusalem,
205 for God is giving you back many
whom the serpent wanted to sunder from you,
who now gleam in a greater brightness
than would have been their state before.

Scene 4

Devil:
Who are you? Where are you coming from? You were in my embrace, I
210 led you out. Yet now you are going back, defying me – but I shall fight
you and bring you down!

Anima (penitently):
I recognised that all my ways were wicked, so I fled you.
But now, you trickster, I'll fight you face to face.
Queen Humility, come with your medicine, give me aid!

Humility:
215 Victory, you who once conquered this creature in the heavens,
run now, with all your soldiery,
and all of you bind this Fiend!

Victory:
Bravest and most glorious warriors, come,
help me to vanquish this deceitful one!

Virtues:
220 Oh sweetest warrior, in the scorching fountain
that swallowed up the voracious wolf –
glorious, crowned one, how gladly
we'll fight against that trickster, at your side!

Humility:
Bind him then, you shining Virtues!

Virtutes:
225 O regina nostra, tibi parebimus,
et precepta tua in omnibus adimplebimus.

Victoria:
48¹va Gaudete, o socii, quia antiquus serpens / ligatus est!

Virtutes:
Laus tibi, Christe, rex angelorum!

Castitas:
In mente altissimi, o Satana, caput tuum conculcavi,
230 et in virginea forma dulce miraculum colui,
ubi filius dei venit in mundum;
unde deiectus es in omnibus spoliis tuis,
et nunc gaudeant omnes qui habitant in celis,
quia venter tuus confusus est.

Diabolus:
235 Tu nescis quid colis, quia venter tuus vacuus est pulcra forma de viro sumpta – ubi transis preceptum quod deus in suavi copula precepit; unde nescis quid sis!

Castitas:
Quomodo posset me hoc tangere
quod tua suggestio polluit per immundiciam incestus?
240 Unum virum protuli, qui genus humanum
ad se congregat, contra te, per nativitatem suam.

Virtutes:
O deus, quis es tu, qui in temetipso
hoc magnum consilium habuisti,
quod destruxit infernalem haustum
245 in publicanis et peccatoribus,
qui nunc lucent in superna bonitate!
Unde, o rex, laus sit tibi.
O pater omnipotens, ex te fluit fons in igneo amore:
48¹vb perduc / filios tuos in rectum ventum velorum aquarum,
250 ita ut et nos eos hoc modo perducamus
in celestem Ierusalem.

²⁴⁷/⁸ virtutes (*between* tibi. *and* O pater) R

Virtues:
225 Queen of us all, we obey –
we'll carry out your orders totally.

Victory:
Comrades, rejoice: the age-old snake is bound!

Virtues:
Praise be to you, Christ, King of the angels!

Chastity:
In the mind of the Highest, Satan, I trod on your head,
230 and in a virgin form I nurtured a sweet miracle
when the Son of God came into the world;
therefore you are laid low, with all your plunder;
and now let all who dwell in heaven rejoice,
because your belly has been confounded.

Devil:
235 You don't know what you are nurturing, for your belly is devoid of the beautiful form that woman receives from man; in this you transgress the command that God enjoined in the sweet act of love; so you don't even know what you are!

Chastity:
How can what you say affect me?
Even your suggestion smirches it with foulness.
240 I did bring forth a man, who gathers up mankind
to himself, against you, through his nativity.

Virtues:
Who are you, God, who held
such great counsel in yourself,
a counsel that destroyed the draught of hell
245 in publicans and sinners,
who now shine in paradisal goodness!
Praise to you, King, for this!
Almighty Father, from you flowed a fountain in fiery love:
guide your children into a fair wind, sailing the waters,
250 so that we too may steer them in this way
into the heavenly Jerusalem.

<*Virtutes et Anime*>:
In principio omnes creature viruerunt,
in medio flores floruerunt;
postea viriditas descendit.
255 Et istud vir preliator vidit et dixit:
Hoc scio, sed aureus numerus nondum est plenus.
Tu ergo, paternum speculum aspice:
in corpore meo fatigationem sustineo,
parvuli etiam mei deficiunt.
260 Nunc memor esto, quod plenitudo que in primo facta est
arescere non debuit,
et tunc in te habuisti
quod oculus tuus numquam cederet
usque dum corpus meum videres plenum gemmarum.
265 Nam me fatigat quod omnia membra mea in irrisionem vadunt.
Pater, vide, vulnera mea tibi ostendo.
Ergo nunc, omnes homines,
genua vestra ad patrem vestrum flectite,
ut vobis manum suam porrigat.

Finale

Virtues and Souls:
In the beginning all creation was verdant,
flowers blossomed in the midst of it;
later, greenness sank away.
255 And the champion saw this and said:
"I know it, but the golden number is not yet full.
You then, behold me, mirror of your fatherhood:
in my body I am suffering exhaustion,
even my little ones faint.
260 Now remember that the fullness which was made in the beginning
need not have grown dry,
and that then you resolved
that your eye would never fail
until you saw my body full of jewels.
265 For it wearies me that all my limbs are exposed to mockery:
Father, behold, I am showing you my wounds."
So now, all you people,
bend your knees to the Father,
that he may reach you his hand.

Explanatory notes

1 Isaiah 60, 8.
6–8 Cf. Isaiah 60, 21.
14 The souls, begging to be carried back to paradise, claim it is most justly theirs (cf. 11).
18 in prima apparitione] I.e. in Anima's first appearance on earth, united to a body.
22 Cf. Luke 7, 47.
24 Cf. Song of Songs, 1, 1.
30 felix instrumentum] Hildegard may have two senses of *instrumentum* in mind: seeing Anima as instrumental in achieving her state of bliss, and as the blissful instrument on which God can play his music.
30–1 I.e. Why are you so tearful at the prospect of crushing sin, which God achieved in the maidenly nature of Mary?
32 in nobis] In terms of the play, Diabolus is in the midst of the Virtues; but the meaning may also be microcosmic: Anima must conquer Diabolus by using the powers (*virtutes*) within herself.
34 As Hildegard uses *induo* with acc. at 39, and with double acc. at 184, she may also have written *quod es induta* here, but been 'corrected', by secretary or copyist, in the light of the (frequent, though not invariable) biblical Latin usage of passive forms of *induo* with abl. (cf. Dronke 1992, pp. 151–2). The reference is to the mortal dress that Anima has to complete (*perficere*, 38) before she can win the heavenly *vestem preclaram* (17).
43 Cf. Genesis 3, 8.
48 Fatue, fatue] These could also be constructed as masc. voc.: Hildegard later treats the masc. forms *fugitivus* and *peccator* (165, 176, 189) as being of common gender, applying them to Anima.
49 amplectetur] The world's 'embrace' is the antitype of the divine embraces (cf. 125, 129, 195, 209).
58 avariciam] Acc. for abl., or perhaps understand <*secundum*> *avariciam*.
59 The syntax is difficult: either understand *que dicit* after *potestas*, or construe *quod* in a sense akin to *quasi*.
60 dabo illi omnia] Cf. Matthew 4, 9.
64–6 The fall of Lucifer (cf. esp. Isaiah 14, 12 ff.; Apocalypse 12, 7–12) is a leitmotif throughout Hildegard's writings.
70 Cf. Luke 15, 8–10.

84   Euge! euge!] The double *euge* is used as a derisive shout in Psalm 34, 21 and 25; 39, 16; 69, 4; Ezekiel 25, 3. Diabolus here mocks both fear of God and love of God. With *Ubi est pugnator* ... he is saying, there is no struggle, and no one to reward the winner in a struggle.

86   To counter his boast that he knows no *timor*, the Virtues remind Diabolus that he *was* afraid of God when he was plunged into the abyss.

90   osculum regis] Cf. Song 1, 1–3.

95   fontem salientem] Cf. John 4, 14.

98   conspectrix viventis oculi] Hildegard probably intends the genitive to have both subjective and objective force: Spes gazes upon God's eye, and she is the gazing of God's eye, 'the life of life' (cf. 101, 103).

104   (and 112) Neither Castitas nor Innocentia declare themselves, like the other Virtues. Hildegard presents them as timid figures, so that Castitas celebrates Maidenhood rather than herself, and Innocentia utters only the briefest words of encouragement, to the *oves* – presumably the audience, or *omnes homines* (267). The expression *oves* foreshadows the allusions to the parable of the lost sheep (Luke 15, 3–7) at the opening of the next scene (160).

109   Flos campi] Cf. Song 2, 1.

126   dilectio in summo deo] The ambiguity may well be deliberate: Amor Celestis exists in the highest God and proceeds from him – or again, is a quality that opens heaven to mortals and comes to rest in God.

127   The name of the Virtue who sings these lines has been erased, and the reading *Caritas* in BL Add. 15102 cannot be right, since she has already declared herself (76–8). I adopt Maura Böckeler's suggestion *Disciplina*, from her edn (*Reigen der Tugenden*, Maria Laach 1927).

138   manum porrigere] Cf. the play's closing line (269).

141   Misericordia's anointing of the poor and weak recalls the action of the Good Samaritan, *misericordia motus* (Luke 10, 33–4).

143   Cf. 1 Kings 17, 50; Genesis 3, 15.

144–5   See the Introduction above, p. 150.

154   Cf. Song 2, 14.

156   Cf. Song 8, 5.

165   fugitive] Hildegard treats *fugitivus* as being of common gender (cf. note to 48 above).

166   fervens ... absorbuit: cf. 144–5.

168   Noli timere] such an expression is characteristically used by angels in Luke: to Zachary (1, 13), to Mary (1, 30), and to the shepherds (2, 10).

169   Cf. John 10, 11 and 14; Luke 15, 4.

184   Cf. Romans 13, 12.

187   Cf. Psalm 37, 6.

193   Cf. Luke 15, 7 and 10.

220–3   The Virtues repeat their acclamation of Victoria (= 144–7).

227   Cf. Apocalypse 20, 2.

229   Cf. Genesis 3, 15, and 143 above.

240–1 Cf. John 12, 32.
249 Cf. Isaiah 60, 9 (*naves maris ... ut adducam filios tuos*).
254 On Hildegard's concept and imagery of *viriditas*, see esp. Dronke 1984, pp. 82–7.

IX Ludus de passione
The Passion Play, from the Carmina Burana (Bressanone?)

Style, meaning and structure

The *Carmina Burana Passion Play* shows in striking ways the contrast – and complementarity – between two radically divergent dramatic styles and uses of dialogue. There are many short scenes in which the presentation is succinctly biblical and the language virtually confined to that of gospels and liturgy; and there are two long scenes, one with Mary Magdalen as heroine in the first half, one with Mary the mother as heroine in the second, that are rich in dramatic and poetic invention, in the portrayal of emotions about which the gospels say nothing, and in captivating non-biblical, non-liturgical language. These scenes include vivid strophes in the vernacular as well as in Latin, strophes that will especially have reached out to and moved the unlearned in the early audiences. If the whole play, reckoning with the miming and *reprises* indicated in the text, took some two hours to perform, these large freely conceived scenes of the two Maries will have occupied at least half that playing-time, and will have dominated the imaginative effect of the whole.

There are some indications that the *Carmina Burana* play, composed probably c. 1180 (cf. Dronke 1992, pp. 457 ff.) but copied a good half-century later, is defectively preserved. The most disconcerting is the initial rubric, which mentions the entry of two characters – Pilate's wife, and the Merchant's wife – who do not in fact appear in the play-text as it survives. Both have parts in the Resurrection-play (*CB* 15*, at 14–17, 88–91) which precedes in the codex, though it was inserted later. There are at least three possibilities: (1) that the scenes which concern the Merchant and Pilate in the *Passion Play* are fragmentary, and once included further strophes that featured the two wives; (2) that the initial rubric here has been garbled under the influence of an earlier copy of *CB* 15* (which includes 'Pilate and his wife' in its opening instructions, and which begins with the same liturgical responsory, 'Pilate having entered ...', as our play); (3) that the rubricator of the *Passion Play*, knowing a version of *CB* 15*, regarded this as a sequel, so that he gave some indications of cast which applied to the two plays together.

In other passages the text of the *Passion Play* is cryptic rather than defective: that is, the copyists frequently give only the cues for the texts needed, and the extent to which such cues should be completed can involve delicate questions of editorial judgement. What we have, in short, is a copy of a working scenario, rather than of a fully recorded poetic and musical text such as the *Ordo Virtutum* (VIII). Yet, given this mode of transmission, the Buranus text also contains remarkably few scribal errors – only a dozen in the course of a long play – and there is a firm dramatic structure, even if many details seem *prima facie* erratic and surprising.

To clarify the articulation, I have divided the text into twenty scenes. The overall structure (cf. Dronke 1992, pp. 458 f.) can be compared to that of a medieval altarpiece, a diptych, each half showing a large central scene surrounded by nine small panels that depict other, related scenes. The first half of the play (Sc. 1–10) concludes, on this analysis, with Judas' betrayal (185–203); its principal scene involves Simon the Pharisee, Jesus and Judas, as well as Mary Magdalen, her companions, and the Merchant (36–151). The second half (Sc. 11–20) has its principal scene (248–93) nearer the close; the only characters in it are Mary, Jesus and John; its focus is on Mary's three rending songs of lamentation.

In Part I, the first scene is a mime presenting the entrance of some of the principal personages; they make their way to their appointed 'places' (*loca*) in the playing-area, probably with instrumental, or perhaps with choral, accompaniment (this detail has not been noted in the rubric). Scene 2 (1–6) involves a mime of a different kind: the choir sings a liturgical responsory that anticipates some of the key phrases in the later exchanges between Pilate and Christ (cf. 218–19) and between Pilate and the Jewish populace (cf. 237–8, 246). Here, that is, we are given the concentrated essence of the play that is to unfold. Whilst we cannot rule out that the actors playing Pilate and Jesus themselves sang the lines ascribed to them in the responsory, it seems to me likelier that the choir (who will later have doubled as the crowd) sang the complete liturgical text, while this premonitory scene was acted out in dumbshow.

Next (Sc. 3) come two more naturalistic moments, using chiefly biblical language. They are flashbacks, recalling two vital episodes in Christ's ministry: the calling of the first apostles (7–9), and the healing of the blind man in Jericho, followed – as in Luke – by the calling of

Zacchaeus (10–16). Emblematically these show Christ's first and last appeals for followers. After this comes a mime of Christ's entry into Jerusalem (Sc. 4), an episode that is here wholly framed by liturgical chants. Four antiphons celebrating that triumphal advent are followed by the words *Gloria, laus* – the incipit of the Palm Sunday processional, in classical couplets, composed by Theodulf of Orléans († 821). Whether this was here confined to one or several couplets, or was sung entire, is not possible to determine.

The fifth, central scene is a vast and original elaboration of the episode of Simon the Pharisee and the sinful woman who anointed Christ's feet in Simon's house (Luke 7, 36–50). In the western Church, unlike the eastern, this woman was identified from early times as Mary Magdalen (who in fact is named two verses later in Luke [8, 2] as the woman from whom Christ had driven out seven demons). The dramatist invents quasi-biblical words for the scene's opening (36), even including a gloss for 'Rabbi' in the way that John does (20, 16) when the risen Christ appears to Mary Magdalen. But from the Pharisee's words to his servant (38 ff.) onwards, invention becomes wholly non-biblical. Mary sings a paean to worldly joy and voluptuousness, in a form and language that seem to echo the witty irreverence of the Archpoet's 'confession', *Estuans intrinsecus* (*CB* 191). She is wealthy, confident of her beauty and seductiveness (a confidence on which the Merchant plays – cf. 54–7). In her German strophes, which begin as if imitating the measure of the Latin but move into a different rhythm, Mary goes on to vaunt her familiarity with the notions of high courtly love, its virtue and its ennobling power (65–8): the dramatist makes a piquant contrast between her lip-service to these refined ideals and the frank hedonism that she reveals in her other declarations.

The rubrics of the scenario do not include all the necessary indications for Mary's thrice-repeated sleep and dream – a repetition that lends the scene an atmosphere of *féerie*. It is only at 107/8, for instance, that a demon is mentioned, as retreating. Yet one can safely reconstruct that, after each message from the angel, this demon is at hand and mimes a contrary message, so that Mary, on waking, resumes her quest for worldly delight and for the cosmetics best designed to help her to achieve it. It is only after her third sleep and dream of the angel (97/8) that the demonic influence is vanquished: she awakes repentant, and her lover (already mentioned in a rubric at 82/3) and the demon withdraw. Both these non-singing rôles must have given scope for mime, in the projecting of Mary's inner conflict. Her change of clothes at this point (107/8) is the visual expression of her change of heart. Then, in her third and last approach to the Merchant, her question and his answer are citations: they use the words (108–14) that the *three* Maries and the Merchant sang at Vic during the buying of an unguent for the dead Christ (see above, pp. 92–4).[1] This is no arbitrary borrowing: for the dramatist conflates the language of the episode in Luke 7, which belongs to the beginnings of Christ's ministry, with that in the house of Simon the leper (Matthew 26, 6 ff.), which immediately precedes Judas' betrayal and the Last Supper. Following John (12, 4–7), he assigns to Judas the words of rebuke (131) that Matthew gives to the disciples in general, and it is Judas who receives Christ's reproachful rejoinder (132 – cf. Matthew 26, 8–10). In the gospels Christ explicitly sees the woman's *unguentum* as a premonition of his burial. The poet, that is, by adapting the widely known strophes of the three Maries after Christ's death, was able to suggest this sense of foreshadowing.

Mary approaches Christ in a Latin strophe filled with imagery of healing akin to Hildegard's (cf. p. 150), and in two German strophes (121–8) of touching simplicity. The rest of the scene – apart from Judas' intervention and Jesus' answer (131–2) – returns to Luke's account of the episode in Simon's house. This, however, is given the freshly invented climax of Mary's lament in German (144–51), in which she lends her own repentance a wider, exemplary force.

The Magdalen episodes conclude (Sc. 6) with a brief scene couched fully in biblical language, the raising of Lazarus (cf. John 11, 1–44), whom John identifies as the brother not only of Martha but of the woman who had anointed Christ's feet. Here the rubrics indicate the combination of narrative, sung by a choir of clergy, and dialogue, sung by Jesus and the two sisters.

The scene between Judas and the Chief Priests (Sc. 7) is the dramatist's free amplification of a brief passage in Matthew (26, 14–15). Where this ends with the indefinite 'Then Judas sought an opportunity to betray him', the playwright gains greater immediacy by compressing time and giving Judas now his later words concluding the betrayal (172 – cf. Matthew 26, 48). He lets the hunt for Jesus (172/3) and the mime of the Last Supper (Sc. 8, *ibid.*) occur simultaneously in different parts of the playing-space. The directions are so unexpected at this point that one might imagine there was textual corruption; yet it seems possible, and dramatically compelling, to suppose that Judas temporarily leaves his crowd in order to take part in the mimed Last Supper scene, and

---

[1] These strophes are used again in the *CB* Resurrection-play (*CB* 15*, 80–3, 88–91), where the second strophe is given to the wife of the Merchant or Pharmacist (Apothecarius).

slinks back to it in the course of Scene 9, which shows Christ on Mount Olivet. Here too a remarkable, probably deliberate, reversal of biblical tradition occurs: Christ's words 'Sleep now and take some rest' (173), which belong to the close of the gospel scene, addressed to the chosen ones who have failed to stay awake (Matthew 26, 45), are here sung at the opening, to the disciples whom Christ leaves behind.

The dialogue in this scene is wholly biblical, as it is in that of Judas' betrayal (Sc. 10), except that Jesus' gospel reply to Judas, 'Friend, for what purpose have you come?' (26, 50) is expanded into a weightier, more lyrical reproach (193–7). The scene continues with Peter's denial of Jesus (cf. Matthew 28, 69–75, here modified by Mark 14, 69 – where the same girl challenges Peter twice – and enriched by John 18, 26 – where the priest's servant speaks of Peter's presence in the garden). Peter's triple disavowal is clear from the words of dialogue as recorded in the Codex Buranus, though, since two rubrics indicating speakers are missing, this episode has defeated previous editors, who have printed it garbled (Young) or incomplete (Vollmann), or have deleted it from the text altogether (Bischoff). The juxtaposition of the two betrayals – by Judas and by Peter – is not direct or immediate in the gospels. But it emerges in all its starkness for instance at the climax of the medieval English ballad of Judas (ed. Carleton Brown, *English Lyrics of the XIIIth Century*, Oxford 1932, no. 25); later, too, Fra Angelico in the Convent of San Marco depicts the faces together – that of Judas kissing Christ is set just over that of Peter, into whose eyes the *ancilla* gazes in wonderment at his denials. This confrontation of Judas with Peter, which concludes the first half of the play, finds its dramatic echo at the close of the second half, in the confrontation of Longinus, who arrives at true belief, with the Jews who persist in their derision (Sc. 20).

Part II begins with the diverse interrogations, before the Chief Priests (Sc. 11), Pilate (Sc. 12), Herod (Sc. 13) then Pilate again (Sc. 14), and the Jewish populace (Sc. 15). The fullest of these scenes is the third and last encounter with Pilate (Sc. 16), who, washing his hands, delivers Christ to be crucified. These scenes are enacted using nothing but gospel words. Only the first (Sc. 11) has an element of choral narration (204, 208), the others are pure dialogue, but there is also a trace of mime in the embrace of Pilate and Herod (215/6 – cf. Luke 23, 12), and in the scourging and mocking of Christ (225/6) – though the wording of the rubric here may indicate that the scourging itself was not presented 'on-stage'.

More freely elaborated (from Matthew 27, 3–5) is the brief scene (Sc. 17) of Judas' despair and end. Judas is here given an impassioned lyrical strophe (241 ff.), the form of which has not been recognised by editors. Where the gospel text says that Judas 'hanged himself by a noose', here a devil leads him to a gibbet, and the passive construction, 'he is hanged' (*suspenditur*, 243/4), implies that it is this devil who performs the hanging. The language, that is, suggests that visually this scene was presented as a precise antitype of Christ's crucifixion (compare *suspendatur* at 244/5). The playwright, boldly changing the gospel order of events, lets the crucifixion (Sc. 18) follow straight upon Judas' hanging. From the many biblical verses he chooses only four (244–7), to evoke this scene in its essence.

The spare, hieratic quality with which the supreme moment of the Passion is presented contrasts markedly with the emotional fecundity of the long scene that follows (Sc. 19), of the lamentations of the Virgin. These, like the profane songs and the *peripeteia* in Mary Magdalen's life in the first half, are a vividly dramatic invention: the gospels do not so much as allude to a lament on the Virgin's part. The chief elements, both of the dialogue between Mary Magdalen and the Merchant and of the German and Latin *planctus* of Mary the mother, can be traced in a corpus of late-antique verse homilies that were attributed to the prodigiously creative Syrian poet St Ephraem († 373). Yet direct affiliations are hard to establish, particularly in the case of the Magdalen dialogue, where the Syriac original has survived and is much closer to our play than are the extant Greek adaptations.[2] In the case of the *Threni* of the Virgin Mary, by contrast, a late-antique Latin text in lyrical prose survives, but its presumed Ephraemic prototype has not been found, either in Syriac or Greek. (For documentation and discussion, cf. Dronke 1992, pp. 466–89). It would seem that we must reckon, both in the eastern and the western Church, with strong popular traditions for these themes, which in the earlier Middle Ages surface only sporadically in written texts.

The German *planctus* of Mary here may well be the learned dramatist's homage to such a popular tradition. At the same time, certain motifs – Mary dwelling on the beauty of her child (252), or begging to be killed in place of him (261–2) – have precise parallels in the late-antique Latin *Threni*. This is likewise true of the motif of the 'sword of sorrows' (cf. Luke 2, 35) that Mary recalls in her first Latin lament (273–7), and of the series of impassioned apostrophes – to her son, to the personified Death (Mors), to the Jewish race, and to the daughters of

---

[2] However, where the play features a devil as well as a lover, in the Syriac homily Satan disguises himself in the shape of Mary's lover (cf. Dronke 1992, p. 468).

Jerusalem who are Mary's fellow-mourners – which structure her resplendent final lament, *Planctus ante nescia* (286). These two Latin compositions, unlike the German one, were not the work of the dramatist himself: they are of French origin, and about a generation older than the play-text (cf. Dronke 1992, p. 458 n. 3). Yet their adaptation is felicitous. The first, *Flete, fideles anime* (265 ff.), is not used complete:[3] after the opening strophes (1a–2b), Mary turns to John, bidding him join her lament, and this half-strophe, which occurs later (5a) in the *planctus* text, is used as a refrain after Mary has sung *Planctus ante nescia*. For this piece only the cue of the opening verse is given, so it is not demonstrable that Mary sang the *planctus* entire. Yet there is an aspect of its content which speaks in favour of this. Mary, after her outcries upon the Jewish race, foretelling its bitter future (11b) and begging the Jews to change heart (12a–b), has a *peripeteia* in which, her sorrow and death-wish notwithstanding, she comprehends the joy of the redemption. Christ's arms are 'wide open', no longer because they are outstretched in pain, but in order to embrace all human beings who love him (13b). Mary's *peripeteia*, the new insight to which she here attains, is the counterpart of Mary Magdalen's in the first half, as she attained insight into her life; it is through the close of *Planctus ante nescia* that the two great freshly conceived scenes in the play, and the presentation of the two heroines, are endowed with a profound imaginative symmetry.

At the end of the scene (291–2) we return to biblical words: the new filial bond between John and Mary, already twice celebrated in the strophe from *Flete, fideles anime*, is here not instituted but rather solemnised by the dying Christ.

The final scene (Sc. 20) interweaves biblical words relating to Christ's last moments with other words and other material: the nameless centurion of the gospels who says 'Truly this was the Son of God' (Matthew 27, 54; Mark 15, 39) becomes the compassionate blind soldier Longinus of medieval legend, who regains sight through a drop of Christ's blood that falls upon his eyes. The rubrics are sparse: at 298/9, for instance, the copyist, and perhaps the dramatist before him, assumed that users of the scenario would know how Longinus was cured, that the actor would mime it appropriately, and that the reason for Longinus' triumphant exclamations (299–300) would be clear. Where in John (19, 34) a soldier pierces the dead Christ's side, Longinus does so in order to release the still living Christ from pain (296–7).

---

[3] It is theoretically possible that sts. 3a–4b were also sung, though there is no indication in favour of this; what is certain from the rubrics in the play is that 5a was the last half-strophe used (i.e. that sts. 5b–6b could not have been included).

Conversely, the mocking by the Jews here (303–5), as against the gospels, takes place when Christ has already died. The dramatic purpose of these changes is to heighten the confrontation between the believer and the unbelievers at the close (cf. Vollmann p. 1292).

It has often been debated whether this close is fragmentary. To me the stark juxtaposition of the joyously rewarded Roman soldier and the grim, uncomprehending Jews seems an arresting conclusion – to a play of the Passion. In a wider religious context, it might be argued, no Passion-play can be self-sufficient: it must reach out towards a play of the Resurrection, even as the Good Friday liturgy is completed by that of Easter Saturday and Easter Sunday. The Resurrection-play in the Codex Buranus (CB 15*) reveals a different poetic and dramatic sensibility, and cannot be regarded as a sequel in any stricter sense. Yet we should not go far wrong in saying that the play edited here, complete and (as I have indicated) meticulously crafted within its limits, will probably have been followed in the Easter days by a Resurrection-play of the *kind* exemplified by its neighbour in the codex.

The relation to the Vienna play

In Scene 5, forty-three Latin lines, sung by Mary Magdalen, the Angel, Simon and Jesus (in the present edition, 42–57, 76–82, 98–101, 104–7, 117–20, 135–42), also occur in a fourteenth-century German and Latin Passion-play from Vienna, a fragment that survives with music in the eight leaves of the Vienna MS 12887.[1] In this later play the Latin verses are at several points more abundant than in the *Carmina Burana* one, and there are further Latin 'goliardic' strophes for Judas, Simon and Christ where our play gives them biblical words (129–34, 143), and for Mary Magdalen where our play gives her a German plea to Christ (121–8) and a German lament (144–51).

The Vienna play, though rich in other German strophes, includes neither this plea and lament nor any of the German *CB* dialogue between Mary and the Merchant (58–75, 83–95). It does not have – even once – Mary's sleep or dream, her demon or her lover. The words the Angel addresses to her in our play (76–82) are sung by 'Simon's messenger'.[2]

---

[1] Text ed. R. Froning, *Das Drama des Mittelalters* (Stuttgart 1891/2, repr. Darmstadt 1964), pp. 302–24; music ed. A. Orel, in *Mitteilungen des Vereines für Geschichte der Stadt Wien* 6 (1926) 72–95.

[2] An angel does, however, address Mary slightly later, when she is awake and busy (*peragat officium suum*), in two Latin strophes, which are followed at once by her repentance (= 98 ff. in our play).

In the view of the distinguished editor Bernhard Bischoff, the *CB* version of what I have called Scene 5 reveals itself as 'only the ruins' of an original Mary Magdalen play that was entirely in Latin (*CB* I 3, p. 166), and that he tries to reconstruct with the help of the extra Latin verses and strophes in the Vienna play (*ibid*. pp. 172–5). In my view this is a mistaken enterprise: the reconstruction is imaginatively far more jejune than what is actually preserved in the Codex Buranus. I do not believe there ever existed a purely Latin original for this scene. On the contrary, it is among the Buranus dramatist's most brilliant achievements to have interwoven the two languages: to delete the German exchanges between Mary and the Merchant, and Mary's plea and lament in German, as Bischoff does in his reconstruction, is simply to impoverish the dramatist's design. Again, to exclude the repetitions – Mary's triple dream and waking – like Bischoff, following the Vienna version – is to deprive the scene of its insistent realism: Mary has been 'chosen' to act as she will do under the influence of her dreams. Finally, the extra Latin verses in the Vienna text, which Bischoff claimed to belong to the lost original, because 'there is no essential difference' between them and those in the *CB* (*ibid*. p. 166), seem to me to be inferior, with the conventional signs of *remaniement* and the wordiness that indicates lost direction on the part of the writer. To give just one example: the first Latin strophe, with which Mary enters and reveals herself (42–5 in the Buranus text), becomes two strophes in Vienna, with the addition of the four verses that are italicised below:

Mundi delectatio   dulcis est et grata,
eius conversatio   suavis et ornata.
In hac tota cupio   mente iocundari,
nil enim iocundius   possum amplexari.

Mundi sunt delicie   quibus estuare
volo, nec lasciviam   eius devitare.
Seculi blandiciis   placet adherere
et concupiscentiis   animum replere.

The world's delight is sweet and lovely,
its way of life is soft and full of grace.
With all my mind I long to take joy in it:
there's nothing more joyous that I can embrace.

For the world's allurements I burn willingly –
I'll not shun their voluptuousness.
I love to cling to the world's blandishments
and to fill my mind with longings.

I would find it hard indeed to believe that this, rather than the Buranus, was the original version; or else, if the Buranus dramatist came upon these eight verses and cut them to four, that itself would be a sign of his decisive poetic skill.

In short, the Magdalen scene in our play, like the later scene of the laments of the Virgin, is bilingual in its conception. In the diversity of language and techniques – in the transitions between biblical words and Latin 'goliardic' strophes and witty or impassioned vernacular ones – we can perceive the playwright's distinctive way of working.

Versification

The non-biblical, non-liturgical parts of the play, Latin and German, deploy a considerable range of rhythms. Occasionally there will be a group of rhyming lines of irregular length: e.g. 8–9, where 3 + 7p is followed by 8 + 7p (cf. also 38–41, 76–82, 162–72, 193–7, 241a–d). Most of Mary Magdalen's Latin strophes (Sc. 5) are in the 'goliardic stanza', 4 × 7pp + 6p, that enjoyed great vogue in Latin from the twelfth century onwards; this is likewise used in the Merchant's Latin strophe (54–7) and in the dialogue between Jesus and Simon (135–42, forming two strophes). The dramatist sometimes uses the monorhymed form of such quatrains, but more often rhymes the verses in pairs.

In her German verses, Mary begins (58–75) with three strophes in which the opening (7 + 6p) is close to a 'goliardic' Latin verse, but which continue with 7 + 10p (refrain 3 + 3 + 6p). In the second group (Mary 83–8, Merchant 90–5) this form, with slight irregularities, is completed by a couplet, 3 + 3 + 7/6p, akin to the previous refrain. Mary's German plea to Christ (121–8) and lament (144–51) are in quatrains in which the verses, carrying four principal stresses, vary from 7 to 10 syllables.

In these German quatrains the verses rhyme in pairs. The same form is used for the German lament of the Virgin (248–64), which comprises four such quatrains, except that the Virgin begins with an outcry of lament (248) which falls outside the strophic pattern. It is at least possible that this line, set at the head of the lament, served as a refrain after each quatrain.

The Virgin's Latin *planctus* (265–85) *Flete, fideles anime* is a classical sequence: each pair of half-strophes shares the same melody, and is identical in syllabic structure, and also (as is usual in classical sequences after 1100) in the structure of the rhythms and rhymes. The complete text (*CB* 4*) has six such pairs of half-strophes, each pair proceeding to a new melody. In the play only sts. 1a–2b and 5a are used.

In Mary's lament (286) *Planctus ante nescia*, though I have followed editors in numbering the pairs of half-strophes consecutively, the architectonics are different in that the forms and melodies of some of these pairs are repeated: thus the form and music of 2 recur in 4, 11 and 12; those of 3 in 5; those of 6 in 10. This variety of sequence form, allowing some irregular strophic and melodic repetition, is often known as a *lai lyrique*.

The manuscript[1]

The Codex Buranus is renowned chiefly for its uniquely large collection of profane Latin lyrics (nearly two hundred all told). At the same time this manuscript includes seven religious plays, and hence is also – with the sole exception of the 'Fleury play-book' (Orléans Bibl. municipale 201, s. XII 3/4), which contains ten – our richest source-book for medieval Latin drama.

The codex, named 'Buranus' because in the eighteenth century it was in the abbey Benediktbeuern (*Benedictobura*), is today preserved in the Bavarian State Library. While most older scholars imagined it was written in Bavaria, this view has been superseded. In 1967, introducing the superb facsimile of the Codex Buranus, Bernhard Bischoff thought Carinthia the likeliest place of origin. Three years later, however (*CB* I 3, xi–xii), he inclined to Styria, and in particular to the episcopal court at Seckau (some 60 km northwest of Graz). In 1983, on the other hand, Georg Steer brought strong arguments in favour of southern Tyrol, and suggested the Augustinian canons' foundation at Bressanone (100 km north of Trento): this is in the area indicated by certain spellings found in the German strophes, by the character of the neums, which is close to north Italian, and by some typically Italian spellings (such as *z* for *c*) in Latin texts. The most recent editor of the *CB*, B. K. Vollmann, has accepted Steer's conclusions, even if with some minor hesitations (p. 900).

The codex consists of 112 vellum leaves (Clm 4660), together with seven further leaves (I–VII, = Clm 4660a), the *Fragmenta Burana*, which had been separated from the main MS and were only rediscovered and edited by Wilhelm Meyer in 1901. The MS was written *c*. 1220–30 (the

---

[1] These notes briefly summarise my provisional conclusions after thirty years' study of the Codex Buranus. While I have nothing to add to my discussion of dating (1962), the other points owe much to the subsequent writing of Bischoff (1967, 1970), Vollmann (1987), and Steer (1983). These references are elucidated under *CB* in the list of abbreviations.

date suggested by Otto Pächt on the basis of the miniatures – see Dronke 1962): this applies to the whole of the principal contents (items 1–228 in the two critical editions); further items (1*–26*) were added from *c.* 1230 till the fourteenth century.

Though the MS was misbound at an early period, the original design of the collection is still for the most part clear. The beginning is lost, and leaves are missing in five other places. In the light of what we know about the composition of medieval Latin lyrical anthologies, it seems at least possible that the 'moral-satirical' section (1–55) was once preceded by a religious one, which is missing today. Next come the love-lyrics (56–186), the 'goliardic' pieces (187–226), in which drinking and gambling are frequent themes, and then the plays.

Within the larger divisions of lyrics, subdivisions by form or content are often apparent. There is, for instance, a group of elaborate art-songs in sequence and related forms (60–73), a group of poems on Trojan themes (98–102), another of songs accompanied by German strophes (135 ff.), which includes many dance-songs. Yet there are also exceptions to the overall design (e.g. 122–5, 127–34 are quite out of place among the love-songs, as is 12 among the moral satires): the classifications, while valid by and large, should not be pressed too hard.

The great majority of the lyrics in the codex were composed in the twelfth century, in France (especially Notre Dame in Paris) and Spain as well as in the German language-area. The latest datable strophe (168a) stems from 1217/19. It is also quite possible that some of the lyrics go back to the eleventh century, as we know to be the case, for instance, with the quantitative verses of 28. Such verses, proverbial or didactic, are frequently interspersed among the songs, and tend to be related to these in their themes (an unusual feature of this MS). Many of the lyrics have been furnished with undiastematic neums. There are also eight miniatures, of which Fortuna (fol. 1r) and Dido's death (fol. 77v) are perhaps the most famous.

Of the plays, the Christmas-play (227) and the play of the King of Egypt (228 – an apocryphal episode on the Holy Family's sojourn in Egypt) belong to the original collection. Three other plays – the Passion-play (16*), which is edited afresh below, the *Peregrinus* (26*), and the fragmentary Assumption-play (26a*) – will have been added not long after 1230,[2] since they have the same rubricator (Bischoff's 'hand 11') as the principal collection. The Easter-play (15*) and the second

---

[2] Bischoff's careful phrase ('may be of a slightly later date than the rest of the main codex', 1967, p. 20) does not warrant Steer's inference' '*c.* 1250' (p. 14): it could as easily be '*c.* 1231'.

Passion-play (13*) were added later, in the period 1250–1300. The plays were provided with undiastematic neums, with only minor omissions, except for 228, 13*, and most of the second half of 227.

Does the Codex Buranus reflect the tastes in profane song and biblical drama of a *weltoffen* group of Augustinian canons in southern Tyrol? Or was it commissioned (perhaps from those canons) by a wealthy patron-collector – a humanistic nobleman or bishop – in the region? How did so international and so varied a repertoire come to be available in that region in the 1220s? These are among the questions we cannot yet solve.

<Ludus de passione>*

I

107r *Primitus producatur Pilatus et uxor sua cum militibus in locum suum.*
Deinde Herodes cum militibus suis. Deinde Pontifices. Tunc Mercator et
uxor sua. Deinde Maria Magdalena.

II

<*Chorus:*>
Ingressus Pilatus <cum Iesu in pretorium, tunc ait illi:
Tu es rex Iudeorum? Respondit: Tu dicis quia rex sum.
Exivit ergo Iesus de pretorio, portans coronam et vestem purpuream.
Et cum indutus fuisset, exclamaverunt omnes:
5 Crucifigatur, quia filium dei se fecit!
(*Versus*) Tunc ait illis Pilatus: Regem vestrum crucifigam?
Responderunt pontifices: Regem non habemus nisi Cesarem.>

III

Postea vadat dominica persona sola ad litus maris, vocare Petrum et
Andream, et inveniat eos piscantes, et dominus dicit ad eos:
7 Venite post me: faciam vos piscatores hominum.

Illi dicunt:
    Domine,   quid vis, hec faciemus,
    et ad tuam voluntatem   protinus adimplemus.

Postea vadat dominica persona ad Zacheum, et obviet ei cecus:
10 Domine Iesu fili David, miserere mei!

---

* The line-numbering for this play has varied according to the editors: it depends on the number and size of the completions they wish to insert, and their choices of line-divisions. Y counts 305 lines (or 321, if like him one adds two German strophes for Joseph of Arimathia and Pilate, which more recently have – rightly – been printed separately, as *CB* 23*). Bi (who also gives Y's numbering) has 284 lines; V (who also gives Bi's) has 323. Rather than institute yet another numerical system, I have followed that of Y. This fits the present edition well enough, with only a few minor anomalies where I have divided lines differently. For *Planctus ante nescia* (286), which I believe should be included in full in the play-text, I have added, in italics, my own separate numbering (for *Flete, fideles anime* I add that of Bi and V). This is a compromise solution, but it means that cross-reference can be made very easily to the eds. of Y and Bi, and with fairly minor divergences to that of V.

The Passion Play

I

First let Pilate and his wife, together with soldiers, be brought forward to their playing-space; next, Herod with his soldiers; next, the Chief Priests; then the Merchant and his wife; after that, Mary Magdalen.

II

Choir:
Pilate, having entered the consistory with Jesus, then said to him:
You are the King of the Jews? He answered: It is you who say I am a king.
So Jesus went out of the consistory wearing a crown and a purple robe.
And when he had been robed thus, everyone shouted:
5 Let him be crucified, for he has made himself the Son of God!
(*Versicle*) Then Pilate said to them: Shall I crucify your king?
The chief priests answered: We have no king but Caesar.

III

After this, he who plays the Lord shall go alone to the seashore to call Peter and Andrew, and shall find them fishing; and the Lord says to them:
7 Come follow me – I shall make you fishers of men.

They say:
  Lord, what you wish, that we shall do –
  we shall at once fulfil your intent.

After this, he who plays the Lord shall go to Zacchaeus, and a blind man shall cross his path:
10 Lord Jesus, son of David, have mercy on me!

B: Munich, Bayerische Staatsbibliothek Clm 4660, fols. 107r–111r
Y: K. Young, *The Drama of the Medieval Church* (2 vols., Oxford 1933) I 518–33
Bi: *Carmina Burana* I 3 (Heidelberg 1970), ed. † O. Schumann, B. Bischoff, *CB* 16* (pp. 149–75)
V: *Carmina Burana*, ed. B. K. Vollmann (Frankfurt am Main 1987), *CB* 16* (pp. 816–59, with German translation; notes pp. 1280–2)

Iesus respondet:
Quid vis ut faciam tibi?

Cecus:
Domine, tantum ut videam!

Iesus dicit:
Respice, fides enim salvum te fecit.

Hiis factis, Iesus procedat ad Zacheum et vocet illum de arbore:
Zachee, festinans descende, quia hodie in domo tua oportet me manere.

Zacheus dicit:
15 Domine, si quid aliquem defraudavi, reddo quadruplum.

Iesus respondet:
Quia hodie huic domui salus facta est, eo quod et tu sis filius Abrahe.

IV

Iesus venit.

<Chorus:>
Cum appropinquaret dominus <Ierosolymam, misit duos ex discipulis suis, dicens:
Ite in castellum quod est contra vos, et invenietis pullum asine alligatum, super quem nullus hominum sedit: solvite, et adducite mihi.
Si quis vos interrogaverit, dicite: Opus domino est.
20 Solventes adduxerunt ad Iesum, et imposuerunt illi vestimenta, et sedit super eum.
Alii expandebant vestimenta sua in via, alii ramos de arboribus prosternebant,
et qui sequebantur clamabant: Osanna!
Benedictus qui venit in nomine domini, benedictum regnum patris nostri David!
Osanna in excelsis! Miserere nobis, fili David!>

Et:
25 Cum audisset <populus quia Iesus venit Ierosolymam, acceperunt ramos palmarum et exierunt ei obviam;
et clamabant pueri, dicentes: Hic est qui venturus est in salutem populi;

Jesus answers:
What do you want me to do for you?

The blind man:
Lord, only let me see!

Jesus says:
Look then, for your faith has healed you.

When these things have been done, Jesus shall go on to Zacchaeus, and call him down from the tree:
Zacchaeus, hurry down, for today I am to stay at your house.

Zacchaeus says:
15 Lord, if I have cheated anyone in any way, I'll pay him back fourfold.

Jesus answers:
For today salvation has come to this house, in that you too shall be a son of Abraham.

IV

Jesus draws near.

Choir:
When the Lord approached Jerusalem, he sent two of his disciples, saying:
Go into the town opposite, and you will find a tethered ass's colt, that no one has yet ridden: untie it and bring it to me.
If anyone questions you, say: The Lord has need of it.
20 Untying it they brought it to Jesus and covered it with their garments, and he rode it.
Some spread their garments on his path, some strewed branches from the trees,
and those that followed shouted: Hosannah!
Blessed is he who comes in the Lord's name, blessed the kingdom of our father David!
Hosannah in the highest! Have mercy on us, son of David!

And:
25 When the people heard, Jesus is coming to Jerusalem, they took palm-branches and went out to meet him;
and children shouted, saying: This is he who is destined to come for the people's salvation;

202 *Ludus de passione*

hec est salus nostra et redemptio Israel!
Quantus est iste, cui throni et dominationes occurrunt!
Noli timere, filia Sion: ecce rex tuus venit tibi, sedens super pullum
    asine, sicut scriptum est.
30 Salve, rex, fabricator mundi, qui venisti redimere nos!>

Et, pueri prosternentes frondes et vestes:
Pueri <Hebreorum, tollentes ramos olivarum, obviaverunt domino,
    clamantes et dicentes: Osanna in excelsis!>

Item:
Pueri <Hebreorum vestimenta prosternebant in via, et clamabant
    dicentes:
Osanna filio David – benedictus qui venit in nomine domini!>

Item:
35 Gloria, laus <et honor tibi sit, rex Christe, redemptor...>

V

Tunc veniat Phariseus et vocet Iesum ad cenam:
Rabi – quod interpretatur magister – peto ut mecum hodie velis
    manducare.

Iesus respondet:
Fiat ut petisti.

Phariseus dicat ad servum:
    Ite cicius:
    preparate sedilia
40   ad mense convivia,
    ut sint placencia.

Maria Magdalena cantet:
    Mundi delectatio   dulcis est et grata,
    eius conversatio,   suavis et ornata.
    Mundi sunt delicie   quibus estuare
45   volo, nec lasciviam   eius devitare.

    Pro mundano gaudio   vitam terminabo,
    bonis temporalibus   ego militabo;

[41/2] cantēt (*i.e.* cantent) B

he is our salvation and the redemption of Israel!
How great he is, he whom thrones and dominations welcome!
Do not be afraid, daughter Jerusalem: look, your King approaches
   you, sitting on an ass's colt, as it was written.
30 Hail, King, fashioner of the world, you who have come to redeem us!

And, as the children are strewing fronds and garments:
The Hebrew children, lifting olive-branches, crowded the Lord's path,
   shouting and saying: Hosannah in the highest!

Again:
The Hebrew children strewed garments on his path and shouted
   saying:
Hosannah to the son of David – blessed he who comes in the Lord's
   name!

Again:
35 Glory, praise and honour to you, Christ, King and redeemer...

V

Then the Pharisee shall come and invite Jesus to supper:
Rabbi – that is, master – I ask that today you consent to eat with me.

Jesus answers:
Let it be as you have asked.

The Pharisee shall say to a servant:
    Go quickly,
    prepare the seats
40   for the banquet,
    to make them pleasing to the eye.

Mary Magdalen shall sing:
    The world's delight is sweet and lovely,
    its way of life is soft and full of grace.
    For the world's allurements I burn willingly –
45   I'll not shun their voluptuousness.

    I'll pursue worldly joy to my life's end,
    I'll enlist to serve all the good things of this moment,

204 Ludus de passione

  nil curans de ceteris,   corpus procurabo –
  variis coloribus   illud perornabo.

Modo vadat Maria cum puellis ad mercatorem, cantando:
50   Michi confer, venditor,   species emendas,
  pro multa pecunia   tibi iam reddenda –
  si quid habes insuper   odoramentorum,
  nam volo perungere   corpus hoc decorum. /

107v *Mercator cantet:*
  Ecce merces optime –   prospice nitorem!
55   Hec tibi conveniunt   ad vultus decorem.
  Hee sunt odorifere –   quas si conprobaris,
  corporis fragrantiam   omne*m* superabis.

Maria Magdalena:
   Chramer, gip die varwe mier,
    div min wengel roete,
60   da mit ich di iungen man
  an ir danch der minnenliebe noete!

Item:
    Seht mich an,
    iungen man –
   lat mich ev gevallen!

Item:
65   Minnet, tugentliche man,
    minnekliche vrǎwen:
   minne tuǒt ev hoech gemǔt;
  vnde lat evch in hoehen eren schǎuven.

Refl.
    Seht mich an,
70   *iunge man*   *et cetera.*

Item:
   Wol dir, Werlt, daz du bist
    also vreudenreiche!
   Ich wil dir sin vndertan
  durch dein liebe immer sicherlichen.

---

[57] omnen B

I'll care for my body, caring naught for other things –
with varied colours I shall beautify it.

Now Mary, with some girls, shall go to the Merchant, singing:
50 Vendor, bring me cosmetics to buy:
a lot of money will now come your way,
especially if you have some perfumes too –
I want to use them on this shapely body.

The Merchant shall sing:
Look, here are my finest wares – see how they glow!
55 This is what is right for you, for your lovely face.
They are laden with scent – if you've tried them once,
you'll surpass all women in your body's fragrance.

Mary Magdalen:
    Merchant, give me the rouge
    to colour my cheeks,
60   so that I may compel young men,
    even against their will, to love!

Again:
    Look at me,
    young men –
    let me captivate you!

Again:
65   Men of excellence, love
    women apt for loving:
    love exalts your inner joy
    and lets others see you in high honour.

Refrain:
    Look at me,
70   *young men*   *etc. (62–4)*

Again:
    Bless you, World, because you are
    so rich in joys!
    I want to be your subject,
    for your love's sake, assuredly forever.

<Refl.>
75   Seht mich an   et cetera.

Postea vadat dormitum, et angelus cantet:
    O Maria Magdalena,
     nova tibi nuntio:
      Symonis hospicio
       hic sedens convivatur
    Iesus ille Nazarenus,
     gratia, virtute plenus,
80   qui relaxat peccata populi;
      hunc turbe confitentur
    salvatorem seculi.

Recedat angelus et surgat Maria cantando:
  Mundi delectatio <...>

Tunc accedat amator, quem Maria salutet, et cum parum locuntur, cantet Maria ad puellas:
    Wol dan, minneklichev chint,
     schăwe wier chrame –
85   chauf wier di varwe da,
    di vns machen schoene vnde wolgetane!
    Er muez sein sorgen vȓi,
    der da minnet mier den leip.

Iterum cantet:
    Chramer, gip di varwe mier <...>

Mercator respondet:
90   Ich gib ev varwe, deu ist guŏt,
     dar zuoe lobelich,
    dev eu machet reht schoene
    vnt dar zuoe uil reht vvunnecliche.
    Nempt si hin, hab ir si:
95   ir ist niht geleiche!

Accepto ungento vadat dormitum. <Angelus cantet:>
    O Maria Magdalena <...>

Et iterum evanescat. Tunc surgat Maria et cantet:
  Mundi delectatio <...>

Et iterum postea obdormiat, et Angelus veniat cantando ut supra, et iterum evanescat. <Maria Magdalena cantet:>

Refrain:
75   *Look at me*   etc. (62–4)

After this, let her go and sleep, and an Angel shall sing:
        Oh Mary Magdalen,
        I have news for you:
        in Simon's lodging
        he sits banqueting,
        the renowned Jesus of Nazareth,
        full of grace, of power,
80   he who frees the people from their sins.
        The crowds proclaim him
        saviour of the world.

The Angel shall withdraw, and Mary shall arise singing:
        The world's delight ...   (42–9)

Then a lover shall approach, and Mary shall greet him; when they have conversed a little, Mary shall sing to the girls:
        Come then, you girls intent on love,
        let us see his wares –
85   let us buy those colours
        that lend us beauty and grace.
        He who loves me for myself
        must be free of cares.

And again let her sing:
        Merchant, give me the rouge ...   (58–61)

The Merchant answers:
90   I'll give you a rouge that's fine
        and deserves every praise:
        it will make you beautiful,
        and what's more, all full of joy.
        Take it, have this one –
95   there's none that can compare!

Having taken the preparation, Mary shall go and sleep. The Angel shall sing:
        Oh Mary Magdalen ...   (76–82)

And again he shall vanish. Then Mary shall arise and sing:
        The world's delight ...   (42–9)

And after that let her again fall asleep, and let the Angel come singing as above, and again vanish. Mary Magdalen shall sing:

208 Ludus de passione

   Heu, vita preterita, vita plena malis,
   fluxus turpitudinis, fons exsicialis!
100 Heu, quid agam misera, plena peccatorum,
   que polluta polleo sorde viciorum?

Angelus dicat sibi:
Dico tibi, gaudium est angelis dei super una pecatrice penitentiam agente.

Maria:
108r Hinc, ornatus / seculi, vestium candores!
105 Protinus a me fugite, turpes amatores!
   Ut quid nasci volui, que sum defedanda
   et ex omni genere criminum notanda?

Tunc deponat vestimenta secularia et induat nigrum pallium. Et amator recedat, et diabolus. Veniat ad mercatorem:
   Dic tu nobis, mercator iuvenis,
   hoc ungentum si tu vendideris:
110 dic precium pro quanto dederis.
   Heu quantus est noster dolor!

Mercator respondet:
   Hoc ungentum si multum cupitis,
   unum auri talentum dabitis,
   <non> aliter u*n*quam portabitis –
115 obtimum est!

Et chorus cantet:
Accessit ad pedes <Iesu peccatrix mulier Maria>.

Accepto ungento, vadat ad dominicam personam, cantando flendo:
   Ibo nunc ad medicum turpiter egrota,
   medicinam postulans: lacrimarum vota
   huic restat ut offeram, et cordis plangores,
120 qui cunctos, ut audio, sanat peccatores.

Item:
   Iesus, troest der sele min,
   la mich dir enpholhen sin,
   vnde loese mich uon der missetat
   da mich deu werlt zuoe hat braht.

---

[114] aliter nusquam B (*for the correction, see above p. 94*)

Alas for my past life, life full of wickedness,
that flood of turpitude, that fount of death!
Alas what shall I do, unhappy, full of sins,
I who abound, polluted, in the filth of vice?

The Angel shall say to her:
I tell you, there is joy among God's angels over one sinful woman
    doing penance.

Mary:
Away with you, worldly glamour, shining robes!
Flee from me instantly, you ignoble lovers!
Why was I ever born, I who had to be disgraced
and marked by every kind of guilty act?

Then let her cast off her society clothes and put on a black cloak, and let her lover and the demon retreat. Let her come to the Merchant:
    Tell us, young merchant,
    if you'll sell us this ointment:
        tell us the price, for how much you will give it.
    Alas, how great is our grief!

The Merchant answers:
    If you want this ointment very much,
    you must pay one talent of gold,
    otherwise you'll never take it with you –
        it is the best!

And the choir shall sing:
She came to Jesus' feet, the sinful woman, Mary.

Having taken the ointment, Mary shall go to him who plays the Lord, singing weeping:
I'll now go to the doctor, I who am vilely sick,
demanding medicine – it's for me to offer
the longings of my tears, my heart's laments
to him who, as I hear, makes all sinners well.

Again:
    Jesus, solace of my soul,
    let me be commended to you,
    and free me from the misdeed
    to which the world has brought me.

Item:
125   Ich chume niht uon den fůezzen dein,
      du erloesest mich von den sunden mein,
      vnde uon der grŏzzen missetat
      da mich deu werlt zuŏ hat braht.

Loquatur Phariseus intra se:
Si hic esset propheta, sciret utique que et qualis illa esset que tangit eum,
130   quia peccatrix est!

Et dicat Iudas:
Ut quid perditio hec? Potuit enim hoc venundari multo et dari
   pauperibus.

Iesus cantet:
Quid molesti estis huic mulieri? Opus bonum operata est in me.

Item statim:
Symon, habeo tibi aliquid dicere.

Symon Phariseus:
Magister, dic.

Dicit Iesus:
135   Debitores habuit   quidam creditorum
      duos, quibus credidit   spe denariorum;
      hic quingentos debuit,   alter quinquagenos,
      set eos pen*uria*   fecerat egenos.

      Cum nequirent reddere,   totum relaxavit.
140   Quis eorum igitur   ipsum plus amavit?

Symon respondet:
   Estimo quod ille plus,   cui plus donavit.

Iesus dicat:
   Tua sic sententia   recte iudicavit.

Item Iesus cantet ad Mariam:
Mulier, remittuntur tibi peccata. Fides tua salvum te fecit. Vade in pace.

108v *Tunc Maria surgat / et vadat lacrimando cantans:*
            Aẃe, aŭve daz ich ie wart geborn:

---

¹³³/⁴ Symon petrus B
¹³⁸ eosdem penitus B (*em. Bi*)

Again:
    I shall not leave your feet
    unless you save me from my sins
    and from the great misdeed
    to which the world has brought me.

The Pharisee shall say to himself:
If this man were a prophet, he would surely know who that woman is, and what kind of woman is touching him – for she is a sinner!

And Judas shall say:
Why this waste? For the ointment could have been sold dear and given to the poor.

Jesus shall sing:
Why are you hostile to this woman? She has done a good deed for me.

And again, at once:
Simon, I have something to say to you.

Simon the Pharisee:
Tell me, Master.

Jesus says:
  A certain creditor had two men in his debt,
  to whom he'd given credit, expecting the money back.
  One owed five hundred denarii, the other fifty,
  but poverty had made both indigent.

  Since they could not repay, he wiped the whole debt out.
  Which of them, then, loved him the more?

Simon answers:
I suppose the one to whom he gave more loved more.

Jesus shall say:
Your answer shows that you have judged aright.

Again let Jesus sing to Mary:
Woman, your sins are forgiven. Your faith has healed you. Go in peace.

Then Mary shall rise and walk lamenting, singing:
    Alas, alas that ever I was born:

212 Ludus de passione

145
        han ich uerdient gotes zorn,
        der mier hat geben sele vnde liep –
        aẘe, ich uil vnselaeich wip!

        Oẘe, aẘe daz ich ie wart geborn,
        suvenne mich erwechet gotes zorn!
150   Wol uf, ir gůte*n* man vnde wip:
        got wil rihten sele vnde leip.

Interea cantent discipuli:
Phariseus iste fontem misericordie conabatur obstruere.

VI

Tunc vadat Iesus ad resuscitandum Lazarum. Et ibi occurrant Maria Magdalena et Martha, plorantes pro Lazaro, et Iesus cantet:
Lazarus, amicus noster, dormit: eamus et a sompno resuscitemus eum!

Tunc Maria Magdalena et Martha flendo cantent:
Domine, si fuisses hic, frater noster non fuisset mortuus.

Et sic tacendo, clerus cantet:
155 Videns dominus flentes sorores Lazari, ad monumentum lacrimatus est coram Iudeis, et clamabat:

Et Iesus cantet:
Lazare, veni foras!

Et clerus cantet:
Et prodiit ligatis m<anibus> et p<edibus>, qui f<uerat> q<uadriduanus> m<ortuus>.

VII

Interim Iudas veniat festinando et querat oportunitatem tradendi, dicens:
        O pontifices,
160   o viri magni consilii,
        Iesum volo vobis tradere.

---

[150] gůetem B (em. Y)
[158] q<uasi> Y q<uadriduum> Bi q<uadriduanus> V (*rightly: cf. John* 11, 39)

145   I have deserved the anger of God
          who gave me soul and body –
          alas, most wretched woman that I am!

          Alas, alas that ever I was born,
          now that God's anger awakens me!
150   Courage, good men and women all:
          God wants to guide body and soul.

Meanwhile the disciples shall sing:
This Pharisee tried to dam up the fount of mercy.

VI

*Then Jesus shall go to raise Lazarus. There Mary Magdalen and Martha
   shall run to meet him, mourning for Lazarus, and Jesus shall sing:*
Lazarus, our friend, is sleeping: let us go and wake him from his sleep!

Then Mary Magdalen and Martha shall sing weeping:
Lord, if you had been here, our brother would not have died.

And so, when they are silent, the clergy shall sing:
155 The Lord, seeing Lazarus' sisters weeping, shed tears at the monument
   in the presence of the Jews, and shouted –

And Jesus shall sing:
Lazarus, come out!

And the clergy shall sing:
And he came out, his hands and feet bound, he who had been four
   days dead.

VII

*Meanwhile let Judas approach in haste and seek an opportunity for
   betraying, saying:*
          You Chief Priests,
160   you men prominent in counsel,
          I want to deliver Jesus to you.

Cui pontifices respondeant:
> O Iuda, si Iesum nobis iam tradideris,
> triginta argenteis remuneraberis.

Iudas respondeat:
> Iesum tradam, credite –
> rem promissam michi solvite!
> Turbam mecum dirigite,
> Iesum caute deducite.

Pontifices cantent:
> Iesum tradas propere:
> hanc turbam tecum accipe
> et procede viriliter –
> Iesum trade velociter!

Iudas tunc det Iudeis signum, cantans:
Quemcumque osculatus fuero, ipse est: tenete eum!

Tunc turba Iudeorum sequatur Iudam cum gladiis et fustibus et lucernis, donec ad Iesum.

VIII

Interea Iesus faciat ut mos est in cena.

IX

Postea assumat quatuor discipulos, et ceteris dicat, quos relinquit:
Dormite iam et requiescite.

Deinde vadat orare, et dicat quatuor discipulis:
Tristis est anima mea usque ad mortem. Sustinete hic et orate, ne intretis in temptationem.

Tunc ascendat in montem Oliveti, et flexis genibus, respiciens celum, petat dicendo:
Pater, si fieri potest transeat a me / calix iste: spiritus quidem promptus est, caro autem infirma. Fiat voluntas tua.

[163/4] Iesum B (*em. Y*)
[174] Sustine B (*em. Y*)

The Chief Priests shall answer him:
> Judas, if you now deliver us Jesus,
> you'll be paid with thirty silver pieces.

Judas shall answer:
> I'll deliver Jesus, believe me –
> pay me what you have promised!
> Send a crowd along with me –
> be on your guard as you take Jesus away.

The Chief Priests shall sing:
> Deliver Jesus without delay:
> take this crowd along with you
> and go forward manfully –
> deliver Jesus speedily!

Then Judas shall give the Jews a signal, singing:
The one that I kiss, he is the man: arrest him!

Then let the crowd of Jews follow Judas with swords and clubs and lanterns, till they reach Jesus.

VIII

Meanwhile, let Jesus act as is customary in the Supper scene.

IX

After that, let him take four disciples, and say to the rest, leaving them:
Sleep now and take some rest.

Then let him go to pray, and say to the four disciples:
My soul is sorrowful to the point of death. Stay here and pray not to be put to the test.

Then he shall climb Mount Olivet, and kneeling, looking up at heaven, he shall beseech:
Father, if it can be done, let this cup go from me. The spirit is indeed willing, but the body weak. Let your will be done.

Hoc facto redeat ad quatuor discipulos et inveniat eos dormientes, et dicat Petro:
Symon, dormis? Non potuisti una hora vigilare mecum? Manete hic donec vadam et orem.

Postea vadat iterum orare ut antea. Tunc iterato veniat ad discipulos et inveniat eos dormientes, et dicat ad eos:
180 Manete hic.

Et iterum dicit:
Pater, si non potest hic calix transire nisi bibam illum, fiat voluntas tua.

Tunc redeat ad discipulos et cantet:
Una hora non potuistis vigilare mecum, qui exhortabamini mori pro me?
Vel Iudam non videtis, quomodo non dormit set festinat tradere me Iudeis?
Surgite, eamus! Ecce appropinquat qui me traditurus est!

X

Veniat Iudas ad Iesum cum turba Iudeorum, quibus Iesus dicat:
185 Quem queritis?

Qui respondent:
Iesum Nazarenum.

Iesus dicit:
Ego sum.

Et turba retrocedat. Item Iesus dicit:
Quem queritis?

Iudei:
Iesum Nazarenum.

Iesus respondet:
190 Dixi vobis quia ego sum.

Item:
Si ergo me queritis, sinite hos abire.

Tunc apostoli dent fugam, excepto Petro, et Iudas dicat:
Ave, Rabbi!

When he has completed this, let him return to the four disciples and find them asleep, and let him say to Peter:
Simon, are you sleeping? Could you not keep watch with me a single hour? Stay here while I go and pray.

Then let him go to pray again as before. Then once more let him come to the disciples and find them asleep, and say to them:
180 Stay here.

And again he says:
Father, if this cup cannot go from me without my drinking it, let your will be done.

Then let him return to the disciples and sing:
Could you not keep watch one hour with me, you who were eager to die for me?
Or do you not see Judas – how he does not sleep but hastens to betray me to the Jews?
Rise, let us go! Look, he who is about to betray me is coming close!

X

Judas shall come to Jesus with the crowd of Jews, to whom Jesus shall say:
185 Whom are you looking for?

They answer:
Jesus of Nazareth.

Jesus says:
I am he.

And the crowd shall edge away. Again Jesus says:
Whom are you looking for?

The Jews:
Jesus of Nazareth.

Jesus answers:
190 I told you that I am he.

Again:
Then if it's me you are looking for, let these men go.

Then the apostles shall flee, except for Peter, and Judas shall say:
Hail, Rabbi!

Iesus illi respondet:
> O Iuda, ad quid venisti?
> Peccatum magnum tu fecisti:
>   me Iudeis traditum
>   ducis ad patibulum
>   cruciandum.

Et Petro sequente Iesum, una ancilla dicit:
Vere tu ex illis es?

Ipse dicit:
Non sum.

Item ancilla:
Vere tu ex illis es, nam et Galileus es. Nam unus ex eis es.

Petrus:
Non novi hominem!

<Servus pontificis:>
Nonne vidi te cum illo in horto?

<Petrus:>
Nescio quid dicis!

Et Iesus dicat:
Tanquam ad latronem existis cum gladiis et fustibus comprehendere me; <quotidie apud vos sedebam docens in templo, et non me tenuistis>.

XI

Et ducatur Iesus ad pontifices. Et Chorus cantet:
Collegerunt pontifices <et Pharisei concilium, et dicebant> –

Et pontifices cantent et cogitent quid faciant:
Quid facimus, quia hic homo multa signa facit? Si dimittimus eum sic, omnes credent in eum.

Et Cayphas cantet:
Expedit vobis ut unus moriatur homo pro populo, et non tota gens pereat.

Jesus answers him:
>Oh Judas, for what purpose have you come?
>You have committed a great sin:
>you are leading me – delivered
>to the Jews – to the gallows
>to be crucified.

And, as Peter follows Jesus, a servant-girl says:
You're really one of them, aren't you?

He says:
I am not.

The servant-girl, again:
You really are one of them, for you're a Galilaean too. For you are one of them.

Peter:
I don't know the man!

The High Priest's servant:
Surely I saw you in the garden with that fellow?

Peter:
I don't know what you're talking about!

And Jesus shall say:
You have come to capture me as if I were a bandit, with swords and clubs; each day I sat among you teaching in the Temple, and you did not lay hands on me.

XI

And Jesus shall be led to the Chief Priests. And the Choir shall sing:
The Chief Priests and Pharisees assembled a council, and said –

And the Chief Priests shall sing and deliberate what to do:
What shall we do, since this man works many wonders? If we let him go free like this, everyone will believe in him.

And Caiaphas shall sing:
It is expedient that one man should die for the people, rather than that the whole nation should perish.

Clerus cantet:
Ab ipso ergo die cogitaverunt <interficere eum, dicentes: Ne forte veniant Romani et tollant nostrum locum et gentem>.

XII

Postea ducitur ad Pilatum Iesus, et dicunt Iudei:
Hic dixit: Solvite templum hoc, et post triduum reedificabo illud!

Pilatus respondet:
210 Quam accusa- / cionem affertis adversus hominem istum?

Iudei respondent:
109v Si non fuisset hic malefactor, non tibi tradidissemus eum.

Pilatus:
Accipite eum vos, et secundum legem vestram iudicate eum.

Iudei:
Nobis non licet interficere quemquam.

XIII

Postea ducitur Iesus ad Herodem, qui dicat ei:
Homo Galileus es?

Iesus vero tacebat. Et Herodes iterum dicit:
215 Quem te ipsum facis?

Iesus non respondet ei ad unum verbum.

XIV

Tunc Iesus induitur veste alba. Et reducunt Iesum ad Pilatum. Tunc conveniunt Pilatus et Herodes et osculantur invicem. Et Iesus veniat ad Pilatum, et ipse dicit:
Nullam causam mortis invenio in homine isto.

215/6 inducitur B (*em.* Y)

The clergy shall sing:
So from that day onwards they plotted to kill him, saying: Lest perhaps the Romans come and take away our holy place and crush our people.

XII

After this Jesus is led to Pilate, and the Jews say:
This man said: Destroy this Temple, and within three days I shall rebuild it!

Pilate answers:
What charge do you bring against this man?

The Jews answer:
If he were not a malefactor, we should not have handed him over to you.

Pilate:
Take him yourselves, and try him by your own law.

The Jews:
We are not allowed to put anyone to death.

XIII

After this Jesus is led to Herod, who shall say to him:
Are you a Galilaean?

But Jesus was silent. And Herod says, again:
Who do you claim to be?

Jesus does not answer him with a single word.

XIV

Then Jesus is dressed in a white robe, and they bring him back to Pilate. Then Pilate and Herod meet and embrace. And Jesus shall come to Pilate, who says:
I can find no case against this man that deserves death.

Iudei dicunt:
Reus est mortis!

Tunc Pilatus dicat ad Iesum:
Tu es rex Iudeorum?

Iesus respondit:
Tu dicis quia rex sum.

Pilatus dicit:
220   Gens tua et pontifices tui tradiderunt te michi.

Iesus paulatim dicat:
Regnum meum non est de hoc mundo.

Pilatus item dicit:
Ergo quem te ipsum facis?

Iesus vero taceat. Et Pilatus dicit ad pontifices:
Quid faciam de Iesu Nazareno?

Iudei:
Crucifigatur!

Pilatus:
225   Corripiam ergo illum et dimittam.

XV

Tunc ducitur Iesus ad flagellandum. Postea Iesus induatur veste purpurea et spinea corona. Tunc dicant Iudei, plasphemando, ad Iesum:
Ave, rex Iudeorum!

Et dent ei alapas:
Prophetiza, quis est qui te percussit?

XVI

Et ducant eum ad Pilatum. Quibus Pilatus dicit:
Ecce homo.

Iudei:
Crucifige, crucifige eum!

[227/8] cui B (*but cf. John 19, 5*)

The Jews say:
He is guilty of death!

Then Pilate shall say to Jesus:
You are the King of the Jews?

Jesus answered:
It is you who say I am a king.

Pilate says:
220 Your people and your Chief Priests have delivered you to me.

Jesus shall say, slowly and deliberately:
My kingdom is not of this world.

Pilate rejoins:
Who then do you claim to be?

But Jesus shall be silent. And Pilate says to the Chief Priests:
What shall I do about Jesus of Nazareth?

The Jews:
Let him be crucified!

Pilate:
225 I shall chastise him, then, and let him go.

XV

Then Jesus is led away to be scourged. After that, he shall be dressed in a purple robe and a crown of thorns. Then the Jews, blaspheming, shall say to Jesus:
Hail, King of the Jews!

And they shall slap him, saying:
Prophesy, who is it who struck you?

XVI

And they shall bring him to Pilate. Pilate says to them:
Here is the man.

The Jews:
Crucify him! Crucify him!

Pilatus:
230 Accipite eum vos et crucifigite! Nullam causam invenio in eo.

Iudei:
Si hunc dimittis, non es amicus Cesaris.

Item:
Omnis qui se facit regem contradicit Cesari.

Pilatus:
Unde es tu?

Iesus tacet. Pilatus:
Michi non loqueris?

Item:
235 Nescis quia potestatem habeo crucifigere te et potestatem dimittere te?

Iesus respondet:
Non haberes in me potestatem nisi desuper tibi datum fuisset.

Pilatus ad Iudeos:
Regem vestrum crucifigam?

Iudei respondent:
Crucifigatur, quia filium dei se fecit!

Pilatus, lavans manus suas cum aqua, et dicat ad Iudeos:
Innocens ego sum a sanguine huius – vos videritis. /

110r *Tunc Iesus ducatur ad crucifigendum.*

XVII

Tunc Iudas ad pontifices vadat cantando, et, reiectis denariis, dicit flendo:
240 Penitet me graviter quod istis argenteis Christum vendiderim.

Item:
    Resumite vestra, resumite!
    Mori volo et non vivere.
    Suspendii supplicio
     me volo perdere!
Peccavi, tradens san<guinem> iustum!

[241c–d] suspendi supplicio volo B (*em.* Bi, *but printing as prose*)

Pilate:
Take him yourselves and crucify him! I find no case against him.

The Jews:
If you release him, you are no friend of Caesar's.

Again:
Anyone who makes himself king defies Caesar.

Pilate:
Where are you from?

Jesus is silent. Pilate:
You are not speaking to me?

Again:
Do you not know that I have power to crucify you and power to release you?

Jesus replies:
You would have no power over me if it had not been given you from above.

Pilate to the Jews:
Shall I crucify your king?

The Jews answer:
Let him be crucified, for he has claimed to be the Son of God!

Pilate, washing his hands in water, shall at the same time say to the Jews:
I am innocent of this man's blood – this is your affair.

Then Jesus shall be led away to be crucified.

XVII

Then Judas shall go to the Chief Priests singing, and, throwing the denarii back, he says, weeping:
I grievously repent that I sold Christ for this silver.

Again:
>Take it back, it's yours, take it back!
>I want to die and not to live.
>In the torment of hanging
>I want to lose myself!

I have sinned, betraying innocent blood!

Pontifices:
243 Quid ad nos, Iudas Scariotys? Tu videris.

Statim veniat diabolus et ducat Iudam ad suspendium, et suspenditur.

XVIII

Tunc veniant mulieres a longe, plorantes, flere Iesum; quibus Iesus dicat:
Filie Ierusalem, nolite flere super me, set super vos ipsas!

Tunc Iesus suspendatur in cruce, et titulus fiat. <Chorus:>
245 Iesus Nazarenus rex Iudeorum.

Tunc respondent Iudei Pilato, cant<antes>:
Regem non habemus nisi Cesarem.

Pilatus:
Quod scripsi, scripsi.

XIX

Tunc veniat mater domini lamentando, cum Iohanne ewangelista, et ipsa accedens crucem respicit crucifixum:

   Awe, awe, mich hiût vnde immer we!
   Awe, wie sihe ich nv an
250   daz liebiste chint daz ie gewan
   ze dirre werlde ie dehain wip.
   Awe, mines shoene chindes lip!

Item:
   Den sihe ich iemerlichen an:
   lat iuch erbarmen, wip vnde man –
255   lat iwer ovgen sehen dar
   vnde nemt der marter rehte war!

Item:
   Wart marter ie so iemerlich
   vnde also rehte angestlich?
   Nv merchet marter, not vnde tot,
260   vnde al den lip von blûte rot.

The Chief Priests:
243 What is that to us, Judas Iscariot? That is your affair.

At once a demon shall come and lead Judas to a gibbet, and Judas is hanged.

XVIII

Then women shall come from afar, mourning, to weep for Jesus. Jesus shall say to them:
Daughters of Jerusalem, do not weep for me, but for yourselves!

Then let Jesus be hung on the cross, and the inscription made. Choir:
245 Jesus of Nazareth, King of the Jews.

Then the Jews answer Pilate, singing:
We have no king but Caesar.

Pilate:
What I have written, I have written.

XIX

Then the mother of the Lord shall come on, lamenting, together with John the evangelist, and, approaching the cross, she gazes on the crucified one:
    Alas, alas for me, today and always!
    Alas, in what state do I now see
250   the dearest child that ever any woman
    in this world bore?
    Alas for the body of my beautiful child!

Again:
    I gaze at him in wretchedness:
    be moved to pity, women and men –
255   let your eyes look there
    and note the torments truthfully!

Again:
    Was ever torment so pitiful
    and so truly full of anguish?
    Now mark the torments, sorrow and death,
260   and all the body red with blood.

228 *Ludus de passione*

Item:
>   Lat leben mir daz chindel min
>   vnde toetet mich, die muter sin,
>   Mariam, mich uil armez wip!
> 264   Zwiv sol mir leben vnde lip?

Item mater domini, omni ploratu exhibens multos planctus, et clamat ad mulieres flentes et conquerendo valde:

1a Flete, fideles anime,	1b Fleant materna viscera
flete, sorores optime,	Marie matris vulnera.
ut sint multiplices	Materne doleo,
doloris indices	que dici soleo
270 5 planctus et lacrime!	5 felix puerpera.
2a Triste spectaculum	2b Dum caput cernu-<um,
crucis et lancee	dum spinas capitis,
clausum signaculum	dum plagas manuum
mentis virginee	cruentis digitis
5 graviter vulnerat:	5 supplex suspicio,
hoc est quod dixerat,	sub hoc supplicio
quod prophetaverat	tota deficio,
275 felix prenuntius –	dum vulnus lateris,
hic ille gladius	dum locus vulneris
10 qui me transverberat!	10 est in profluvio.>

111r *Tunc Maria amplexetur Iohannem et cantet, eum habens inter brachia:*

>   5a Mi Iohannes, planctum move:
>   plange mecum, fili nove,
> 280   fili novo federe
>   matris et matertere;
>   5   tempus est lamenti:
>   immolemus intimas
>   lacrimarum victimas
> 285   Christo morienti.

---

[265] (1a 4) dolores B (em. Y)
[275] (2a 8) felix prenuntius] Simeon was happy that his life was fulfilled 'in peace' (Luke 2,29); the reading felix here need not be rejected in favour of senex (sic Bi, V), the lectio facilior of other MSS of the planctus.
[277] (2b 1) Fol. 110r ends with Dum caput cernu, 110v contains an unrelated German text. (CB 17*), the play resumes on 111r (Tunc Maria).

Again:

> For my sake let my little child live
> and kill me, his mother,
> me, Mary, most wretched woman!
> To what end should I have life and being?

Again the mother of the Lord, bringing forth many laments amid all her tears, also cries out to the women weeping in deep mourning:

1a Weep, loyal souls,
    weep, peerless sisters,
    so that the plaints and tears
    may be the manifold
 5 tokens of grief!

1b May wombs of mothers weep
    the wounds of the mother Mary.
    As mother I sorrow,
    I who am wont to be called
 5 happy childbearer.

2a The dismal spectacle
    of cross and lance
    deeply wound
    the sealed enclosure
 5 of the maiden mind:
    this is what he had said,
    what he had prophesied,
    the happy harbinger –
    this is the long-known sword
10 that now transpierces me!

2b The head bowed,
    thorns on the head,
    wounds in the hands,
    fingers bleeding –
 5 when, imploring, I see them,
    in this torment
    I grow all faint,
    as the wound in the side
    and the place of the wound
10 become a torrent.

Then Mary shall embrace John and sing, holding him in her arms:

5a My John, release your plaint:
    lament with me, my new son,
    son through a new alliance
    of the rôles of mother and of aunt.
 5 It is the time for threnody:
    let us offer sacrifices,
    inner ones, of tears,
    for the dying Christ.

Et per horam quiescat sedendo. Et iterum surgat et cantet:

1a Planctus ante nescia
    <planctu lassor anxia,
      crucior dolore:

1b orbat orbem radio,
    me Iudea filio,
      gaudio, dulcore.

2a Fili, dulcor unice,
    singulare gaudium,
    matrem flentem respice,
    conferens solatium!

2b Pectus, mentem, lumina
    tua torquent vulnera:
    que mater, que femina
    tam felix, tam misera?

3a Flos florum,   dux morum,
    venie vena,
    quam gravis   in clavis
    est tibi pena!

3b Proh dolor,   hinc color
    effugit oris,
    hinc ruit,   hinc fluit
    unda cruoris.

4a O quam sero deditus,
    quam cito me deseris!
    O quam digne genitus,
    quam abiecte moreris!

4b O quis amor corporis
    tibi fecit spolia –
    o quam dulcis pignoris
    quam amara premia!

5a O pia   gratia
    sic morientis,
    o zelus,   o scelus
    invide gentis!

5b o fera   dextera
    crucifigentis,
    o lenis   in penis
    mens patientis!

6a O verum eloquium
    iusti Simeonis:
    quem promisit gladium
    sentio doloris.

6b Gemitus, suspiria
    lacrimeque foris
    vulneris indicia
    sunt interioris.

7a Parcito proli,
    Mors, michi noli –
    tunc michi soli
    sola mederis.

7b Morte, beate,
    separer a te,
    dummodo, nate,
    non crucieris.

8a Quod crimen, que scelera
    gens commisit effera:
    vincla, virgas, vulnera,
    sputa, spinas, cetera
5   sine culpa patitur.

8b Nato, queso, parcite –
    matrem crucifigite
    aut in crucis stipite
    nos simul affigite!
5   Male solus moritur.

---

286 Planctus ante nescia] *Completed from* CB 14* (Bi), *with some changes of line-arrangement and punctuation.*

And for a time let her rest, seated. And then let her rise again and sing:

286 1a I who knew no lament before,
anguished, am worn with lament,
agonised by pain:

1b Judaea robs the world
of its light, me of my son,
my joy, my sweetness.

2a Son, my one-and-only sweetness,
my unique joy,
look upon your weeping mother –
bring her solace!

2b Your wounds torment my heart,
my mind, my eyes:
what mother, what woman
so blissful, so wretched?

3a Flower of flowers, prince of courtesy,
stream of forgiveness,
how grievous on those nails
is your suffering!

3b The grief of it – from your face
the colour drains,
from it streams, from it flows
a wave of blood.

4a Oh how lately given to me,
how quickly you desert me!
Oh how nobly begotten,
how abjectly you die!

4b Oh what love has caused
the despoiling of your body –
oh for so sweet a child
how bitter a reward!

5b Oh compassionate grace
of him who dies thus!
Oh jealousy, crime
of an envious race!

5b Oh fierce the right hand
of the crucifier,
oh gentle in pain
the mind of the sufferer!

6a Oh truthful utterance
of Simeon the just:
the sword of sorrows
he promised, I feel.

6b Moaning, sighing
and tears without
are the manifest signs
of the wound within.

7a Spare my son, Death,
do not spare me –
then you alone
heal me who am alone.

7b May Death part me
from you, blessed one,
if only you are not
tormented, my son.

8a What crimes, what evil deeds
the savage race has done:
chains, rods, wounds,
spitting, thorns, all else
5   he, without guilt, endures.

8b I beseech you, spare the son,
crucify the mother,
or else to the cross-beam
fasten us together!
5   It is bad to die alone.

9a Reddite mestissime
    corpus, vel exanime,
    ut sic minoratus
    crescat cruciatus
5   osculis, amplexibus.

10a Quid stupes, gens misera,
    terram se movere,
    obscurari sidera,
    languidos lugere?

11a Homicidam liberas,
    Iesum das supplicio:
    male pacem toleras,
    veniet seditio.

12a Gens ceca, gens flebilis,
    age penitentiam
    dum tibi flexibilis
    Iesus est ad veniam.

13a Flete, Sion filie,
    tante grate gratie:
    iuvenis angustie
    sibi sunt delicie
5   pro vestris offensis.

9b Utinam sic doleam
    ut dolore peream –
    nam plus est dolori
    sine morte mori
5   quam perire citius.

10b Solem privas lumine –
    quomodo luceret?
    egrum medicamine –
    unde convaleret?

11b Famis, cedis, pestium
    scies, docta pondere
    Iesum tibi mortuum
    Barrabamque vivere!

12b Quos fecisti, fontium
    prosint tibi flumina:
    sitim sedant omnium,
    cuncta lavant crimina.

13b In amplexus ruite
    dum pendet in stipite:
    mutuis amplexibus
    se parat amantibus
5   brachiis protensis.

14 In hoc solo gaudeo,
    quod pro vobis doleo.
    Vicem, queso, reddite:
    matris damnum plangite. >

Tunc iterum amplexetur Iohannem et cantet:
            Mi Iohannes...   *et cetera.*

Iohannes ad hec:
        O Maria, tantum noli
        lamentare tuo proli –

9a In my utmost sorrow, give me back
   the body, even without life,
   that so the torment
   may grow less
   through kissing, through embracing.

9b If only I could grieve so much
   as to die of grief –
   for there's more grief in dying
   without dying
   than in perishing more swiftly.

10a Why are you amazed, unhappy race,
   that the earth quakes,
   the stars grow dark,
   the sick mourn?

10b You deprive the sun of light –
   how then should it gleam?
   You take the medicine from the sick –
   how should they get well?

11a You set the murderer free,
   hand Jesus over to torture:
   you find peace hard to tolerate –
   turbulence will come.

11b You'll know, taught by the heaviness
   of famine, slaughter, plagues,
   that for you Jesus is dead
   and that Barabbas lives!

12a Blind race, lamentable race, do penance

   while Jesus may be swayed
   to grant you pardon.

12b Let the streams of fountains
   you made flow now give you aid:
   they slake the thirst of everyone,
   they wash away all guilt.

13a Weep, daughters of Jerusalem,
   for such joyous grace:
   the young man's pains
   are his delights,
5 offered for your sins.

13b Rush into his embrace
   as he hangs upon the beam:
   he waits to share the embrace
   of those who love him,
5 with arms wide open.

   14 I rejoice only in this,
      that I grieve on your behalf.
      Make exchange, I beg you:
      lament the mother's loss.

Then she shall again embrace John and sing:
   My John ...   etc. (278–85)

At this, John says:
   Oh Mary, do not lament
   your child so much –

290   sine me nunc plangere,
      que vitam cupis cedere!

Et Iohannes teneat Mariam sub humeris. Et dicat Iesus ad eam:
Mulier, ecce filius tuus.

Deinde dicit ad Iohannem:
Ecce mater tua.

Postea vadant Maria et Iohannes de cruce.

XX

Et Iesus dicat:
Sitio.

Statim veniant Iudei prebentes spongiam cum acceto, et Iesus bibat:
295 Consummatum est.

Tunc Longinus veniat cum lancea et perforet latus eius, et ille dicat aperte:
   Ich wil im stechen ab daz herze sin,
   daz sich ende siner marter pin.

Iesus, videns finem, dicit clamando:
Ely, Ely, Lema sabactany? Hoc est: Deus, Deus meus, ut quid dereliquisti me?

Et inclinando caput emittat spiritum. Longinus:
Vere filius dei erat iste!

Item:
300 Dirre ist des waren gotes sůn!

Item:
   Er hat zaichen an mir getan,
   wan ich min sehen wider han.

Et unus ex Iudeis dicat ad Iudeos:
Elyam vocat iste. Eamus et videamus si Elyas veniens liberet eum an non?

Alter Iudeus:
Si filius dei es, descende de cruce!

Item alter:
305 Alios salvos fecit – seipsum non potest salvum facere!

290   let me mourn now,
            you who long to give up life!

And let John hold Mary steady, supporting her shoulders. And Jesus shall say to her:
Woman, look: your son.

Then he says to John:
Look: your mother.

After this Mary and John shall move away from the cross.

XX

And Jesus shall say:
I am thirsty.

At once Jews shall come offering a sponge soaked in vinegar and Jesus shall drink, saying:
295 It is fulfilled.

Then Longinus shall come with a lance and pierce his side, and say aloud:
            I want to pierce his heart,
            so that his torments end.

Jesus, seeing the end, cries out:
Ely, Ely, Lema sabactany? That is: God, my God, why have you abandoned me?

And, bowing his head, he shall give up his spirit. Longinus:
Truly this was the Son of God!

Again:
300 This is the Son of the true God!

Again:
            He has worked miracles for me,
            since now I have my sight again.

And one of the Jews shall say to the others:
He is calling for Elijah. Shall we go and see whether or not Elijah comes to set him free?

Another Jew:
If you are the Son of God, come down from the cross!

Again another:
305 He saved others – he cannot save himself!

Explanatory notes

Before 1: 'Pilate and his wife ... the Merchant and his wife' – see above, p. 185.
1   Ingressus Pilatus] Responsory and versicle from Hesbert 6966. In completions here and below, where B gives only the incipits of responsories and antiphons, I follow Hesbert's *Corpus* throughout, slightly modifying his punctuation and (classical) spelling, and arranging the lines so as to indicate their articulation.
7   Cf. Matthew 4, 19; Mark 1, 17.
10–13   Cf. Luke 18, 35–42.
14–16   Cf. Luke 19, 5–9.
17–24   Cum approprinquaret dominus] Hesbert 1976.
25–30   Cum audisset] Hesbert 1983.
31–2   Pueri] Hesbert 4415.
33–4   Pueri] Hesbert 4416.
35   Gloria, laus] Theodulf of Orléans's hymn, which was used as a Palm Sunday processional, is ed. and tr. by F. Brittain, *The Penguin Book of Latin Verse*, pp. 139–40. It is not possible to determine how much of the hymn was sung here.
36   Cf. Luke 7, 36.
42–9   Cf. Archpoet, *Estuans intrinsecus* (CB 191), sts. 4–6, and above p. 187.
82/3   (and 96/7) When the angel withdraws, the *diabolus* who is mentioned as retreating, along with Mary's lover, at 107/8, must appear to Mary in her sleep and influence her by his mime in such a way that she heeds him and not the angel, and thus returns to her song in praise of *Mundi delectatio* (83, 97). The demon's earlier rubrics are missing, but his first entrance must precede that of the lover (83/4).
97/8   Here too the transition presupposes a mime for the *diabolus*, this time showing his frustration and defeat.
102   Cf. Hesbert 2208.
108–14 Verses adapted from the Vic Resurrection-play (v 15 ff.); on the passage of the Vic play to the Germanic language-area, see p. 87. Cf. also CB 15*, 76–91.
116   I adopt Bi's completion, based on the text of an antiphon used in later German plays.
129–30 Cf. Luke 7, 39.
131–2   Cf. Matthew 26, 8–10; Hesbert 4527 (Mark 14, 4–6; John 12, 6–7).
133–43 Cf. Luke 7, 40–8.
153   Cf. John 11, 11; Hesbert 3603.

154   Cf. John 11, 21 (and 32).
155–8 Cf. John 11, 33–44.
159–71 Cf. Matthew 26, 14–15.
172   Cf. Matthew 26, 48.
172/3 turba ... cum gladiis et fustibus] Cf. Matthew 26, 47.
173   Cf. Matthew 26, 45; Mark 14, 41.
174–84 Cf. Matthew 26, 38–46; on liturgical versions of 174–8 (= Bi 185–7), cf. Bi p. 171.
182   mori pro me] Cf. John 11, 16.
185–91 Cf. John 18, 4–8.
192   Cf. Matthew 26, 49.
193–7 Possibly tu in 194 is hypermetric and should be deleted; but as B has no neums for these verses, or for Peter's denials (198–203), this remains uncertain.
197–8 Cf. Matthew 26, 73; John 18, 25; Luke 22, 58.
199/200 Item ancilla] Cf. Mark 14, 69.
200   Cf. Luke 22, 59.
201   Cf. Matthew 26, 72.
202   Cf. John 18, 26.
203   Cf. Matthew 26, 70; Luke 22, 60.
203b–c Tanquam ... tenuistis] Cf. Matthew 26, 55.
204–8 (Sc. 11) Cf. Hesbert 1852.
209   Cf. Matthew 26, 61.
210–13 Cf. John 18, 29–31.
215   Cf. John 8, 53.
215/16 Cf. Luke 23, 9 and 12.
216   Cf. Luke 23, 22.
217   Cf. Matthew 26, 66.
218–21 Cf. John 18, 33–7.
222   Cf. John 8, 53.
223–4 Cf. Matthew 27, 22–3.
225   Cf. Luke 23, 22.
225/6 (and 226) Cf. John 19, 1–3; Mark 15, 17–18.
227   Cf. Luke 22, 64.
228–38 Cf. John 19, 5–15.
239   Cf. Matthew 27, 24.
240–3 Cf. Matthew 27, 3–5.
244   Cf. Luke 23, 28.
245–7 Cf. John 19, 19, 15, and 22.
265 ff. Flete, fideles anime] Complete text in *CB* 4* (Bi – followed here for 2b).
292–5 Cf. John 19, 26–30.
295/6 Tunc Longinus] Cf. John 19, 34, and above p. 191.
298   Cf. Matthew 27, 46; Mark 15, 34.
299–300 Cf. Matthew 27, 54; Mark 15, 39.
303   Cf. Matthew 27, 47–9; Mark 15, 36–7.
304–5 Cf. Matthew 27, 40–2.

Printed in the United Kingdom
by Lightning Source UK Ltd.
129626UK00001B/247/P